Walt Whitman
and the
Body Beautiful

Harold Aspiz

WALT WHITMAN
and the
BODY BEAUTIFUL

UNIVERSITY OF ILLINOIS PRESS

Urbana   Chicago   London

LIBRARY OF CONGRESS CATALOGING IN PUBLICATION DATA

Aspiz, Harold, 1921–
  Walt Whitman and the body beautiful.

  Includes index.
  1. Whitman, Walt, 1819–1892—Criticism and interpre-
tation.   2. Body, Human, in literature.   3. Beauty,
Personal, in literature.   I. Title.
PS3242.B58A84   811'.3   79-28280
ISBN 0-252-00799-9

The sublime vision comes to the pure and simple soul in a clean and chaste body

—Emerson, "The Poet"

Contents

Preface

THE POET MUST TRANSMUTE WORDS into flesh and infuse them with the fire of life, but at the same time he must transmute flesh—the human body—into the magic of words. This striking metaphor which Whitman uses to show that poetry involves the reciprocal relation between language and the human body may be illustrated by a pair of complementary quotations. "A perfect writer," he declares in *An American Primer*, is the one who "would make words sing, dance, kiss, do the male and female act, bear children, weep, bleed, rage, stab, steal, fire cannon, steer ships, sack cities, charge with cavalry or infantry, or do any thing, that man or woman or the natural powers can do." But such a writer, he implies in "A Song of the Rolling Earth," is also the one who can create poetry and poetic language out of the physical body:

> Human bodies are words, myriads of words,
> (In the best poems re-appears the body, man's or woman's, well-
>   shaped, natural, gay,
> Every part able, active, receptive, without shame or the need of
>   shame.)

Whitman certainly concurred in Emerson's statement that "a good deal of our politics is physiological," but he believed that a good deal of our poetics is physiological, too.

Whitman's depictions of the body may be seen as celebrations of his zestful engagement with life, as revelations of his psyche, or as expressions of his feeling of centrality in the cosmic order. These interpretations are valid, of course, for the poet often makes the body the emblem or indicator of spiritual or personal truths. But how are we to confront Whitman's treatment of the human body as such—the physical, physiological body—without consideration of which our reading of *Leaves of Grass* must remain partial and incomplete? What does Whitman "mean" by the body? What does the body connote in the context of his thinking and his cultural milieu? Relatively little attention has been focused on his physiological ideas, on their provenance and their workings in, and through, the poems. As the following pages illustrate, however, his interest in the body and the physiological and medical lore of his day was an essential element in shaping *Leaves of Grass*, its themes, its metaphors, its vision of a splendid new race of men and women, and its portrayal of the Whitman persona.

Whitman's candor and his wholesome acceptance of the dignity of all bodily functions may create the impression that he treats the body in a modern and, perhaps, a timeless fashion. Nevertheless, a closer look reveals that his utterances about the physique and about physical well-being derive from his keen observation of the health practices of his time and from his amateur acquaintance with medicine, popular eugenics, and health fads. Whenever possible, therefore, the present study has tried to relate his writings to those nineteenth-century "physiological" contexts which help to clarify the implications, or "meanings," of his poetic treatment of such matters as physical beauty, sexuality, personal magnetism, or even the nature of poetry. Examining the transmutation into poetry of scientific and quasi-scientific medical lore (some of which now appears old-fashioned or discredited) helps us to understand the poet, his poetic practice, and his world. It illuminates the personal, social, and philosophical relevance of his writings about the body and his achievement in making the body an exalted poetic theme.

This study examines five areas in which Whitman's concern with the body is particularly relevant. Chapter 1 contrasts the sequence of poses which the Whitman persona assumed in portraying the man of perfect physique with a more nearly historic reconstruction of Whitman's physical self. Chapters 2 and 3 chronicle Whitman's involvement with, and his reactions to, medical practice and hospitals and his attempts to evangelize a gospel of health among the masses, particularly as these are related to the first three editions of *Leaves of Grass* (chapter 2) and to *Drum-Taps*, the later writings, and his mature attitudes toward the healing arts (chapter 3).

Chapters 4 and 5 examine Whitman's use of medical pseudo-sciences, particularly phrenology, physiognomy, and pathognomy (body language), with their attendant perfectibilian doctrines (chapter 4), and electrical biology, magnetism, and electro-spiritualism, with their relevance to the persona's dynamism, his healing powers, and his clairvoyant inspiration (chapter 5).

Chapters 6 and 7 discuss Whitman's sexual-eugenic credo in terms of secular evolution, marriage, and the Whitman persona's role as a sexual-genetic prototype (chapter 6) and in terms of the physical soundness and capacity for perfect motherhood which form the basis of his feminine aesthetic (chapter 7).

Chapter 8 summarizes Whitman's gospel of the body as the essential complement of his gospel of the soul.

As Whitman revised *Leaves of Grass* during its half-dozen editions, he changed or deleted some passages and altered the physiological relevance of many poems. Whenever convenient, therefore, this study follows the "Comprehensive Reader's Edition" of *Leaves of Grass* (New York University Press, 1965), based on Whitman's final edition, so that the poet may be given the last editorial word. But earlier editions are cited whenever they appear to be more applicable to the argument.

In quoting from Whitman's poems, I have used asterisks to indicate omissions (three asterisks to indicate the omission of less than a sentence, four to indicate the omission of a sentence or more). This practice is needed to avoid confusion, inasmuch as the poet used two, three, or four dots to punctuate the first edition of *Leaves of Grass*.

For a key to the abbreviations used in the notes, please see page 249.

Acknowledgments

MANY PEOPLE HAVE HELPED ME in the course of preparing this book. (I like to think that they were motivated, as I was, by an affection for Whitman.) Thanks to Dr. Harold D. Barnshaw, Jonathan Ray Bishop, John B. Blake, the late Thomas L. Brasher, the late Emory Holloway, Mrs. Lisabeth M. Holloway, Mrs. Katherine Molinoff, Dr. Fred B. Rogers, Miss Madeleine B. Stern, my son Ira, and many librarians and other helpful persons.

Thanks to the Long Beach California State College Foundation for supporting my project in its early stages.

Thanks to my colleague Arnold T. Schwab for reading early drafts of this work and for wise counsel; Elizabeth G. Dulany, George Hendrick, and Noel R. Parsons for sound editorial criticism and advice; and Howard H. Kerr for a critique which was, in fact, a labor of painstaking scholarship. Particular thanks to Frank O. Williams of the University of Illinois Press for cheerful and unflagging encouragement and for valuable aid in shaping this book.

I am especially indebted to three persons without whom this project might not have been consummated: Charles E. Feinberg, for sharing his vast knowledge of Whitman and some of his choice Whitman materials; William White, for providing me with information about Whitman and much sagacious guidance and assistance; and, above all, my wife, Sylvia. Her selfless participation in these labors, even when the Body Beautiful seemed likely to become a full-fledged member of our household, has made this a genuinely collaborative effort. This is her book as much as it is mine.

The Whitman Persona
and Whitman's Physical Self

"A Perfect and Enamour'd Body"

1

IN SHAPING THE PHYSIOLOGICAL FACTS of his life into the myth of the superman-poet and transforming the author of *Leaves of Grass* into the persona of that work, Whitman scored an artistic triumph. Although aware of the flawed condition of his flesh-and-blood self, he invented a physical-culture hero—a figure of matchless physique and the prototype of future American manhood. His social, physical, and psychic motivations for doing so are shrouded in uncertainty. But in these literary-mythic projections of himself, his true physical history is darkly mirrored.

Whitman's "constantly retouched self-portrait" shows him as the model of untainted masculinity, the manly comrade, and the galvanic personage whose body attracts men and women like a magnet and infuses then with health and the electric life force.[1] For Whitman contended that genuine prophecy and poetry can originate only in the man of perfect body. In opposition to those he termed effete dilettantes, unfit for great creative deeds, he chose to mythologize himself as the superb male who radiates health and spirituality—the only sort of poet who could create a work like *Leaves of Grass*. The mythic Whitman persona sometimes appears to be a plausible extension of Whitman's flesh-and-blood self, sometimes a barely recognizable shadow of physical reality, and sometimes the product of pure invention or the deliberate thwarting of fact. For Walt Whitman never enjoyed the unexampled health with which he endowed his mythic self in poems, self-written reviews, and the "authorized" biographical sketches that he helped to create. Some of his contemporaries were skeptical, too. Henry James, the elder, felt that the perfect health Whitman boasted about could only limit his achievement as a poet, because profound poetry must be written by those who have endured sickness and suffering.[2] William Rossetti cautiously speculated that the ideas in *Leaves of Grass*, which appeared to be "throughout those of a man in robust health . . . might alter much under different conditions." And a friend of Rossetti's guessed perceptively that Whitman's bluster and "blatant ebullience of feeling and speech" disguised the fact that his "great fault is a fault of debility, not an excess of strength."[3] And, indeed, the poet's body failed him completely in his fifty-fourth year, after he had already completed his major work.

As the living poet grew older, the mythic persona was embellished in successive editions of *Leaves of Grass*. The first three editions of the work blended fact and invention to shape a man who is fiercely vain of his magnificent body. The image of the poet-hero as "one of the roughs" in the first (1855) edition was expanded, in the second edition (1856), to include the magnetic folk-evangelist to the city masses. The third edition (1860) showed him also as the reincarnated Adam, the lusty camerado "singing the phallus," an anthem intended to "fetch bully breeds of children" for a future-perfect America and to lure male lovers to his irresistible self. Despite its elements of shock and bravado, the 1860 edition softened and "spiritualized" its hero and made him more distinctly Christ-like. The fourth edition (1867) introduced the healer-camarado of hospital and campground—the unifier of war-torn America. This edition, with its extensive editorial changes, coincided with the beginning of the poet's physical decline. The persona's physical excellence now became less tangible in the poems, the allure of his body less powerful. The athlete-hero of quenchless physical vitality mellowed into a "national" poet—a spiritualized reconciler and prophet. In "Starting from Paumanok" the persona had appeared "free, fresh, savage . . . self-content . . . lusty-begotten and various" (1860), but in the 1867 edition his bearing became less proud and more respectable. In "Behold This Swarthy Face" (1860) he had offered himself as a physical and moral model to be emulated by the young men of the nation; in 1867 he deleted this offer along with the poem's reference to his presence in a "public room." The introductory poem of the 1867 edition presented its readers with "ONE'S-SELF—that wondrous thing, a simple, separate person." However, "one's-self" is not the astonishing "myself" of the earlier poems. The perfect body has

Walt Whitman and the Body Beautiful

become an abstraction; no longer is it the poet's own "enamour'd body."[4] In contrast to the first three editions of *Leaves of Grass*, which comprise a mythopoetic diary of Whitman's self and the world he confronts, the editions which appeared after the Civil War chronicle his former glories and the spiritual lessons which may be learned therefrom. *Democratic Vistas* (1871), his most ambitious prose work, stresses a sound physiology as the basis of all individual and national virtues, but unlike the 1855 preface to *Leaves of Grass*, the essay draws little sustenance from Whitman's physical biography. And the writings of his last two decades are often backward-looking and wistful.

With mythic bravado and a cavalier disregard for whatever facts might contradict his self-portrait, Whitman originally proposed his idealized person as the nation's poet and the model of American masculinity. Behold him in "Walt Whitman, a Brooklyn Boy," an anonymous self-review of the 1855 edition:

> Of American breed, of reckless health, his body perfect, free from taint from top to toe, free forever from headache and dyspepsia, full-blooded, six feet high, a good feeder, never once using medicine, drinking water only—a swimmer in the river or bay or by the seashore—of straight attitude and slow movement of foot—an indescribable style evincing indifference and disdain—ample limbed, weight a hundred and eighty-five pounds, age thirty-six years [1855]—never dressed in black, always dressed freely and clean in strong clothes, neck open, shirt-collar flat and broad, countenance of swarthy transparent red, beard short and well mottled with white, hair like hay after it has been mowed in the field and lies tossed and streaked—face not refined or intellectual, but calm and wholesome—a face of an unaffected animal—a face that absorbs the sunshine and meets savage or gentleman on equal terms—a face of one who eats and drinks and is a brawny lover and embracer—a face of undying friendship and indulgence toward men and women, and of one who finds the same returned many fold—a face with two gray eyes where passion and hauteur sleep, and melancholy stands behind them—a spirit that mixes cheerfully with the world—a person singularly beloved and welcomed, especially by young men and mechanics. . . .[5]

The statement resembles certain passages in the 1856 and 1860 versions of "Starting from Paumanok," wherein the persona sarcastically contrasts his rugged self to his effete literary rivals:

No dainty dolce affectuoso I,
Bearded, sun-burnt, gray-neck'd, forbidding, I have
arrived * * * *6

Whitman lauded his looks in many poems. His face, he declared, is "the programme of all good," his "manly beard" a sign of his virility, and his rosy body an emblem of his soundness. For the glow of animal health, physiologists commonly asserted, results from the proper circulation of the blood, which suffuses the skin with a pinkish tinge. The skin of gross sensualists was alleged to be fiery red; that of enervate and sedentary persons, pale; but the man of perfect physical and mental vigor was characterized by a rosy skin. Typically, in "Song at Sunset" (1860), Whitman dotes upon his idealized body and his "fine skin—that criterion of condition *in man and horse*."7 He declares it wonderful

* * * to look on my rose-color'd flesh!
To be conscious of my body, so satisfied, so large!
To be this incredible God I am!
To have gone forth among other Gods, these men and women I
love.8

In a pair of self-reviews, published in 1855, Whitman contrasted the college-bred, "tea-drinking," and furtively licentious British poets (New England poets, he probably meant) with himself—the inspired paragon of American manhood: "one of the roughs, large, proud, affectionate, eating, drinking, and breeding. . . ." Proclaiming himself the equal of any man, he proposed to instill the joy and wisdom of sexuality into literature, behavior, and the begetting of "healthy and powerful breeds of children." This self-crowned "insolent unknown" declared that if he were less than perfect in body and spirit he would be "the very harlot of persons." Citing his superb genealogy as a proof of his fitness to write great poetry, he asserted: "All beauty comes from beautiful blood and a beautiful brain." Establishment poets—the feebly inspired "shoats and geldings," "rhymesters, melancholy and swallow-tailed," and the "confectioners and upholsterers of verse"— were warned that they were about to confront "the tan-faced man here advancing . . . the natural and proper bard."9

Whitman also attempted to strike the pose of a natural aristocrat—like that of Epicurus in Frances Wright's novel *A Few Days in Athens* (1822)—a physically superb prophet-teacher of inoffensive sensuality and Lamarckian evolution who does not concede that he is a philosopher and who relishes the companionship of young male disciples, whom he often touches and caresses.[10] But the cloak of Epicurus proved less comfortable than the garb of a carpenter-poet and spokesman for the urban masses who could display a life-style like the one that Emerson attributed to Thoreau—knowing "how to be poor without the least hint of squalor or inelegance." Whitman boasted: "Mine are not the songs of a story teller, or of a voluptuous person, or of an enuyeed person, but of an American constructor, looking with friendly eyes upon the earth and man and beholding the vistas of the great missions of these States."[11] In a lighter vein, he described his appearance as the carpenter-persona, sauntering along Broadway, hale, contented, and with haunting-mesmerizing eyes: "Tall, large, rough-looking man, in a journeyman carpenter's uniform. Coarse, sanguine complexion; strong, bristly, grizzled beard; singular eyes, of a semi-transparent, indistinct light blue, and with that sleepy look that comes when the lid rests half way down over the pupil; careless, lounging gait. Walt Whitman, the sturdy, self-conscious, microcosmic, prose-poetical author of that incongruous hash of mud and gold—'Leaves of Grass.'"[12]

The poems Whitman wrote and the propaganda pieces he composed or those he inspired in friendly publicists boasted of his proletarian simplicity; yet it was alleged that the self-styled carpenter-poet could not build houses or handle a saw and hammer well enough to earn a living. The everyday Whitman was something of an aesthete, a friend of artists, and an amateur art collector, whose typically bourgeois pursuits in the 1850's included keeping store, editing newspapers, and what he called successful "house building speculations." Nevertheless, he cherished his mythic roles of carpenter-poet and physical-culture hero and augmented them with that of the compassionate healer who produces cures by his electrifying, but nonetheless "homely and accustomed," physical presence and his healthy emanations.[13]

The Civil War years gave rise to the myths that transfigured Whitman's real self into the matchless healer-hero. Although the agonizing hours the poet spent in the military hospitals of the Washington area sapped his health and produced the symptoms of an impending paralytic stroke, he bore the risk stoically. He whom Burroughs called perceptively "a great tender mother-man" was motivated by a sympathy for suffering that had for many years drawn him to the hospitals and prisons in New York—experiences out of which he had created the Christ-like healer of the "Messenger Leaves" poems (1860).[14] However, it required his dedicated service in the Washington hospitals to lay the groundwork for the realized literary image of the good gray poet—simply dressed, fatherly, and magnetic—who moves "with bent knee" through the pages of Whitman's *Drum-Taps* (1865); through Burroughs's quasi-biography, on which Whitman collaborated,[15] and through the later prose works. These productions transfigure Whitman into a saintly healer, possessing "the perfection of physical health," and depict his labors among the disabled soldiers in the wards of the military hospitals as physical-spiritual wonder rituals:

> [His] principles of operation, effective as they were, seemed strangely few, simple, and on a low key,—to act upon the appetite, to cheer by a healthy and fitly bracing appearance and demeanor; and to fill and satisfy in certain cases the affectional longings of the patients, was about all. He carried among them no sentimentalism nor moralizing; spoke not to any man of his "sins," but gave something good to eat, a buoying word, or a trifling gift and a look. He appeared with ruddy face, clean dress, with a flower or a green sprig in the lapel of his coat. Crossing the fields in summer, he would gather a great bunch of dandelion blossoms, and red and white clover, to bring and scatter on the cots, as reminders of out-door air and sunshine.
>
> When practicable, he came to the long and crowded wards of the maimed, the feeble, and the dying, only after preparations as for a festival,—strengthened by a good meal, rest, the bath, and fresh underclothes. He entered with a huge haversack slung over his shoulder, full of appropriate articles, with parcels under his arms, and protuberant pockets. He would sometimes come in summer with a good-sized basket filled with oranges, and would go round for hours paring and dividing them among the feverish and thirsty.[16]

Whitman and his friends fashioned the myth of a hospital visitor endowed with limitless health, spirituality, and "incredible and exhaustless" magnetic-curative powers. "It is no figure of speech, but a fact deeper than speech," Burroughs asserted, that the "lusterless eye [of the suffering soldiers] brightened up at his approach, his commonplace words invigorated; a bracing air seemed to fill the ward and neutralize the bad smells." Indeed, Whitman was said to possess a "new and mysterious" bodily quality which was indescribable, "but which none who come into his presence can escape, and which is, perhaps, the analogue to the intuitive quality of his intellect." [17]

Whitman's efforts to arouse the soldiers' recuperative powers were consistent with the nineteenth-century medical theory of vitalism, according to which every person possesses, in addition to his physical and chemical organization, an electric life force that is linked to his will and that governs his ability to overcome sickness. It is true that Whitman helped soldiers to survive essentially by rallying their *will* to overcome illness. But the well-publicized charisma of the healer-persona was compounded, in part, of mystical elements and seasoned with a generous dash of poetic imagination. In sentiments, if not words, that are the poet's own, Bucke's *Walt Whitman* (1883), a joint venture in mytho-biography, declared that Whitman had buoyed up the ailing soldiers "with a few words, with caresses, with personal affection; he bends over them, strong, clean, cheerful, perfumed, loving, and his magnetic touch and love sustain them." Whitman's touch, Bucke explained, had "a charm that cannot be described, and if it could, the description would not be believed except by those who know him either personally or through *Leaves of Grass*. This charm (physiological more than psychological), if understood, would explain the whole mystery of the man, and how he produced such effects not only upon the well, but among the sick and wounded." [18]

As part of the campaign to defend the poet's nobility and purity against the slander that he was a dirty old man and a lascivious writer, his friend William Douglas O'Connor composed two emotional ripostes. His polemic *The Good Gray Poet* (1866) pictures an idealized Whitman with gray "Homeric" head, powerful, impeccably clean, magnetically radiating "an unexcluding friendliness and goodness," and "exhaling faint fragrance; the whole form surrounded with manliness as with a nimbus, and breathing, in perfect health and vigor, the august charm of the strong." His Dickensian saint's legend, "The Carpenter" (1868), casts Whitman as a Christ-like carpenter-nurse whose reconciling of a household divided by its wartime loyalties symbolizes the poet-healer's power to restore unity to postwar America. O'Connor's gray, gentle reconciler, "with that heavy-lidded, draining gaze," establishes himself "in close *rapport* with every one, as only a man of powerful intuition, vivid impressions, and great magnetic force and dignity could have done, and leaving them with a sense as if something very electric and sweet had passed through them." This former confidant of Lincoln (a groundless embellishment of the myth), this saint who had walked the wards of the military hospitals, this "strange, gray man," assuages pain, allays guilt by his charmed touch, and foretells the future.[19] The tale idealizes Whitman at the end of the period which he himself described as "the flush of my health and strength, from the age of 30 to 50 years. . . ."[20]

To counteract the allegations that the poet was sensual or coarse, Whitman and his supporters now stressed his resemblance to spiritual aristocrats rather than his affinity to farmers and artisans. Typically, Burroughs claimed that "the impression he makes upon you is that of the best birth and breeding" and that he is "fastidious as a high-caste Brahmin in his food and personal neatness." He compared Whitman's physiognomy to that of the ancient Greeks—a conceit with which the poet loved to toy. Perfect himself and inspiring perfection in others, the creator of Leaves of Grass was said to be able to establish a wonder-working electric contact with his readers, whom the very poems, the pages of the book, could charge with physical and spiritual health. "One who has the volume for a daily companion," Burroughs commented, "will be under a constant invisible influence toward physiological cleanliness, strength, and gradual severance from all that corrupts and makes morbid and mean."[21] Several of Whitman's "Inscription" poems imply that Leaves of Grass can indeed transmit the poet's beneficial emanations to any reader who will submit to their powers. And, as if to confirm the book's influence over the lives of its readers, the English writer John Addington Symonds testified that simply by reading Leaves of Grass in the 1860's he had been cured of his former physical debility.[22]

As a reflection of the poet's physical decline and the shattered health that culminated in his paralytic collapse in 1873, after the strain of his hospital labors had taken their heaviest toll, the poet developed the Whitman-Columbus myth. It was inspired by Washington Irving's Life and Voyages of Christopher Columbus, by the frequent invocation of Columbus's name in association with the laying of the Atlantic Cable, and perhaps by Thoreau's admonition to "be a Columbus to whole new continents and worlds operating

within you, opening new channels, not of trade, but of thought."
Alcott had, in fact, praised Whitman as "the American Columbus."[23] In this incarnation, the Whitman persona emerges as a
spiritual explorer, shattered in body and subjected to scorn by his
detractors, but unshaken in his faith. Having exhibited matchless
devotion to his country and ventured into new worlds of the
human soul, Whitman-Columbus now consecrates himself to instill hope and courage in the masses and to embark on death's voyage. Like the hero of Tennyson's "Ulysses," a poem that Whitman
admired, the persona voices a passionate readiness for life's final
adventure. In the fifth section of "Passage to India," composed in
1868, he assures everyone that the hearts of old Adam's "fretted
children shall be sooth'd" by this "true son of God, the poet," who
will one day reconcile "Nature and Man." And in the sixth section
of the poem, written in 1871, he dons the mantle of the "sad
shade" of "the chief histrion" of modern times, a tragic Columbus
with imposing body and haunting Whitmanesque eyes:

> Gigantic, visionary, thyself a visionary,
> With majestic limbs and pious beaming eyes,
> Spreading around with every look of thine a golden world,
> Enhuing it with gorgeous hues * * * *
> (History's type of courage, action, faith) * * * *[24]

In "Prayer of Columbus," written late in 1873, the dying and
paralytic "batter'd, wreck'd old man," intoxicated with the thought
of "newer better worlds, their mighty parturition," which he has
helped to bring about, personifies a physically prostrated Whitman, still firm in his faith:

> My hands, my limbs grow nerveless,
> My brain fells rack'd, bewilder'd,
> Let the old timbers part, I will not part,
> I will cling fast to Thee, O God, though the waves buffet me,
> Thee, Thee, at least I know.

Mrs. Anne Gilchrist, the poet's devoted English friend, confirmed
the fact the true hero of this "sacred Poem" was Whitman, a man
who had achieved greatness despite mockery and had "paid the
great price of health—our Columbus!" And Ellen O'Connor
(Mrs. William Douglas O'Connor), another Whitman devotee,
stated that the poet had "unconsciously put a sort of auto-

biographical dash" into the poem.[25] Whitman related the actualities of his life to the Columbus role by declaring that he had himself attempted, in the heyday of his career, "to irradiate buoyancy and health. But it came to me in time that I was not to attempt to live up to the reputation I had, or to my own idea of what my programme should be, but to give out or express what I really was, and, if I felt like the devil, to say so! And I have become more and more confirmed in this!"[26] But the decline in Whitman's physical and poetic powers, as Quentin Anderson observes, was "not accompanied by a retreat from the claim he makes for the experiencer and shaper of *Leaves of Grass*."[27]

In retrospect, Whitman often pictured himself as a latter-day Columbus who perceived his prostrating Civil War labors as an imperative duty to be performed regardless of the consequences. Unlike Prufrock, he had never asked himself during these trying years, "And would it have been worth it, after all?" He chose to picture himself as one who had surrendered his enamoured body and his matchless health for something greater than health, and he asserted his satisfaction with the bargain. Defiantly, he declared that he had received a vast return for the sacrifice of his body, insisting that his wartime service had furnished the capstone for his career and for the purportedly completed architecture of *Leaves of Grass*:

> What did I get?—Well—I got the [soldier] boys, for one thing: the boys: thousands of them: they were, they are, they will be mine. . . . then I got Leaves of Grass: but for this I would never have had Leaves of Grass—the consummated book (the last confirming word). . . . All the wise ones said: "Walt, you should have saved yourself." I did save myself though not in the way they meant: I saved myself in the only way salvation was possible to me. You look on me now [1889] with the ravages of that experience finally reducing me to a powder. Still I say: I only gave myself: I got the boys, I got the Leaves. My body? Yes—it had to be given—it had to be sacrificed: who knows better than I do what that means? . . .[28]

Although Columbus is named in only one other poem ("A Thought of Columbus," 1891), Whitman-Columbus looms darkly in the many songs of farewell and setting sail across the uncharted Atlantic of death. Such old-age lyrics as "Tears," "Patrolling Barnegat," and "With Husky-Haughty Lips, O Sea!" revisit the nightmare image of an old man standing on death's seashore, confronting the storm and gloom of death's fearful ocean of tears, and hint at the repressed terror with which the would-be Columbus sometimes faced the prospect of his own dying.

Neither disease, debility, nor death stayed the tide of myth-making about the aging poet's body. Whitman and his friends persisted in the tale that he had never known a day's illness before he became prostrated as a result of his devotion to the soldiers. O'Connor described him limping up the stairs at a ceremony to commemorate Edgar Allan Poe, looking "grand in his old age and infirmity, like a crippled eagle."[29] After the paralytic stroke, his "enamour'd body" was portrayed as a splendid ruined temple. Burroughs alleged that Walt's "rosy, godlike, yet infantile face . . . is incomparably the grandest face I ever saw—such sweetness and harmony, and such strength—strength like the Roman arches." He asserted that Whitman's superb manhood was visible in his classically handsome body, his phrenology, his physiognomy, his glance, and his immense emotional fires.[30] William Sloane Kennedy, another ardent disciple, praised Whitman's Greek bearing, his "proud but kindly native-aristocratic temper and carriage," his "large personality, the rich, supple-sweet fulness of flesh, delicacy on a basis of rugged strength," and his uncanny effect on others. "I never knew a person to meet him for the first time who did not come under his spell; most people going away in such a curious state of exaltation and excitement as to produce a partial wakefulness, the general feeling not wearing off for a fortnight."[31]

Whitman's own *Specimen Days*, a bittersweet evocation of his young manhood and his wartime labors, reports his slow recovery from the prostration that followed his paralytic stroke and his physical condition during his sixty-fourth year. If his body no longer inspires great and sustained poetry, as it had during his more vigorous years, its former grandeur still serves to illuminate the theme that life remains piquant to the fully developed man even after his physical powers have been diminished. Similarly, Bucke's *Walt Whitman* presents the image of a once-powerful, irresistibly masculine being. In helping Bucke to fashion the portrait of his idealized self, the poet excised from Bucke's manuscript unflattering references to himself as excitable, "a sort of male castrato, a false soprano," a compassionate nurse with "an almost feminine order of mind," and "a motherly soul." But he augmented the volume's references to his uncouthness, his athleticism, his friendliness, and his cleanliness.[32]

The poems added to *Leaves of Grass* in the closing years of Whitman's life chronicle his rare moments of joy and well-being, his despair and his memories of ancient agonies, and, like the closing pages of a saint's legend, his readiness for holy dying. In "A Twilight Song" the crippled hero conjures up visions of the dead and tormented soldiers who file before him in the flickering firelight. In "Death's Valley" he mingles resignation and pride to sum up his lifelong intimacy with sickness and death:

> For I have seen many wounded soldiers die,
> After dread suffering—have seen their lives pass off with smiles;
> And I have watch'd the death-hours of the old; and seen the infant
>   die;
> The rich, with all his nurses and his doctors;
> And then the poor, in meagreness and poverty;
> And I myself for long, O Death, have breath'd my every breath
> Amid the nearness and the silent thought of thee.

In "Carol Closing Sixty-nine" he sings of the vigorous spirit still lingering in his failing body:

> Of me myself—the jocund heart yet beating in my breast,
> The body wreck'd, old, poor and paralyzed—the strange inertia
>   falling pall-like round me,
> The burning fires down in my sluggish blood not yet extinct,
> The undiminish'd faith—the groups of loving friends.

And in "Halcyon Days," one of the noblest lyrics on the cheerful acceptance of death in our language, the persona compares himself to a "really finish'd and indolent-ripe" apple hanging on the bough in the "brooding and blissful" autumnal sunshine, waiting to be plucked for higher uses.[33]

Inevitably, a post-mortem apotheosis of Whitman's physical self appeared—Bucke's *Cosmic Consciousness* (1901). Among the rare humans who are said there to be so highly evolved that they have attained the stage of "cosmic consciousness," or complete spiritual illumination, Bucke included Christ, Saint Paul, Dante, Bacon-Shakespeare, and beyond all compare in modern times, Walt Whitman! Bucke called Whitman "the best, most perfect example the world has so far had of the Cosmic Sense . . . the man

Walt Whitman and the Body Beautiful

in whom the new faculty has been, probably, most perfectly developed" and one whose writings are manifestly inspired by this "interior consciousness." The man who possesses this extraordinary faculty necessarily "has an exceptional physique—exceptional beauty of build and carriage, exceptionally handsome features, exceptional health; exceptional sweetness of temper, exceptional magnetism." Bucke drew upon his (and Whitman's) 1883 biography to depict a Whitman of unruffled temper, beautiful face, rose-colored body, "extraordinary attractiveness," small but remarkable eyes, and uncanny sensitivity: "I have heard him speak of hearing the grass grow and the trees coming out in leaf." [34]

If Walt Whitman of the beautiful quenchless body radiated a charisma that was no less physical than spiritual, Walter Whitman, Junior, whose reality was refracted in the multifaceted myth, was from the beginning afflicted with many ills of the flesh. The records of his historic physical self, which are deplorably scanty for the first half of his life, lend little support to the cherished myths of his matchless ancestry, invulnerably healthy youth and athletic manhood, and sound middle age. The causes of the successive strokes and the physical prostration which he later endured were rooted essentially in his physical and emotional makeup. His triumph over physical shortcomings, massive tubercular infection, and other afflictions was apparently based on an awareness of his condition and on a fierce desire to survive.

Perhaps no part of the myth was more lovingly rehearsed than that of the superb ancestry and the ecstatic coupling of the perfect parents who engendered the poet. And no part of the myth rested on weaker foundations. Whitman insisted that the parental stock from which he was descended "corresponds with the theory of this book [Leaves of Grass] and his own character": "I started well—am built up bodily on a good base: I had a good father and mother, just as my father and mother again had good fathers and mothers." He wrote or editorially approved the statement in Bucke's biography that from "father and mother alike, he derived his magnificent physique, and . . . his almost unexampled health and fulness of bodily life. Walt Whitman could say with perhaps a better right than almost any man for such a boast, that he was 'Well-begotten, and rais'd by a perfect mother.'" [35] This claim was grounded on the popular belief that great men—and great poets, in particular—are descended from physically sound ancestors, and notably from extraordinary mothers. The probability that a poetic genius like Whitman could be the child of a semiliterate mother was thus explained by a contemporary writer: "All talented and great men had great mothers, who, even if they were uneducated, still possessed the elements of original greatness." And Whitman unhesitatingly applied this concept to his mythic self: "Unfolded only out of the inimitable poem of the woman, can come the poems of man—only thence have my poems come * * * *"[36]

He praised both parents. His mother was revered by him as the model of "the perfect woman and mother" and the source of his "chief traits." He memorialized and transfigured her and her forebears in *Leaves of Grass* and in various prose writings. These maternal ancestors of Dutch descent, he claimed, were "broad, solid, practical, materialistic, but with the emotional fires burning within—their women, too, as much as the men—they exemplify my theory of physiological development underlying all else; just as we come from the earth ourselves, however much we may soar above it." And he also paid affectionate tribute to his father and his paternal forebears in his later prose writings. The elder Whitman is pictured in Bucke's quasi-official biography as "a large, quiet, serious man" from whom chiefly "must have come [the poet's] passion for freedom, and the firmness of character which has enabled him to persevere for a lifetime in what he called 'carrying out his own ideal.'" Whitman set forth the glories of these paternal ancestors of English stock—"a stalwart, massive, heavy, long-lived race . . . of democratic and heretical tendencies."[37] (Both his grandfather's friend Elias Hicks, the heretical Quaker preacher, and the New England Whitmans had been cited as examples of longevity and piety in Orson S. Fowler's *Hereditary Descent*, a book which specified the type of parentage from which great bards are descended.)[38] That the ancestral Whitmans were "long-lived" or "heretical" may be true, but Walt's father died at sixty-six and his paternal grandfather at fifty-four, and Walt himself was obsessed by the idea of living to an old age.

What is known about Walt's ancestry does not support the cherished myth that his poetic endowments are traceable to his inherited physical excellence. His massive, if not sluggish, physique seems to have been inherited from both birth stocks. In later life he

Walt Whitman and the Body Beautiful

conceded that "there is apoplexy or paralysis in the family." His mother's alleged perfection, as Quentin Anderson observes, "doesn't account for the poems, nor does it qualify the poems." Indeed, no visitors to the Whitman home in Brooklyn are known to have been overwhelmed by Mrs. Whitman's physical or mental presence. Her photograph, probably dating from her late fifties, reveals a heavy-set, full-faced, clear-complexioned, bright-eyed woman. If she enjoyed exemplary health in her youth, as her son boasted, she suffered in her old age from arthritis, dizziness, head pains, loss of teeth, lameness in her right arm, and possible bronchial tuberculosis. And like all members of the Whitman family, she was incapable of understanding her son's poetical aspirations.[39]

Long after the death of his father, Whitman admitted the affinities in their physical makeup. The elder Whitman's photograph, taken when he was about sixty years old, reveals a pain-wracked and asymmetrical face, its distortion a probable indication of hemiplegia, the paralysis of one side of the body which would one day victimize the poet and at least two of his brothers. (Such facial asymmetry can be seen in photographs of Walt, where it is softened by the famous manly beard, and of his brother Jeff.) Toward the end of his life the father was subject to migrainelike spells resembling those which afflicted the poet and some of his siblings. A few days after the first appearance of *Leaves of Grass*, following three years of exhausting illness, Whitman's father died of "paralysis due to cerebral hemorrhage" (according to one medical assessment of the evidence).[40] Walt may have been thinking of the senior Whitman's qualities as a father when he called "the institution of the father a failure," and, whether from a sense of his father's shortcomings or a fear of his own inadequacies, he did not emulate his father's example by becoming the head of a family. Rather ambiguously, he declared that he had stayed unmarried for "a set purpose" and that he had "had an instinct against forming ties that would bind me . . . the instinct of self-preservation."[41] The poems of the first edition include the "strong, self-sufficient, manly, mean, anger'd, unjust" image of the father in "There Was a Child Went Forth," which many biographers have seen as an image of the elder Whitman, and the allusion to the phallic Lucifer in "The Sleepers," which may suggest a father-son hostility. Other vignettes of the satanic father figure occur in Whitman's short story "Bervance" (1841), in which a maddened son calls his father "Flint Serpent," and in the poem "Chanting the Square Deific" (1865–66).[42]

Walt's parents simply did not produce unusually healthy or well-poised children. One of Walt's brothers died before completing his first year of life. Jesse, one year older than Walt, was "excitable, jealous, and hysterical, even from infancy," possibly the result of a blow or a fall. According to Dr. Josiah C. Trent's study of the Whitmans' medical history, Jesse apparently suffered from "cardiovascular and nervous system syphilis." By his mid-thirties he had become increasingly violent; when he was forty-eight the poet was obliged to commit him to the Kings County Lunatic Asylum, where he died, aged fifty-two, of the rupture of an aneurysm, possibly attributable to the syphilis. Walt's younger brother Eddie, whom he supported and helped to care for, seems to have been feeble-minded, epileptic, and emotionally disturbed, his crippled left hand and paralyzed left leg indicating that the poet's paralysis, like his dizzy spells and his appearance of being prematurely old, had a complex family history. Walt's brother Andrew died, aged thirty-six, apparently of tuberculosis of the throat. George Washington Whitman, ten years Walt's junior, and Thomas Jefferson ("Jeff") Whitman, fourteen years Walt's junior, were said by the poet to be "both of them big hearty preserved fellows." However, George returned from his war service with "lung fever" (another possible instance of tuberculosis in the Whitman family); by 1865 he was afflicted, like Walt, with headaches; like his mother, he developed arthritis; and two years before his death, in 1901, he, too, became paralyzed. Jeff, Walt's favorite brother (the poet remarks on their strong resemblance), died in 1890 at fifty-eight of "typhoid pneumonia" (tuberculosis once more?); his photograph suggests debility and a poor physique. Walt's death certificate attributed his own death to pneumonia and general miliary tuberculosis.[43] The observation appears just that the source of Walt's massive tubercular infection "was probably within his own family, and it is likely that the germs were implanted in one or both lungs during his childhood or early adolescence."[44] However, the disease may have been arrested during his young manhood.

Apparently, Jesse, Eddie, and Walt all had volatile temperaments. The poet tells of trying to control this dangerous element in his character, and his composure, whether in the Washington

Walt Whitman and the Body Beautiful

hospitals or on his Camden sickbed, represented the triumph of a determined mind over an emotional, sometimes morbid, disposition. He recalled his first adolescent thrill to the magic of the theatre as "a fat-cheeked boy . . . trembling with expectation and excitement" and his terror when, as a lad, he saw a man falling from a haystack. Bliss Perry, an early Whitman biographer, remarks that the latter incident demonstrates "an excess of emotional endowment, to which the tragic fate of his oldest and youngest brothers gives significance," and (possibly influenced by the poet's mytho-biography) that "it was a fortunate instinct which drove him so early into the open air and into contact with self-contented, strong-muscled men."[45] But if Walt usually succeeded in curbing his emotionalism, his favorite sister Hannah, for example, the longest-lived of the Whitman children, seems to have remained temperamentally unstable all her life. Her husband Charles L. Heyde scored a hostile bull's-eye on Whitman's poetic-physiological theories when he complained to the poet that Hannah's lassitude and erratic behavior "must be in the blood."[46]

Wistfully recalling the observation made by the dyspeptic Carlyle that "the healthy know not of their health, but only the sick," Whitman asserted on his Camden sickbed that he had been a perfectly healthy animal most of his days. Burroughs's biography, with a generous assist from the poet, alleged that young Walt, "in perfect bodily condition," had experienced all "passions, pleasures, and abandonments of life."[47] He must have developed slowly as a child, for he says in "Who Learns My Lesson Complete" that he "passed from a babe in the creeping trance of three summers and three winters to articulate and walk."[48] He claimed to have been a big, vigorous adolescent. As a teen-aged country schoolteacher, he appeared to be easygoing, serious, perhaps even "magnetic" to his boy pupils, but he did not seem attracted to girls. A student remembered him as "a rugged, healthy-looking fellow with clear eyes, firm lips, and a fine red color in his face." And he said about his physical condition during his twenties, thirties, and forties: "I doubt if a heartier, stronger physique lived from 1840 to '70. My greatest call (Quaker) to go around and do what I could among the suffering and sick was that I seemed to be so *well* I considered myself invulnerable."[49] Colleagues of the twenty-three-year-old reporter on the *New York Aurora* called him "tall and graceful," but the articles he wrote for the journal showed little interest in physiology and athletics.[50] As editor of the *Brooklyn Daily Eagle*, 1846–48, however, he displayed a strong desire to be accepted by his readers as a household counselor on matters of physical exercise and health, for these were the years in which he apparently conceived his abortive projects—lecturing to young men about their health and writing articles or a popular book about the subject.

The evidence of Whitman's physical condition toward the end of his third decade has a certain consistency. An 1846 photograph reveals a pale young man affecting an effete pose and characterized (to use Whitman's sarcastic term) by a condition of "delicatesse." The wavy hair is streaked with gray, and the lips have a rather feminine fullness. But in approving his application for a life insurance policy in May, 1847, an insurance company medical examiner described him in these words: "About six feet tall, full, healthy, sedantary [*sic*] as an editor. Heart action slow and regular, pulse rather slow but regular, full and soft. Healthy, risk good."[51] A rival newspaper called him "well-built." Discharged as editor of the *Eagle* in 1848, the twenty-nine-year-old Whitman was described by the now-hostile paper as "slow, indolent, heavy, discourteous." Another newspaper called him "a pretty fair specimen of . . . a polished *Aborigine*," but also observed his "remarkably indolent" expression.[52] Early that year he had gone to work on the *New Orleans Daily Crescent*, returning to New York after four months. During that period, he subsequently recalled, he had maintained "perfect health—enjoyed perfect physical nonchalance, in fact: was moved by nothing: was absolutely season and climate proof. . . ."[53]

Further evidence of his physical condition may be gleaned from his phrenological examination by Lorenzo Niles Fowler the following year. Despite the fulsome ambiguity of some of Fowler's comments, the phrenologist carefully described Whitman as an intellectual man, given to inertia, overeating, and possible emotionalism, and, ominously enough, one whose physical and recuperative powers could remain sound only if he obeyed "the laws of health, of life and mental and physical development." He told Whitman: "You have much energy when you are aroused but you are not easily moved at trifles. . . . You choose to fight with tongue and pen rather than with your fist. . . . Your courage is probably more *moral* than *physical*." Fowler judged his client to be

Walt Whitman and the Body Beautiful

introspective, just, sympathetic, unorthodox, and well-endowed with memory, language skills, and a mechanical eye (the examination chart identified Whitman as a printer).[54]

Whitman liked to recall his athletic prowess. He declared that he used to enjoy playing "foot and a half" as well as baseball, remarking in 1889 that "I still find my interest in the [latter] game unabated." (George Whitman said that Walt was "an old-fashioned ball-player" and moderately athletic.)[55] He rambled extensively about Long Island, and later, in and near Washington, he and Peter Doyle walked "sometimes ten miles at a stretch," he claimed. In the last year of his life, he recalled: "F'm 25 to 45 [years of age], I c'd hop on & get up front a stage [a horse-drawn streetcar] while going a good trot—also put my hand on a six-barr'd fence & leap over at once—(terrible reminiscences now). . . ."[56] He told his newspaper readers how much he liked "to sail all day on the river amid a party of fresh and jovial boatmen," and he spoke of himself as an occasional fisherman but a poor sailor. Several poems celebrate his adventures as a seine fisher, spearer of eels, or catcher of "blue-fish off Paumanok." Behold him, in "A Song of Joys," digging clams alongside the clam diggers: "I laugh and work with them, I joke at my work like a mettlesome young man * * * *"[57] Experience and homoerotic dreams seem to merge in this image of the poetic persona who, in the midst of his youthful male companions, is proud to be a "mettlesome" (sexually charged) man.

Of all sporting activities, Whitman seems to have loved swimming best, but his swimming, too, was characteristically lethargic. He told Bronson Alcott that he bathed at the seaside from the onset of warm weather until midwinter. "Bathing in this clear, pure salt water, twice every day, is one of my best pleasures," he informed his newspaper readers, joking that he "must have the [phrenological] bump of 'aquativeness' large." In the early 1840's, he swam in the Knickerbocker Hotel pool in New York City and later apparently attended Edward Gray's swimming establishment in Brooklyn each summer over a period of several years.[58] He testified, however, that "I was never what you could call a skillful swimmer but was quite good. I always hugely enjoyed swimming. My forte was—if I can say it that way—in floating. I possessed almost unlimited capacity for floating on my back—for however long: could almost take a nap meanwhile. . . . That is to say I was very much at home in the water. I never could do any of the surprising stunts of the other boys when I was young but I was a first-rate aquatic loafer." [59]

Asked in 1877 whether he had cultivated his body in youth as he had in middle age, he answered: "More so, oh! And I used to be more proud when I went to the [swimming] bath and someone would say that I was the finest-shaped youngster in the bath, than I have been of all my literary admiration since." The pride and emotional excitement of Whitman's handsome self floating among the nude young men is evident in several of his poems. Thus the persona proclaims: "And who possesses a perfect and enamour'd body? for I do not believe any one possesses a more perfect or enamour'd body than mine * * * *" [60] The line occurs in "Excelsior" (1856), a poem with the very title Longfellow had used for his celebrated lyric about the nebulous Anglo-Saxon culture hero who climbs the transcendental Alps of human progress. In shaping the persona of *Leaves of Grass*, Whitman Americanized Longfellow's hero, gave him brawn and a suntan, and appropriated the role for his idealized self.

Testimony about Whitman's physical condition following the initial appearance of *Leaves of Grass* was provided by four contemporaries—Fanny Fern, Henry David Thoreau, Bronson Alcott, and Moncure Daniel Conway. Fanny Fern's intemperate praise of Whitman's face, his "fine, ample chest," and "his voice! rich, deep, and clear, as a clarion note," could hardly be called objective. [61] But the testimony of the two inquisitive Transcendentalists who came to Brooklyn in 1856 to have a look at the poetic phenomenon appears to be reliable. Thoreau found Whitman a man of "remarkably strong, though coarse, nature, of a sweet disposition, and much prized by his friends. Though peculiar and rough in his exterior, his skin (all over (?)) red, he is essentially a gentleman." The celebration of sensuality in Whitman's poems disturbed him, because he felt that men have not been ashamed of their animal natures without reason. But to his credit Thoreau concluded: "He is awfully good. . . . He is a great fellow." Alcott was impressed by Whitman as a "God" and as "broad-chested, rouge-fleshed, Bacchus-browed, bearded like a satyr, and rank. . . ." He found Whitman to be a slow talker and "swaggy in his walk." "He has never been sick, he says, nor taken medicine, nor sinned; and so is quite innocent of repentance and man's fall. A bachelor, he professes a great respect for women. . . . Age 38." [62]

Walt Whitman and the Body Beautiful

Conway, a Unitarian minister, wrote to Emerson that Whitman looked like the 1855 photograph but was "rather narrow behind the eyes." That detail might imply that the poet's cephalic index—the ratio of the breadth of the head above the ears to the length of the head—was low, signifying an unsophisticated intellectual development. (Conway later amended this impression, alleging that Whitman's head was "oviform in every way," thus anticipating the soon-to-be-familiar boast of the poet's perfect Nordic physiognomy.) He described Whitman—"his gray clothing, his blue-gray shirt, his iron-gray hair, his swart, sun-burnt face and bare neck"—sunning himself on a little grassy square in Brooklyn. Another time, observing Whitman swimming at the seashore, he was puzzled by "the reddish tanned face and neck of the poet [which] crowned a body of lily-like whiteness and a shapely form"—hardly the specifications of a bronzed and well-muscled athlete—and by the "strange contrast" between the grizzled hair and beard and "the almost infantine fulness and serenity of his face." Conway, the biographer of Thomas Paine, made note of Whitman's "insouciance" as they "sauntered along the streets" and observed that Whitman was not the proletarian he affected to be, but, like Paine, had been deluded by his Quaker heritage to believe that by living simply he had entered into the working class spirit.[63] Conway's insight into Whitman's bourgeois pride is confirmed in the poet's celebrated public letter to Emerson (1856), which declares that "a profound person can easily know more of the people than they know of themselves." And a "Calamus" poem ingenuously admits that the poet is uneasy in his affected proletarian role:

> *After to-day* I inure myself to run, leap, swim, wrestle, fight, * * *
> To speak readily and clearly—to feel at home among *common*
> *people* * * * *[64]

The diminishing bravado with which the poet showed off his mythic body in the third edition of *Leaves of Grass* may betray an awareness that his health was not altogether sound. The frontispiece portrait of Whitman, based on a painting by Charles Hine, depicts a refined face with sunken eyes and puffy but delicate features; photographs taken during this period confirm a pronounced stoutness. Nevertheless, the flesh-and-blood Whitman impressed many. For example, Helen Price, a family friend since 1856, commented on his "superabundant vitality and strength." A Boston printer who recalled the poet's appearance at the time he was seeing the 1860 volume of poems through the press, told of "his splendid health and impressive physique," his rugged outdoor look, and his sunburned neck. Beholding the poet in "Pfaff's Cave," the gathering place of literary Bohemians, William Dean Howells was impressed by his "fine head, with a cloud of Jovian hair upon it, and a branching beard and mustache, and gentle eyes. . . ." But Whitman's literary enemy, William Winter, who observed the allegedly "eccentric" poet in the same restaurant, poked fun at his tippling "a little brandy and water," his "bovine air of omniscience," the vulgar display of his "brawny anatomy," and his "hirsute chest and complacent visage." Another literary enemy, Thomas Wentworth Higginson, sneeringly labeled this appearance Whitman's "Boweriness."[65]

The condition of the poet's health at the end of his fourth decade tends to belie the myth of his quenchless vigor. In 1858 he suffered his first known episode of "sunstroke," which Dr. Philip Marshall Dale interprets as "a small cerebral hemorrhage," one of the many he was destined to endure.[66] Many of his newspaper articles in the *Brooklyn Daily Times*, 1857–59, demonstrated an interest in consumption and in the methods used to effect its cure; others dealt with the care of the sick and injured, the availability of healthful food and pure water, and the need for exercise. Moreover, his frequent visits to patients in the New York hospitals and his careful observation of medical care showed a sympathy with physical suffering which could have stemmed from an apprehension of his own imperfect health as well as a psychological need to be close to men who live in agony and on the verge of death.

A notebook jotting dated two days after the onset of the Civil War suggests that the personal crisis which the poet apparently experienced before going to Washington in 1862 may have been aggravated by his poor physical condition: "I have this day, this hour, resolved to inaugurate for myself a pure, perfect, sweet, clean-blooded robust body, by ignoring all drinks but water and pure milk, and all fat meats, late suppers—a great body, purged, cleansed, spiritualized, invigorated body." Could the poet, as he approached his forty-fourth birthday, have been thinking seriously of conditioning himself for war service? The Whitman who left for Washington later that year was overweight, ruddy, and gray bearded, and, as he subsequently remarked, "I was no spring chicken then."[67]

Evidence of Whitman's physical condition during the last three decades of his life—a period of continual physical decline—is more ample than that for the earlier years. Much of it is based on the observations of competent physicians.

Three devoted friends provide testimony about his health after he settled in Washington. John Burroughs, whose friendship with the poet began in 1863, was impressed by the magnetic and "broad-chested old fellow," who usually dressed like a farmer or sailor, by his "gray beard and moustache radiating from a broad, ruddy face," and by his "absorbing and devouring" eyes. After looking on as Whitman bathed, Burroughs observed: "such a handsome body, and such delicate-rosy flesh I never saw before. . . . he looked good enough to eat." He then judged the poet's physique to be "superb,"[68] but he later reflected that it was "curiously the body of a child; one saw that in its form, in its pink color, and the delicate texture of the skin. He [Whitman] took little interest in feats of strength, or in athletic sports. He walked with a slow rolling gait, indeed moved slowly in all ways; he always had an air of infinite leisure."[69] Thomas Donaldson, an employee of the Indian Bureau and later a Philadelphia attorney, observed that "Mr. Whitman, when in full health was physically slow of movement, and walked with a perceptive, heavy drag. I saw him many times in Washington in the sixties. At that time he used no cane, and his walk was always lazy-swaggy; and his response to questions very deliberate." (What Helen Price called his "elephantine roll"—a walk typical of persons whose legs are of uneven length—antedated his arrival in Washington; the poet himself alludes to it in his self-reviews of the fifties.)[70] Ellen O'Connor reported favorably on Whitman's physical appearance, his sturdiness, his daily bathing, and a purported physical fastidiousness that matched his loathing of coarse thought and speech; but she confirmed the fact that his stroke in 1873 had been preceded, over a span of many years, by the excruciating "occasional headaches" which the poet ingenuously attributed to his frequent "exposure to the fierce midday sun." She wrote in her recollections of Whitman: "He told us that his physician also held that the unusual combination that existed in his case, of a rapidly moving brain in a slow-moving body, was unfortunate. . . . Even the ability to stop thinking at will, and make his brain 'negative,' as he described a gift of his at that time of almost perfect health, did not insure him against those attacks of headache."[71] Her husband, William Douglas O'Connor, recalled that Whitman survived during the 1866–71 period only because of his "masterly composure" and his knack of taking things easy. "He would come in [to his job] of a morning," O'Connor said, "sit down, work like a steam engine for an hour or so, then throw himself back in his chair, yawn, stretch himself, pick up his hat, and go out."[72]

Whitman's paralytic stroke and the invalidism which ensued had been preceded for more than a decade by premonitions that he was taxing his health and endangering his life. Physical and emotional stress forced him to withdraw from his hospital labors a few months after he undertook them in 1863. He began them again in January, 1864, working, as he said, with the most "lamentable cases," his system "doubtless weakened by anxiety" and infected by "hospital malaria." According to Dr. Dale's analysis, his condition had become noticeably worsened:

> . . . he was well except for occasional sensations of "fullness in the head" and attacks of faintness. These annoying symptoms increased both in frequency and severity until mid-July when he was "prostrated," undoubtedly by a small cerebral hemorrhage. . . . It is likely that [his] blood pressure was somewhat elevated but unlikely that it was very high. Certainly the capillaries and the smallest arteries of the brain were in a condition of fragility, the result of degenerative changes, and it was this condition that prompted the headache and fullness of the head which caused him so much discomfort. . . .[73]

Following another breakdown, early in 1865, he admitted to a correspondent that he no longer "had the unconscious and perfect health I formerly had. . . . It is my first appearance in the character of a man not entirely well." According to Dr. Dale, he "continued to have small strokes until the autumn of 1869 when he was stricken so severely that he was partially paralyzed. He recovered well, however, and remained in reasonably good condition until 4 January 1873, when he awoke one night to find his arm and leg partially paralyzed. The leg was worse involved than the arm—the face and organs of speech hardly at all."[74]

As Gay Wilson Allen remarks, Whitman's "emotional up-

Walt Whitman and the Body Beautiful

heaval might well have helped bring on the physical decline that became obvious in 1871–72; or, on the other hand, his physical condition, which had not been good for several years, could have been mainly responsible for his emotional state a year earlier. Who can say which was cause and which effect?"[75] The flood tide of poetic creation between 1854 and 1872 had taxed the poet's emotional resources, and there is some plausibility in his explanation that the "volcanic emotional fires" in his poems represent "about the largest emotional element that has appeared anywhere" and that if this tendency had not been "controlled by a potent rational balance," it would have "wrecked him as disastrously as ever storm and gale drove ship to ruin." It was these passions, he said, "aroused to intense activity and unnatural strain during the four years of the War, and his persistent labors in the hospitals, that have resulted in his illness and paralysis since."[76] His emotional reaction to the carnage and suffering and his efforts to control his passionate nature obviously lay close to the root of his physical breakdown. "I am faithful, I do not give out," exclaims the persona in "The Wound-Dresser," trying, like Whitman himself, to rein in his turbulent emotions. The troubles within the Whitman family, the uncertain future of *Leaves of Grass*, and the poet's unresolved erotic impulses all added to his emotional pressures and speeded his collapse.

Dr. Daniel Longaker, who attended Whitman during the last year of his life, attributed the postwar breakdown to "blood poisoning absorbed from certain gangrenous wounds in patients whom he had at that time [1863–65] closely attended" and "the emotional strain of those terrible years." He noted the general worsening of the poet's health, culminating in the 1873 paralytic attack, which was "greatly aggravated" by the death of his mother that same year. "This paralysis more than once brought him to death's door. It let up a little in the late seventies and early eighties, and steadily deepened until the end." In his more dispassionate moments, Whitman concurred in these views. He blamed his physical breakdown on his "overstrained labors from 1862 to '65, in army hospitals and after battles, and on the field," where he had nursed and "ministered to 100,000 persons," on "hospital malaria," and on a gangrenous infection originating in 1863 from "a bad cut or abrasion of the hand" when he had assisted the doctors in an amputation. But he conceded that his collapse had also come about through "the excessive labors and worriments of that period." These factors, he admitted, "no doubt thoroughly entered and partially sapped, even Whitman's splendid physique." Following the war, he recalled, he had managed to overcome "some three or four" major attacks, "till, at last the culminating stroke of paralysis which though relieved by a few favorable lulls, struck deep, and has prostrated him since, 20 years." [77]

Dr. William Beverly Drinkard, a European-trained Virginian who visited the invalid almost daily after his collapse, attributed his patient's "markedly serious" condition to a combination of physical and emotional stresses. In April, 1873 (for "a couple of weeks' trial," according to Whitman's recollection), Dr. Drinkard, an electrical specialist, treated him by inducing a mild current into the afflicted areas of his body through the use of Gaiffe's battery. The poet seemed to derive a slight improvement of the circulation in his leg from this therapy, but his locomotion remained impaired for the rest of his life. Dr. Drinkard, whom Whitman later called "one of my true friends whose affection was something to be recked of," prescribed bromides for the poet's headaches, "the phosphate of iron, quinin, and strychnia" as a tonic, a mild laxative to relieve the constipation which would eventually become chronic, and the body massage that the poet continued to receive during his remaining years. Above all, he encouraged the invalid to struggle against despair and his habitual lassitude and brooding, and in this manner, according to the poet, saved his life. [78] And in view of the persistent questionings of Whitman's essential soundness by two generations of scholars, serious attention must be paid to Dr. Drinkard's apparently dispassionate testimony that Whitman was essentially free from physical and psychic abnormalities: "Mr. Whitman's physical mould, his habits of life, tastes and mental constitution, are I think, the most natural I have ever encountered." [79]

The massive stroke that felled the poet left him for the remainder of his life, as he said, "a *half-paralytic.*" [80] He removed to Camden where, despite some periods of respite, his body deteriorated steadily during the last nineteen years of his life. Dr. Matthew Grier, the first of his Philadelphia-based physicians, who attended him in 1873 when he suffered a physical setback, generally concurred in Dr. Drinkard's diagnosis, maintaining that the invalid suffered chiefly from gastrointestinal ailments, cerebral anemia, and the aftermath of prolonged emotional strain. "He thinks it has been coming on for many years," the poet told Mrs. O'Connor, "says I need rest, rest for a long time & social exhilaration." The brusque-mannered Dr. Grier prescribed small amounts of whiskey, the "injecture syringe," and asafoetida pills (commonly used as a stimulant for the sympathetic nervous system and as a carminative to relieve flatulence) and employed the battery to stimulate the nerves in the poet's sacrolumbar region and lower limbs. (Battery treatment for a very broad range of ailments was in the mainstream of medical practice in the seventies and eighties.) But Whitman later claimed that such therapy, whether administered by Dr. Grier or other (unspecified) doctors, had never benefited him.[81] One medical historian asserts that Whitman generally improved under Dr. Grier's care, but it is not known whether Dr. Grier was still attending him when he suffered another paralytic stroke in 1875.[82]

Whitman was able to announce the next year that he had enjoyed "partial recovery (a sort of second wind, or semi-renewal of the lease of life) from the prostration of 1874–75" and that he had "got over the worst of it." In 1876 he began the practice of spending some weeks each year not far from Camden at the farm of George Stafford at Timber Creek, New Jersey, where he relaxed in the open air. He explained the secret of his physical survival with a stoicism that was worthy of Samuel Johnson's Rasselas: "The trick is, I find, to tone your wants and tastes low enough, and make much of negatives, and of mere daylight and the skies."[83] In the prose preface to the 1876 edition of Leaves of Grass, the crippled poet informed his readers of his tedious attacks of paralysis but assured them that he was "without serious pain" at the moment. Nevertheless, he bade farewell to his former state of rugged health: "At the eleventh hour, under grave illness, I gather up the pieces of Prose and Poetry . . . nearly all of them (sombre as many are, making this almost Death's book) composed in by-gone atmospheres of perfect health. . . ."[84]

For the next several years his health was not seriously altered. Edward Carpenter, the young English author, was impressed by the elderly-looking man who dragged his paralyzed leg and could barely walk but was cheerful, free of mannerisms, and brighteyed. Grace Gilchrist recalled that at fifty-eight Whitman looked seventy, was clear-complexioned, walked with a stick, and recited and sang in a rather harsh "high baritone voice."[85] Dr. S. Weir

Mitchell, the famed novelist, poet, and neurologist who began caring for the poet in the 1870's, examined him in March, 1878, another of Whitman's low periods, and found no heart trouble, sunstroke, or worsening of the paralysis, as the poet had feared. Camden, the doctor declared, was a bad place for him; he needed the mountain air. The next year the poet left on his celebrated journey to Denver.[86] Although the strain of travel brought about his collapse at his brother Jeff's house in St. Louis on the return trip, he was well enough the following year to visit Dr. Bucke in Canada and to deliver a lecture on the death of Lincoln in Boston in 1881. The press described him on the latter occasion as a gray-haired man who "walked haltingly" and was distinguished by "venerable hair and beard, but sturdy presence." A year later, Thomas Donaldson sketched him as immaculate and rosy-hued, "his mouth and teeth good, his figure that of an athlete."[87]

The poet's physical decline was gradual but steady. *Specimen Days* implies that these years are filled with seldom-abated agonies. "About two-thirds of the time," he admitted laconically, "I am quite comfortable."[88] In 1882, Dr. Dowling Benjamin, whose offices were near George Whitman's house in Camden, where the poet resided, diagnosed the poet's chief complaint as a liver condition and prescribed the strong medicinal dosages which Whitman abhorred and which generally disagreed with him. In July, 1885, his increasing debility culminated in another "sunstroke" attack. He became cranky and overweight; his digestion and bladder seemed to be failing; his blocked urinary tract necessitated the use of a catheter. Daily, his feeble body was lowered into a triangular metal tub, about four feet long and one foot deep, in the bedroom of his little house on Mickle Street, where he then lived.[89]

In 1886 the brilliant Canadian physician William Osler first visited the poet, and the doctor continued to attend Whitman over a three-year period that lasted until he was appointed professor of the principles and practice of medicine at Johns Hopkins University. In the midst of the characteristic clutter in which the poet lived, Dr. Osler beheld a pleasant, handsome, and hirsute old man, whom he admiringly described as "a fine figure of a man who has aged beautifully, or more properly speaking, majestically." He continued to visit the poet, sometimes in the company of Dr. Bucke or other physicians. In October, 1886, he took Whitman to consult

Walt Whitman and the Body Beautiful

with the distinguished Philadelphia ophthalmologist Dr. William Fisher Norris.[90] Although the poet repeatedly complained that no one appreciated how critically ill he was, Dr. Osler understood that his patient's crankiness masked a tenacious will to live, and he predicted that Whitman might survive "for months, even years." He gained the invalid's esteem by respecting his deep dislike of medicines. And, comprehending like Dr. Drinkard that the poet's habitual torpor and despair were dangerous, he counseled him to take "carpe diem" for his motto. This advice was part of the creed by which Dr. Osler shaped his own life, for he believed that finding one's work and pursuing it day by day was the noblest and most healthful of personal dedications.[91]

The old poet lingered on, yielding only an inch at a time. To a young friend he declared typically: "I am still here in my shanty in Mickle Street—probably *let down a peg or two* from when I saw you last, but not much different—mentally the same—physically a sad wreck. . . ."[92] Dr. Bucke, who for many years made sure that Whitman was receiving the best possible medical care, personally attended the poet during the nearly fatal crisis of 1888. Whitman declared that he was "quite sure Dr. Bucke this time saved my life; that if he had not been here to roll up his sleeves and stay and work and watch, it would have been a final call. . . ." When Dr. Bucke was at home in London, Ontario, the poet sent reports almost daily to him in the form of letters and postal cards: "they are all about my bowels, head, symptoms, diet—the professional facts which a doctor knows what to do with," he remarked. Following a visit by Dr. Osler and Dr. Henry Redwood Wharton, of Philadelphia, in 1888, when he appeared to be suffering from diabetes and a prostate condition, he wrote Bucke: "Drs: [*sic*] Osler and Wharton have been here—it is as we tho't the enlarged prostrate [*sic*] gland incident is senilia—A short visit not much talk—Wharton was very good. . . ." He also informed Dr. Bucke regularly of visits by Drs. James Francis Walsh, Alexander McAlister, and Daniel Longaker, of Camden, and John Kearsley Mitchell, of Philadelphia, and of the succession of male nurses who tended him as his strength ebbed away. Besides keeping Dr. Bucke and his many correspondents posted, during the 1880's, on the state of his bowels, fevers, and headaches, Whitman told the public about his physical condition in brief verses, biographical writings, prefaces, newspaper releases, and conversations with visitors.[93] As one critic irreverently remarks, "certainly there never was and never will be a more explicit record of a major poet's excretory problems."[94]

During the invalid's last four years, Horace Traubel, the poet's Boswell, chronicled the steady worsening of the old man's hearing and vision, the slowing of his speech, the failing of his locomotion, the souring of his temperament, and his tedious bedridden days.[95] At times he was consoled by the fact that he had been left with a modicum of energy: "Well, it's a comfort to think I'm not as ill as I might be," he quipped. But in recognition of his diminishing strength, he admitted: "It is time for another peg to be taken out. . . ."[96] Peg after peg was taken out. But as Dr. Osler had foreseen, the old poet had staying power.

An anonymous self-review of Whitman's final Lincoln lecture mingles myth and reality in the description of his appearance: "hoarse and half blind . . . physically wreck'd. But his voice and magnetism are the same."[97] Some of the final verses record his physical distress. One lyric complains of his "ungracious glooms, aches, lethargy, constipation, whimpering, *ennui*." "The Dismantled Ship" compares his "rusting, mouldering" self to an "old, dismasted, gray and batter'd ship." "To the Sun-Set Breeze" pictures him "old, alone, sick, weak-down, melted-worn with sweat." A year before his death he told William Sloane Kennedy: "I realize perfectly well that definition Epictetus gives of the living personality and body, 'a little spark of a soul dragging a great lummox of a corpse body clumsily to and fro about.'" And in the same year the old paralytic wrote:

> I sing of life, yet mind me well of death:
> To-day shadowy Death dogs my steps, my seated shape, and has
>   for years—
> Draws sometimes close to me, as face to face.[98]

Six months before his death, he told his sister Hannah: "I am half blind and deaf." The following month he explained to Dr. Bucke: "My disease is now called *progressive* paralysis."[99] Thereafter, the decline was precipitous.

The best assessment of Whitman's physical condition toward the end of his life, Dr. Josiah C. Trent's evaluation based on the autopsy report and other medical data, indicates that the old poet's body had become massively infected and confirms a long history

Walt Whitman and the Body Beautiful

of physical deterioration. Tubercles pervaded much of his system. A left adrenal cyst might have contributed to his lifelong "lassitude and inertia" or even to his paralysis. His body bore evidence of excessive fatty tissue, "hypertrophy of the prostate," and possible brain damage. According to Dr. Trent, a plausible diagnosis of the poet's maladies just prior to his death should read:

> Pulmonary tuberculosis, far advanced, right; atelectasis of left lung; tuberculous empyema, left; bronchopleural fistula, left; disseminated abdominal tuberculosis; tuberculous abscesses of sternum, fifth rib and left foot; cyst of left adrenal gland; chronic cholecystitis and cholelithiasis [inflammation of the gall bladder and the tendency to form gallstones]; cerebral atrophy; cerebral arteriosclerosis; benign prostatic hypertrophy; pulmonary emphysema; cloudy swelling of kidneys; history of hypertension (?).[100]

Medicine, Health, and Hospitals

"I Am He Bringing Help for the Sick"

2

NOT LONG AFTER HE SETTLED IN Camden, Whitman told some
friends: "If I had to choose, were I looking about for a profession, I
should choose that of a doctor. Yes; widely opposite as science and
the emotional elements are, they might be joined in the medical
profession, and there would be great opportunities for developing
them. Nowhere is there such a call for them. . . . Oh, a doctor
should be a superb fellow. He does not approach at present what
he should be."[1]

This opinion was not capricious. For decades, Whitman had
been a fascinated observer of doctors and medicine. He had read
and reviewed books and articles on medical topics. Before the
Civil War, he had numbered physicians among his friends. As a
resident of Brooklyn, long before he visited the disabled soldiers in
and near Washington, he had frequented hospitals and observed
the treatment of the sick. During the war, he served as a volunteer
hospital aide. And because he required much medical attention following the war, he remained keenly interested, according to Dr.
Longaker, in "medical men and matters medical."[2] Consequently,
Dr. Bucke's assertion that Whitman absorbed medical truths by intuition understates the poet's knowledge of the body. Bucke argued that Whitman probably knew little or nothing of technical
physiology" but nevertheless "recognized and acted upon one of
the deepest of all physiological truths," *i.e.*, the dignity of man's
bodily and sexual instincts; and, as a consequence, he probably did
more for "the future of the human race than all the physiologists
and doctors of this generation."[3]

In fact, Whitman had a better-than-average layman's acquaintance with physiology and medicine at mid-century. His news-paper pieces devoted to medical and health topics—many of them hardly more than the digests or "scissorings" of nontechnical writ-ings—reveal no great expertise. Nevertheless, he acquired a con-siderable knowledge by extensive but unsystematic reading of popular medical writings, observation of doctors, and visits to hospitals. Some of his medical ideas now appear to have been for-ward-looking, some seem to have been medical platitudes, and others reflect the medical aberrations of the day. He advocated fresh air, adequate exercise, the full and rounded development of the physical and mental self, and the treatment of patients in terms of their total personality and organic being. But many of his no-tions about the physiology of sex, the healthy person's immunity to infection, and the function of the skin, for example, were out-dated during his lifetime and now seem quaint or ingenuous.

To comprehend Whitman's medical standards and his skepti-cism toward conventional medical practice, one must recall the unsophisticated state of the healing arts in the years before *Leaves of Grass* appeared. Formally trained physicians generally pre-scribed an awesome array of medicines. According to one re-spected doctor, "whiskey in some form was the most popular medicament in the Pharmacopoeia as in the saloon" but calomel was the physicians' "sheet-anchor of hope."[4] According to a doc-tor whom Whitman knew, "Within the last fifty years no less than four different methods of treating ordinary fevers have prevailed: the bark and wine practice, the cold effusion practice, the bleeding and saline practice, and the mercurial and opium practice." The physician complained that many allopathic physicians (those who believed in the use of agents—chiefly chemical—to counteract the effects of disease) still bled their patients, although most of them could not justify the practice on pragmatic grounds.[5] Allopathic treatments for a broad range of ailments, according to another doctor with whose views Whitman was familiar, included "bleed-ing, cupping, leeching, scarifying, setoning [inserting a thread beneath the skin to create a discharge], blistering, causticizing, or creating lesions by other chemical or mechanical means," and pre-scribing huge dosages of purgatives and cathartics.[6] The wrong-headedness that characterized the usual treatment of illness was il-lustrated by Dr. John M. Galt in *The Treatment of Insanity* (1846),

Walt Whitman and the Body Beautiful

an anthology of essays and case histories which Whitman reviewed in the *Daily Eagle*. In the volume, the medical superintendents of asylums in several countries described the care (often involving harsh drugs, "the straight waistcoat," solitary confinement, and needless surgical procedures) of those whom they considered insane, including persons confined for the "disease" of masturbation. Whitman, who visited patients at the King's County Lunatic Asylum and who believed, like some of his enlightened contemporaries, that most victims of mental illness could be rehabilitated by timely and adequate institutional care and a balanced regimen, remarked that "the ailments of mind" are "no less deserving of compassion than a broken leg or fever." [7]

The "advent of strictly modern medicine," as a present-day scholar calls it, may be reckoned only from the 1820's, when the "Paris school," by applying the scientific method, began to isolate and identify specific diseases and their causes. [8] Four decades later, Dr. Oliver Wendell Holmes, the poetic professor of anatomy at the Harvard Medical College and a product of the "Paris school," declared that anatomy, which "studies the organism in space," had become firmly established in medical training but that physiology, which "studies it in time," was just beginning to profit from the use of the microscope and new scientific techniques. He remarked that "if the whole materia medica, *as now used*, could be sunk to the bottom of the sea, it would be all the better for mankind,—and all the worse for the fishes." [9] As late as the Civil War, the typical surgeon still performed operations in unsanitary surroundings; he usually wore an apron over his street clothes and used the same knife and marine sponge (after rinsing them in tap water) upon successive patients, who were seldom properly cleansed before being operated on, and, perhaps trusting to the ancient fable of "laudable pus," he helped to spread gangrene and to transmit infection from patient to patient. Not until the 1860's did Dr. Stephen Smith of New York's Bellevue Hospital initiate Lister's antiseptic techniques in America—the use of carbolic acid and cotton wool to cleanse wounds and the sterilization of surgical instruments. And not until the 1870's was there any marked progress in etiology, the identification of the bacterial and viral causes of disease. [10]

Understandably, Whitman was intolerant of the more brutal

medical practices of his formative years. Bleeding he considered "full of nonsense, to the very brim." The physician who has once "begun his purging, blistering, prostrating career," he complained, will continue to do so out of prejudice and greed. His newspaper pieces in the *Daily Eagle* kept up a steady barrage against drugs and druggists. After what must have been a traumatic experience, he charged a Myrtle Street druggist with nearly poisoning him by selling him oxalic acid rather than the tartaric acid that was needed for Mrs. Whitman's baking. He accused medical men of persevering in their harsh treatments and of prescribing harmful drugs simply because the remedies may presumably have worked in the past: "Blindly thus, they sacrifice human life to their own miserable vanity." [11] Speculating on the claims of the rival schools of medicine—allopathy, homeopathy, and hydropathy, he approvingly quoted "the great French physiologist and pathologist Magendie" to the effect that experiments in the treatment of typhus and malignant fevers had proven that patients who are given "the common simples of domestic practice" do better than those who are treated with the remedies of the pharmacopoeia, and that those patients fare best who are left "to the common-sense management of the nurses, without any medicines at all." [12]

Without denying altogether the merits of the orthodox physicians, Whitman was offended by what he considered their slavish adherence to precedent and their willingness to short-circuit the natural process of healing by ignoring the fact that diseases often have hereditary causes or develop through a long and complex chain of circumstances. That physicians, whatever their book learning, should prescribe some half-understood medicines after asking the patient a few routine questions was to Whitman the most arrogant presumption. Indeed, he insisted that genuine cures can result only from a careful investigation of the whole person— an attitude to which he clung for the rest of his life. In response to a physician who had, not unreasonably, taunted him with "being tinctured with the dangerous [medical] ultraism of the age," editor Whitman accused the orthodox doctors of "dogmatism," the failure to investigate novel medical systems, and an insufficient reverence for the human body. [13]

Although he became more appreciative of scientific medical practice as he grew older and as he observed the dedicated labors

Walt Whitman and the Body Beautiful

of trained physicians, his medical ideas remained a mixture of the orthodox, the semiscientific, and the intuitive approaches to health.

The self-reliant healer-persona in *Leaves of Grass* exemplifies the principle that some men are gifted with the instinctive power to heal others. Particularly in the first three editions, he resembles an unorthodox dispenser of people's medicine who teaches every sufferer to rely on his inborn resiliency and on the kindly powers of nature. In the decade before the poems first appeared, Whitman had apparently intended to disseminate the gospel of health in the form of popular lectures or manuals of instruction. But sensing that his gospel should become an integral element of his poetic programme, he created the compassionate healer-persona who articulates the message, throughout the poems, that bodily health is a key to spirituality. In his dual role of healer and onlooker, the persona discloses Whitman's own attitudes toward health and the health sciences. Physiological concepts derived from the poet's observation of conservative and unorthodox medical practices enrich the poems. Whitman's reading about health matters, his increasingly frequent hospital visits, and his growing appreciation of trained doctors are objectified in the *persona*'s sharpened powers of observation and his revelations of acute physical suffering. The development of the healer-persona in the poems parallels Whitman's own development as an observer of "matters medical"—a process climaxed during the Civil War by the near fusion of Walt Whitman the military hospital attendant with Walt Whitman the healer-persona of the *Drum-Taps* poems.

Among the medical unorthodoxies that helped Whitman to fashion this healer-persona in the earlier editions of *Leaves of Grass* were homeopathy, Thomsonianism, and hydropathy, the practitioners of which distrusted medical professionalism and maintained that they alone could cure the bodies and spirits of the masses. (The distinctions between various medical heresies and orthodox practice often proved to be quite nebulous.) These schools of healing regarded most illness as a derangement of the total organism; they supposed nature and the sufferer's own vital powers to be the essential sources of cure. Therefore they believed that the medical practitioner's intuition and compassion were more important to successful healing than any formal training.[14] A similar faith in nature's curative forces and in the wonder-working power of personal sympathy is, of course, an attribute of Whitman's healer-persona.

Fundamental to these schools of healing was the ancient therapeutic dogma: Nature cures; physicians treat. Nature, it was assumed, works constantly to repair and regulate a disordered organism through the agency of the *vis medicatrix naturae*—the individual's vital, health-giving force which Whitman's contemporaries sometimes equated with bodily electricity. Unorthodox practitioners denounced the supposed neglect of this vitalistic principle on the part of allopathic physicians, whose "heroic" dosings and potent remedies they also deplored. Thus, Dr. Samuel C. F. Hahnemann, the founder of homeopathy (the practice of dispensing an infinitesimal quantity of "what ails you" in what Dr. Holmes mockingly described as oceans of water), argued that disease is not ordinarily a localized condition affecting a specific organ but "a derangement of the 'immaterial vital principle' pervading and animating the body." He believed that a sufferer, encouraged by the healer, can get well because "the native army" (the patient's indwelling recuperative powers) will respond to his own *and* the practitioner's faith in God and in nature's laws.[15] Dr. Edward H. Dixon declared that homeopathy is to be thanked "for the great truth it has helped to teach us [physicians], of the utter uselessness of medicine in most cases." For by dispensing sugar pills and a measure of hopefulness, and intervening seldom in the operation of nature's own healing powers, he felt, the homeopaths had done as much to cure the sick as had their allopathic brethren. These were Whitman's sentiments, too. Half-humorously, the poet said that the "excellence" of the hydropathic and homeopathic schools of medicine "is nearly altogether of a negative kind.—They may not cure, but neither do they kill. . . ." Moreover, the American practice of homeopathy, as Martin Kaufman observes, was tinctured with Swedenborgianism and Transcendentalism—two ideologies that were familiar to the healer-poet of *Leaves of Grass*.[16]

Whitman had ample opportunity to learn about homeopathy. The "homeopathic system" had been established since 1825 in New York, where some three hundred homeopathic physicians were in practice at mid-century. His old friend and occasional walking companion William Cullen Bryant had become a convert

Walt Whitman and the Body Beautiful

to homeopathy in the 1830's and in 1869 was elected president of the board of the Homoeopathic College in New York City. Whitman recalled Bryant as "a great homeopathist—a great Unitarian," who had delivered "two or three lectures on the subject" of homeopathy—a probable reminiscence of Bryant's lectures "in defence of the system" in 1842 when, as Bryant observed, homeopathy seemed to be "carrying all before it."[17] If Whitman shared the homeopathists' distrust of heroic dosages and their reliance on the body's inherent ability to cure itself (he, too, called it the *vis*),[18] he did not endorse their well-publicized methodology.

The assumption that formal medical training is not necessary to the physician's art was strenuously urged by the Thomsonians—the "steam doctors" and herbalists whose botanical prescriptions were based on folk medicine and, rather loosely, on Justus Liebig's equation of bodily heat with physical vitality. Thomsonian practitioners, together with the eclectics, or "reformed" Thomsonians, had treated as many as four million American patients by 1840. Contending that the trained professional physician is a member of a privileged caste and therefore is "superfluous" to the healing arts in a democratic society, Thomsonians urged each person to become his own doctor and each family to become its own medical center. Rejecting the "ostentatious verbiage" and the "meaningless taxonomy" of the medical colleges, they insisted that only those individuals who "had a special knack" for healing could be successful healers.[19] This very "knack," raised to a godlike power, characterizes the healer-persona of *Leaves of Grass*.

Hydropathy, which combined internal and external water therapy, dietary reforms, personal hygiene, and a hodgepodge of medical techniques, was yet another deviant health practice that affected Whitman's medical outlook. In an era when most Americans were an unwashed people who feared that frequent bathing could lower their resistance to disease and when indoor plumbing was only an innovation, hydropathists publicized the benefits of personal and public sanitation, reasoning that the skin's capillary action draws off impure liquids within the body and that pure water, internally imbibed or externally applied, restores the body's wholesomeness and chemical balance. The practice of hydropathy had an immense international vogue. When *Leaves of Grass* first appeared, hydropathy in New York boasted half a dozen journals, two hospitals, and about one hundred practitioners.[20] Advocates of the cult included Catharine Beecher, who implied that three glasses of water each day and a daily bath could hasten the millennium; Bronson Alcott, who suggested that drinking water and eating vegetables could help transform men into gods; and the English novelist Edward Bulwer-Lytton, who asserted that a course of water therapy had cured him—without painful aftereffects—of being a hopelessly debilitated literary man.[21]

Among the hydropathists whom Whitman knew was Dr. O. K. Sammis, who practiced medicine in New York and Brooklyn for a couple of decades before the Civil War and whom the Whitman family apparently consulted about Andrew Whitman's tuberculosis of the throat. For even though Walt had, in an 1858 editorial, sympathetically quoted a *Scalpel* article denying that the inhalation of water improves the functioning of the respiratory system, he apparently changed his mind five years later in approving Dr. Sammis's treatments. Like one who valued his own medical expertise in the curative arts, he wrote to his mother that Andrew's infection was "Dr. Sammis's *mucous membrane*, you know," and instructed her that Andrew's delicate throat lining should be left to heal itself without medication but with the help of a common-sense diet, warm water or vapor baths, gentle care, and the merciful workings of nature. Eight months later, however, Andrew Whitman was dead.[22]

Other water-cure practitioners whom Whitman knew were associated with the extensive water-cure enterprises of Fowler and Wells. Dr. Lydia (Mrs. Lorenzo) Fowler, the second woman in America to earn a medical degree and a popular lecturer on physiology to female audiences, was a hydropathic consultant to ladies. Dr. Joel Shew, a medical doctor who conducted a water-cure practice in New York City and was a member of the Fowler and Wells stable of authors, served, from 1848 until his death in 1855, as the founding editor of their *Water-Cure Journal and Herald of Reforms*, which the *New York Post* called "the most popular Health Journal in the world."[23] From this periodical, Whitman clipped articles on various phases of health and physiology. Dr. Russell Thacher Trall, called "the high priest of the water-cure system," founded Trall's New York Hydropathic and Physiological School in 1853. His *Hydropathic Encyclopedia* (1851), a bulky opus covering a broad spectrum of physiological, medical, and pseudo-medical topics, was apparently known to Whitman. Among the encyclopedia's laudable features were an insistence on personal hygiene, a skepticism toward drugs, an advocacy of gradualism in the treatment of disease, a knowledgeable discussion of female physiology, and the same sort of hostility toward impure foods and the "swill milk" obtained from cattle who were fed on "distillery slops" that could be found in Whitman's newspaper pieces. The poet also reviewed Trall's *The Illustrated Family Gymnasium* (1857), an encyclopedic handbook of exercises, games, and calisthenics, in the *Brooklyn Daily Times*. And he may have examined Trall's *Sexual Physiology* (1866), which expresses many opinions on physical and sexual development that are very close to his own views. Moreover, Trall was an assistant editor of Fowler and Wells' *Life Illustrated* when that weekly paper published some of Whitman's best essays under the curiously medical title "New York Dissected" (1855–56).[24]

Dr. Trall's hydropathic establishment was a gathering place for reformers, spiritualists, and literati. During the period when they first visited Whitman, Thoreau and Alcott stayed there, and Alcott conducted a series of his celebrated "conversations" on such subjects as health, temperance, and purity. Although Alcott was untrained in medicine or physiology, his acceptance by Dr. Trall's hydropathic students as an oracle of health delighted him: "I find myself esteemed as the best Doctor under the sun, if not Esculapius, the very God of Healing to soul and body both," he told his wife.[25] A decade later, Whitman would experience a somewhat similar acceptance, by doctors and ailing soldiers, of his own efforts as a healer.

Whitman's columns in the *Daily Eagle* were generally favorable to hydropathy. The poet declared that James M. Gully's *Water Cure in Chronic Diseases*, a Fowler and Wells book, "deserves the good will of the whole community" and praised another water-cure volume, "edited by a water patient." He declared that drinking pure Croton River water, swimming, and bathing could curb dysentery and the appalling summertime death rate among children and infants. He called the People's Wash and Bath House in Manhattan, where baths could be purchased for a few cents, a benefactor of the poor, and he extolled Edward Gray's Brooklyn Swimming Bath, recommending that Brooklynites patronize its "salt Baths, hot and cold," because "most slight attacks of illness, and quite all fits of hypochondria, and such nervous diseases, are curable by a good bath." [26] Whitman, who regularly spent twenty minutes a day at Gray's Bath, perhaps to combat his own torpor, latent hypochondria, or feelings of sexual distress, prescribed a daily bath to overcome the universal tendency to consumption and to open the pores of the populace. "Every body knows, or ought to know, that the skin is a breathing apparatus," he told his readers. Warning them to avoid "the vile nostrums of the day" and urging the claims of hydropathy above those of conventional medicine, he advocated the bath, because "it will send the blood coursing quickly through the highways, by-ways, streets and lanes of your dull carcass, and mantle the cheek with a roseate hue, not to be imitated by carmine or rouge." [27]

Together with many enlightened contemporaries who were concerned with eliminating the apparent sources of diseases whose pathological cause they could not discover, Whitman campaigned, in his newspaper columns, to obtain a supply of pure drinking water and to promote sanitation and adequate sewage disposal. (He remained very proud of this phase of his journalism.) He also advocated bathing as a wholesome sport. Despite legal restrictions against bathing in certain public places, he expressed his outrage in 1858 when some New Yorkers were arrested at the beach "for the frightful crime of bathing." [28] But like Melville, who mocked the follies of the "wretched Soakites and Vapourites," [29] Whitman was irritated by the zeal of the hydropathic fanatics—"cold-water worshippers," he called them—for subjecting themselves to shower baths and hip baths and foot baths in all weathers and for insisting that those who failed to do likewise were unclean. Indeed, their sanctimonious stress on cleanliness may have been on his mind when he poetically mocked "those wash'd and trimm'd faces" or when he announced: "Washes and razors for foofoos . . . . for me freckles and a bristling beard." And in a private jotting, he demanded: Why should "the freckles and bristly beard of Jupiter [tokens of his godliness] be removed by washes and razors under the judgment of genteel squirts?" [30]

Whitman's writings contain refractions of water-cure lore. His self-reviews disparage the effete custom of tea drinking. (Had not Dr. Trall and Dr. Dixon declared that tea injures the brain, particularly in nervous persons? that it is a sedative resembling foxglove? that it stimulates perverse sensuality and onanism? and that imbibing warm tea is partly to blame for the prevailing debility among women?)[31] Small wonder that the heroic personages of *Leaves of Grass*, like so many paragons of health in Romantic literature, drink only the universal temperance beverage! The clear-skinned heroes in Whitman's poems who imbibe nothing but water include the carefree homosexual duo in "We Two Boys Together Clinging," the stalwart paterfamilias in "I Sing the Body Electric," the prophets of the future in "Mediums," and the poet-persona himself in "Starting from Paumanok." In various poems the persona bathes in the swimming-bath, on the shores of Manhattan, and on both seacoasts. He bathes to prepare himself for sleep with his beloved companion and to celebrate "the fitness and equanimity of things." Symbolically, the act of bathing represents personal and national well-being, sexual love, the cosmos, healing, death, inspiration, spiritual purification, and the sanctification of the body.[32]

Early in 1862, when his memories were stirred by frequent visits to New York hospitals, Whitman reminisced about his childhood impressions of the room behind Dr. J. W. Vanderhoef's drugstore on Fulton Street in Brooklyn Village: "Dr. [Charles] Ball (father of the later Police Physician [George Ball]), had his office there; and Dr. [Matthew] Wendell, too, we believe. Those two were the court physicians then; more omnipotent than eastern Pachas. Can any body who reads this call to mind having a tooth drawn, or any surgical operation performed in Vanderhoef's back room? It makes the writer shudder, even now, to think of the diabolical array of cold steel that room presented!"[33] Perhaps Whitman was reliving his own brief stint, at the age of ten, as an errand boy in the drugstore and office of Dr. Joseph G. T. Hunt, the picturesque village health officer who had served as ship's surgeon in the North African campaigns of Commodore Decatur. These scenes, and possibly Dr. Hunt's tales of heroism and carnage on shipboard, must have etched themselves into the boy's memory and ultimately have become part of the magic panorama of *Leaves of Grass*. (Because of the skepticism toward formally trained physicians which the adult Whitman often expressed, it is noteworthy that Drs. Wendell, Ball, and Hunt—the most prominent practitioners in Brooklyn Village—were not graduates of medical schools, but merely licentiates.)[34]

Out of his experiences between 1840 and 1855, Whitman once told some physicians, "came the physiology of *Leaves of Grass*, in my opinion the main part." In these years, he demonstrated an interest in public health, medicine, and the medical pseudo-sciences and visited dispensaries and operating rooms. According to Bucke's biography, he was acquainted with doctors as well as "hospitals, poorhouses, prisons, and their inmates" and was gladly received, because of his personal "magnetism," in the most squalid parts of the city.[35]

This interest in caring for the sick appears in some of his early fiction. In the first version of "The Child and the Profligate" (1841), a melodramatic parable about the redemptive power of a man's love for a boy, the profligate is a trained physician. Another profligate-healer redeemed by his love for a fatherless youth is Philip Marsh, in the first version of "Revenge and Requital" (1845). This tale pays tribute to the self-sacrificing men and women who, during the New York cholera epidemic of 1835–36, "went out amid the diseased, the destitute, and the dying, like merciful spirits—wiping the drops from hot brows, and soothing the agony of cramped limbs—speaking words of consolation to many a despairing creature, who else would have been vanquished by his soul's weakness alone—and treading softly but quickly from bedside to bedside, with those little offices which are so grateful to the sick, but which can so seldom be obtained from strangers." In the "noisome alleys and foul rear-buildings, in damp cellars and hot garrets . . . threading the dirtiest and wretchedest section of the city, between Chatham and Centre streets," Philip Marsh brought food, medicines, and consolation to the afflicted. His "gentle words, and gentle smiles," and "the sight of his pale calm face and his eyes moist with tears of sympathy, often divested death of its severest terrors," according to the tale. Like other examples of Whitman's early fiction, this story suggests his intimate encounters with physical suffering and demonstrates his ability to make literary use of such experiences.[36]

Thomas L. Brasher has cautioned that "Revenge and Requital" may intrigue "those who like to see adumbrations."[37] Philip Marsh, the story's "nurse, the friend, and the physician of the sick," seems to foreshadow the healer-persona of *Leaves of Grass*, whose presence allays pain and eases the onslaught of death; he prefigures the poet who walked the army hospitals a score of years

Walt Whitman and the Body Beautiful

after the story was written, comforting the young men who loved him for his goodness. In "Revenge and Requital," Whitman projects himself both as Philip Marsh, the guilt-ridden healer and befriender of young boys (an ambivalence in which one is indeed tempted "to see adumbrations"), *and* as Adam Covert, the son of Philip Marsh's victim. Young Adam, whose father had been slain and supplanted by Philip Marsh, is described as "a lad of about eighteen," or roughly Whitman's own age at the time of the cholera epidemic which forms the story's backdrop. Moreover, it is hard to resist the feeling that the lad's name is an augury: Adam Covert—the covert Adam of the New World who will surface in 1855, the birth-year of *Leaves of Grass* and the death-year of Walter Whitman, senior.

In 1845, Whitman also published "Some Fact-Romances," a group of five brief sketches based on quasi-medical themes. In the first of these a man who chooses to rescue his drowning sweetheart rather than his drowning sister subsequently dies of no known disease that is "treated in the medical works." In the second a deaf-mute girl is nursed by an old black woman, who labors to earn enough money to send the girl to "a certain New-York institution" for the deaf and dumb. (The Deaf and Dumb Asylum had existed in New York since 1816, and Whitman, as his newspaper pieces reveal, was concerned with the treatment of physically handicapped children.) In the third sketch (which further attests to Whitman's serious respect for medical institutions), a woman invalid dies during an arduous carriage ride home from the hospital after her husband has spurned the advice of her physicians and removed her from their care. In the fourth, a maudlin account of a visit to the Tombs prison, the nascent poet show his ability to transform his presence at hospitals and prisons into literary capital. In the last sketch, harking back to the days "when my mother was a girl" (and anticipating similar moments in "Song of Myself" and "The Sleepers"), Whitman tells a tale of psychological terror.[38]

In the years preceding *Leaves of Grass*, Whitman had apparently planned to present the gospel of physical improvability to the favorite target of his reformistic age, the young men and boys of America. His programme for attaining and preserving health was variously projected as a series of popular lectures, a manual of instructions, and a group of weekly magazine articles. The choice of a youthful male audience, whatever it might imply in terms of his known attraction to boys and young men, was consistent with the practice among reformers of addressing nontechnical (and essentially nonmedical) appeals for health, temperance, and good morals to American youth.[39] Beginning in the 1840's, he clipped and collected articles about health and hygiene from journals of general interest, health reform, water cure, and phrenology.[40] Early in 1849, he signed a note "to pay $25 as rent of store in Granada Hall," apparently in connection with an abortive plan to deliver a series of lectures on physical culture and thus supplement his meager earnings from journalism.[41] As to the projected volume, one notebook entry reads: "A Book for American Boys." Another entry reads: "American boys. A Book. Containing the Main Things—for the formation, reading, reference, and study for an American Young Man—for schools—for study—for individual use—one for the upper classes of every school in the United States."[42] Did Whitman hope to compile a textbook on health, like one of the potboilers put together by the Fowler and Wells stable of authors? Or did he hope to turn out a volume for the firm's successful "How To" series—fifty-cent manuals like *How To Do Business* and the several others of which he published favorable short notices in the *Brooklyn Daily Times*? His precise plans are unknown.

A manuscript outline of a prospectus or placard, dating from the 1840's or 1850's, labels a proposed series of articles "A first Class Original Work on *Manly Training*" and promises that it will be an "engrossing," nontechnical work which is original, "goes into full practical details," is written in a masterly manner, and is intended mainly "for American young men." The reward for faithfully heeding its advice "would be, for every man who reads it / *A Noble and Manly Physique*." It is alleged to be "of priceless value" to men in all walks of life. "For what can be more to a man than a *perfect condition of health and strength*?" Among the captions in the outline are these: "Could there be an entire nation of vigorous and sound men?" and "Strength of future Americans." One of Whitman's fragmentary jottings, possibly associated with this enterprise, seems to relate to these captions:

> I have now to conclude my New Suggestions of America, [with a picture and portrait I have rapidly drawn or model of an American young man of these States] by placing before myself here the portait of the future ideal or model young man of These States,

Walt Whitman and the Body Beautiful

and rapidly transcribing some of its features for you.— The portrait is mental and spiritual, as well as physical.—It represents a young man, such as we must in time copiously see in any city of America, in the [?] or shops, or on any farm, or upon the lakes or rivers, or along the sea-coast. Of this ideal American, the physique—now that we see such a one—to mark the genius of These States * * * *43

By juxtaposing the evidence of the outline with some of the comments in Whitman's notebooks, the clippings that he collected, and the newspaper pieces that he wrote, one may approximate the nature of his project to instill "Athleticism" in American young men. It would have elaborated upon Horace Greeley's slogan: "a due regard for health may justly be accounted a moral duty."44 It would have reflected what Thomas L. Brasher has summarized as the "cardinal tenets" of Whitman's "philosophy of health" during his tenure as editor of the Daily Eagle, 1846–48: "frequent bathing, temperance in eating, and abstinence from medicine," together with a plentiful supply of fresh air.45 It would have warned against chewing tobacco, taking unproved drugs, "excessive brain action," the insalubrity of city life, "angry passions and wicked desires," and such habits as "masturbation, inordinate going with women," overeating, and drunkenness. It would have urged plentiful exercise and well-ventilated public buildings to help prevent the many "attenuated forms and shrunken limbs and pallid faces in our streets." In keeping with Whitman's preoccupation, and that of his age, with the stomach as the key to health, it would have stressed the importance of a hearty diet ("beef, rice, fruit[,] potatoes, bread—these in plenty become a man, twice a day—perhaps even thrice a day; they are to be plain and rude"). It would have commended marriage, temperance, the vitalizing properties of clean air, the cultivation of all faculties, and the healing powers of nature.46 In order to encourage what the prospectus called "Fine Animal Man," it would have sounded the themes, later echoed in the Brooklyn Daily Times, that "a little too much of the animal physique, with its accompanying propensities," is better than being "narrow in the chest, shaky in the legs and pusillanimous in self-defence and self-assertion" and that "the teachers themselves should be athletes!" It would have justified vigorous, even violent, sports because they may help to "awaken in our people a proper sense of the utility, the importance and the beauty of full development of a physical man."47 The proposed work on manly training would have urged that an "American young man should carry himself with the finished and haughty bearing of the greatest ruler and proprietor."[48] But in an effort to please a broad audience, it would have avoided the heterosexual and homosexual Adamism that the poet later articulated in "Children of Adam" and "Calamus."

One manuscript note is significant because the glorification of a serene old age vibrates like an iron string throughout *Leaves of Grass*. On the back of a tax collector's form, the poet recorded the same ideal of mature American manhood that he voiced in the health projects, the newspaper editorials, and the poems. Although thirty is often alleged to be the age at which life loses its savor, it is, according to ancient Jewish lore, "the age of strength." Midway in the fourth decade of his own life, Whitman proclaimed that the prime of life begins in the thirties:

> Between the ages of thirty-five and eighty may be the perfection and realization of mortal life; rising above the previous periods in all that makes a person better, healthier, happier, more commanding, more beloved and more a realisee of love. The mind matured, the senses in full activity, the digestion even, the voice firm, the walk untired, the arms and chest sinewy and imposing, the hip joints flexible, the hands capable of many things, the complexion and blood pure, the breath sweet, the procreative power ever ready in man and the womb power in woman, the inward organs all sweetly performing their offices—during those years the universe presents its riches, its strength, its beauty, to be parts of a man, a woman. Then the body is ripe and the soul also and all the shows of nature attained and the production of thought in books.[49]

The passage may owe something to the opinions of Ludovico Cornaro, the sixteenth-century aristocrat whose celebrated treatise on achieving longevity through temperance was reissued by Fowler and Wells. The Venetian nobleman's declaration that "the regular and temperate life . . . is the true medicine of nature and best suited to man" could serve as Whitman's motto, and Cornaro's citation of the venerable saying that "a man cannot be a perfect physician save of himself alone" reveals how deeply rooted in human history are the attitudes of the hero–healer of "Song of Myself."[50] Whitman's poems idealize the healthy life which culminates in a hearty and serene old age. His notebooks record his admiration for the alert and splendid old man of ninety-four who had been a chaplain in Washington's army and who had never been

Walt Whitman and the Body Beautiful

sick—the apparent model for "The Centenarian's Story" (1865).[51] Echoing the very keynote sounded in many popular medical works at mid-century, his "Old Poets" essay (1890) declares that serene old age is the true mark of the healthy life: "Completed fruitage like this comes (in my opinion) to a grand old age, in man or woman, through an essentially sound continuated physiology and psychology (both important) and is the culminating glorious aureole of all and several preceding. Like the tree or vine just mention'd, it stands at last in a beauty, power and productiveness of its own, above all others, and of a sort and style uniting all criticisms, proofs and adherences."[52]

Whitman's long passage on "the perfection and realization of mortal life" was apparently copied or adapted from a newspaper or magazine. Likewise, his manuscript notes on the consequences of drinking alcohol, which his literary executor Thomas B. Harned cited as an example of the striking originality in Whitman's ideas about physiology, were essentially derived from a clipping which the poet pasted in one of his scrapbooks.[53] Nevertheless, such reliance on popular sources does not substantially diminish the importance of his utterances about health or physical well-being. Emerson remarks that "as the human body can be nourished on any food, though it were boiled grass and the broth of shoes, so the human mind can be fed by any knowledge." Evidently, Whitman's coarse medical fare nurtured his understanding of mankind, sustained his faith in mankind's future health and happiness, and helped to supply the language which he needed to depict his world.

In the decade before the Civil War, Whitman softened his skepticism toward trained physicians and showed a deepening respect for medical professionalism. This shift of attitude, which coincided with the growing prestige of physicians in American society, was to become visible in the persona's role of heroic hospital visitant. Whitman's editorials in the *Brooklyn Daily Times* maintained that the prescribing of medicines by unqualified persons harmed the community and deserved to be punished. They attacked medical imposters, advertisers of spurious health cures and dietary panaceas, and the "ninety-nine quacks" in New York City who professed to be able to cure tuberculosis. Writing in the depression year of 1858, when "scores of well-educated professional men, who had devoted the best years of their lives to the study of disease and its remedies, are at this present moment reduced almost [to] the starvation point," the poet deplored the charlatans who fill the public press "with advertisements of filthy and deleterious drugs, put up in the shape of pills, mixtures, ointments, and we know not what all." Equally indignant about the quacks who preyed on persons who were too fearful or too gullible to seek competent professional advice, he declared that "untold mischief has been done to the minds and morals of the young by reading books on 'Physiology,' so termed, causing apprehensions which have acted as a ceaseless torture to multitudes, until by consultation with honorable physicians, the groundless apprehensions have been removed, which had been excited by plausible fallacies and brazen-faced untruths." He advised these deluded individuals to practice moderation in all phases of their daily lives and to take as little medicine as possible.[54]

As for the poetic use of materials or subjects derived from medicine and physiology, Whitman's attitudes were rather ambiguous. Excited by the rich language of medicine, he declared: "*Medicine* has hundreds of useful and characteristic words—new means of cure—new schools of doctors—the wonderful anatomy of the body—the names of a thousand diseases—surgeon's terms—hydropathy—all that relates to the great organs of the body.—The medical art is always grand—nothing affords a superior scope for superior men and women.—It, of course, will never cease to be near to man, and add new terms."[55] Actually, medical themes and medical language embellish many poems in *Leaves of Grass* and are essential elements in a few of them. On the other hand, Whitman was cautious about translating the terminology and concepts of the health sciences into the language of poetry. He wanted *Leaves of Grass* to be a personal utterance, without linguistic barriers between himself and the reader. Although he realized that there is an associative or "poetic" value in technological language (he updated specific references to science and invention in the successive editions of "A Song for Occupations" in order to reflect the progress of American industrialization), he chose to avoid lavish displays of technical terms. He reminded himself to curtail "scientific and similar allusions" in the poems, because "the theories of Geology, History, Language, &c., &c., are constantly changing," and he added: "Be careful to put in only what *must* be appropriate centuries hence."[56]

Walt Whitman and the Body Beautiful

Like Emerson, he felt that poetry includes and transcends science: "The [scientific] facts are useful and real—they are not my dwelling—I enter by them to an area of the dwelling," declares "Song of Myself." John Burroughs, who hinted that Whitman's considerable knowledge of science had been "transmuted into strong poetic nutriment," implied that the poet viewed science and poetry as "parallel roads." In words that were probably inspired by Whitman, Burroughs wrote: "The poet will always pause when he finds himself in opposition to science; and the scientist is never more worthy of the name, than when he escapes from analysis to synthesis, and gives us living wholes."[57]

Whitman may have made some abortive attempts to create poems on "medicated" themes before he prepared the first edition of *Leaves of Grass*. For example, one notebook entry reads, "Poem of the Trainer," but his only published poem on athletic training is "The Runner" (1867), the dusting off of a longer trial piece in which the trained runner is compared to a graceful ship and to an agile woodcutter.[58] Among the interesting fragments which never evolved into published poems, the following is the most closely related to physical training:

Pure water, sunshine, space unclosed[;]
I stifle in the confinement of rooms
The flesh of animals, wheat, rye, corn, rice,
Give me that I have a clean, sweet, resistless body to myself[.][59]

The first edition of *Leaves of Grass* (1855) incorporates many themes and details from the health sciences. In "The Sleepers," the persona views the rheumatic, the epileptic, "the consumptive, the erisypalite, the idiot," and "the insane in their strong-door'd rooms." (Following a vist to the Kings County Lunatic Asylum in 1846, editor Whitman had described "the iron-barred violent ward" and some of its pathetic inmates.)[60] In "Faces" he beholds an epileptic seizure and also "the face of the most smeared and slobbering idiot they had at the asylum," whom he calls "my brother" (and whom he specifically identified with his brother Eddie).[61] In "A Song for Occupations" he alludes to exercise, boxing, the gymnasium, to diseased and rheumatic persons, and to

The etui of surgical instruments, and the etui of the oculist's or
aurist's instruments, or dentist's instruments * * * *[62]

The most important development of medical themes and observations, however, occurs in "To Think of Time" and "Song of Myself."

"To Think of Time," a brilliant variation on Bryant's "Thanatopsis" theme, portrays the dying driver of a Broadway stagecoach, his death chamber with its smell of camphor, the shelf of useless medicines, the grieving family, and the helpless physician. During his final illness, the driver is "helped by a contribution"—a detail which links the poem to Whitman's bedside visits and his charitable devotion to the stage drivers, prisoners, and disabled soldiers for whom he solicited financial aid and spent his own funds. Long before "To Think of Time" was composed—and possibly because he was drawn to helpless young men and to "rough" types—the poet had begun his visits to hospitals and to Sing Sing and the Tombs, where the prisoners confided in him, as Moncure Conway explained, because he was "that sort of man." [63] The compassionate persona in "To Think of Time" affirms his love for all the rejected persons of the earth, including "the infected in the immigrant hospital." Here the poet apparently refers to the Emigrant Refuge Hospital on Ward's Island, the largest hospital facility in the United States at the time, where thousands of slum dwellers, victims of the cholera epidemic of 1854, were treated and where many of them perished, together with a number of physicians and attendants. [64] Whitman, who visited the finest hospitals in New York and Washington, may well have been familiar with "the immigrant hospital."

"Song of Myself" balances its many pictures of suffering against a dramatization of the Christ-like persona, who foresees a healthy human race and performs curative miracles. In section 41, wherein he identifies with all the gods, the persona declares:

> I am he bringing help for the sick as they pant on their backs,
> And for the strong upright men I bring yet more needed help.

The poem reveals Whitman's keen observations of human agonies. Section 4 alludes poignantly to "the sickness of one of my folks—or of myself." Section 8 depicts the litter of the sick man carried to the hospital and the "groans of over-fed or half-starv'd who fall on the flags sunstruck or in fits." (Whitman's own episodes of "sunstroke" may date from this period of his life.) Section 15 pictures the reclining opium eater "with rigid head and just-open'd lips,"

Walt Whitman and the Body Beautiful

whose real-life counterparts the poet had observed in rural Long Island, where addiction was common, and possibly in the city, too.[65] Section 15 also reminds us that the poet, who witnessed some amputations in the years before he departed for Washington, was familiar with the horrors of nineteenth-century surgery:

> The malform'd limbs are tied to the surgeon's table,
> What is removed drops horribly in a pail * * * *

Section 33 pictures a wounded slave who cries out, "my gore dribs, thinn'd with the ooze of my skin," and once again reveals the keen student of wounds and afflictions. The section shows the Whitman persona standing by "the cot in the hospital reaching lemonade to a feverish patient" and identifying with "the mash'd firemen"—autobiographical motifs which are repeated in other poems. Section 43 shows the persona offering his healing balm to "him in the poor house tubercled by rum and the bad disorder," a probable allusion to the Kings County Hospital, which was operated in conjunction with a penitentiary, a poorhouse, and a lunatic asylum.[66] The implication that drinking rum causes tubercles (ulcerations resembling those produced by syphilis) may seem antic, but the ulcerative nodules covering the pauper's face and body are grim evidence of his secondary-stage syphilis.[67] And the sensuous imagery of section 49 reveals the persona as he observes an "accoucheur" bringing forth mortal and immortal life.

After relating an old-time sea fight, section 36 describes a surgical operation performed without anesthesia—a scene that has the bitter savor of first-hand observation:

> The hiss of the surgeon's knife, the gnawing teeth of his saw,
> Wheeze, cluck, swash of falling blood, short wild scream, and
>   long, dull, tapering groan,
> These so, these irretrievable.

These "irretrievable" moments of human anguish excited the poet's sympathies and nourished his imagination. Although he had abandoned his doubts about the efficacy of anesthesia in 1847, after witnessing a dental extraction and the setting of a child's dislocated thumb performed with the use of ether,[68] these "irretrievable" recollections of a cruder medical practice lingered in his memory to haunt his tranquil moments. In a similar way, the sufferings of the Civil War soldiers would haunt him and goad him into composing the *Drum-Taps* poems.

Section 37, which depicts the misery of prisoners, revisits the agonies of the cholera patients:

> Not a cholera patient lies at the last gasp but I also lie at the last gasp,
> My face is ash-color'd, my sinews gnarl, away from me people retreat.

Together with the allusions to the cholera victims in "To Think of Time," in "Revenge and Requital" composed a decade earlier, and in his newspaper columns which advocated sanitary measures to check the scourge, these lines attest to Whitman's having observed the disease at first hand during the epidemics of 1835–36, 1849, and 1854. The cholera patient "at the last gasp," typically a poor immigrant, was particularly frightening since his diarrhetic discharges could be lethal to those whom they contaminated. Whitman's poetic vignette accurately reflects the symptomatology of cholera: the patient in the final stages of the disease takes on the appearance of impending death, his body becomes shriveled and shrunken from dehydration, his skin and mucous membranes become dry and wrinkled, his face appears pinched, his eyes are sunken, and his limbs become cold and cyanotic (bluish and discolored from lack of blood). In identifying with the cholera victim, the persona asserts his empathy with the most repulsive and helpless human being of all.

An intriguing passage in section 23 of "Song of Myself" appears to contain a cryptic roster of several New York medical personalities who may have been numbered among Whitman's acquaintances. Despite its patronizing suggestion that poetry appeals to higher reaches of the imagination than does science, the passage implies a fellowship between Whitman and the physicians:

> Hurrah for positive Science! Long live exact demonstration!
> Fetch stonecrop, mixt with cedar and branches of lilac,
> This is the lexicographer—this the chemist—this made a grammar of the old cartouches,
> These mariners put the ship through dangerous unknown seas,
> This is the geologist—this works with the scalpel—and this is a mathematician.

> Gentlemen! I receive you, and attach and clasp hands with you,
> The facts are useful and real—they are not my dwelling—I enter by them to an area of the dwelling.[69]

Walt Whitman and the Body Beautiful

Although the poet himself dabbled with the notion of making a dictionary, the "lexicographer" could have been the celebrated Dr. John Wakefield Francis, the "chemist" could have been one of several physicians,[70] he who "made a grammar of the old cartouches" was Whitman's English friend Dr. Henry Abbott, and "he who works with the scalpel" was in fact the editor of *The Scalpel*, Dr. Edward H. Dixon. The identities of the "geologist" and the "mathematician" are unknown.

The most likely model for the "lexicographer," the eminent Dr. Francis, was sketched by Whitman in a "New York Dissected" article as "old gentleman in carriage. A well-built, portly old man, full ruddy face, abundant wavy—almost frizzly—white hair, good forehead, kindly, intelligent look. Dr. Francis, the encyclopedia of historical information, especially in local history and genealogy." At sixty-seven New York's outstanding obstetrician; a distinguished medical professor; a founder of hospitals, asylums, and the New York Academy of Science; and a contributor to, and patron of, Duyckinck's *Cyclopaedia of American Literature* and Allibone's *Dictionary of American Authors*, Dr. Francis deemed it "the highest privilege of his profession" to be associated with artists and literary personages. His medical antiquarianism is charmingly represented in *Old New York; or, Reminiscences of the Past Sixty Years* (1857), wherein he pleads for the preservation in New York of Dr. Abbott's Egyptian collection (as Whitman had done the year before in a "New York Dissected" article) and draws a lively picture of the New York Hospital (as Whitman was to do five years later in his "City Photographs" series).[71]

Before coming to New York to open his Egyptian Museum on Broadway, Dr. Henry Abbott had served for more than twenty years as the only English physician in Cairo. Whitman described the museum and its collection, which he visited several times, in another "New York Dissected" article. Once, for the poet's pleasure, Dr. Abbott dressed up in an Egyptian costume. At the museum, Whitman enriched his store of Egyptian lore and probably discovered the legendary figure of Sesostris, whom he introduced in trial passages of *Leaves of Grass* as the embodiment of the moral-physical-phallic superman before he decided to assign that distinction to the Whitman persona.[72]

Dr. Dixon was of Quaker stock like Whitman, a genito-urinary surgeon, the founder of his own medical college, the inventor of many surgical instruments in general use, and a stubborn opponent of the alleged "trades-unionism" of the New York Academy of Medicine. The popular doctor had written *Woman and Her Diseases* (1847), a volume addressed to women and dealing with health, uterine ailments, and the debilitating effects of soft living and prudery. Whitman's sympathetic review of the book attributed the rarity of a "well-developed, healthy, *naturally* beautiful woman" in America to women's false sense of shame and their ignorance of physiological facts, but his comments displayed an almost Victorian reticence toward Dixon's clear treatment of menstruation and other medical topics.[73] When Whitman entered into a pocket notebook the address of Dixon's residence and office nine years later,[74] he may have been cognizant of Dixon's *Scenes in the Practice of a New York Surgeon* (1855), an anthology of selections from *The Scalpel*, a magazine whose medical pronouncements and vignettes of New York life (most of them written by Dixon) were reprinted and praised in many American newspapers and applauded in the London *Lancet*. Editor Whitman reviewed many issues of *The Scalpel* in the *Brooklyn Daily Times*, and even though he chided Dr. Dixon's "zealous, hap-hazard, often-sound, often-heated and extreme assertion, regarding the causes of disease and the means of health," he occasionally made up a column of "Health Hints" by borrowing liberally from *The Scalpel*. He justified the practice of excerpting Dr. Dixon's "too intense and ardent" statements about health care "not because we endorse them," but "to arouse suggestions in the mind of the reader." And in a bantering tone that suggests his comfortable relationship with the physician, he observed archly: "There is no mistaking the earnestness and sincerity which dictate every word that Dr. Dixon writes; and we cannot help thinking that if he wields his scalpel as unsparingly and energetically in his surgical practice as against the abuses of society, we should dread to have him perform an operation for us."[75]

Whitman's reactions to Dr. Dixon's once-popular articles confirm the poet's attitudes toward health and medicine. He was indignant at Dr. Dixon's wholesale condemnation of pork, beer, and various other foods because they are supposedly unhealthful; he was amused that Dixon, like a medical Jonathan Edwards, should try to instill a morbid fear of illness into people in order to frighten them into health; and, during the period when Andrew

Walt Whitman and the Body Beautiful

Whitman suffered the ravages of consumption, he criticized the eclectic mixture of common sense and wrongheadedness in Dr. Dixon's articles about tuberculosis.[76] But he shared Dr. Dixon's belief in the therapeutic value of fresh air and exercise, his faith in the hereditary transmission of weakness and deformity, and his animosity toward the producers of drugs and of "swill milk." Approvingly, Whitman quoted *The Scalpel*'s epigraph in his newspaper columns: "Nature is ever busy, by the silent operation of her own forces, endeavoring to cure disease. Her medicines are air, warmth, light, food, water, exercise, and sleep. Their use is directed by instinct, and that man is most worthy of the name of physician, who most reveres its unerring laws." However, he qualified his agreement with Dr. Dixon's formula in a manner that suggests his growing respect for orthodox medical practice. Conceding that nature's forces, "joined with simplicity, ought to be inculcated by the physician, as the main reliance—on all ordinary occasions," he expressed a serious doubt that sane living and the operation of the *vis medicatrix naturae* (the foundation stones of Dixon's *and* Whitman's medical edifices) could suffice to preserve or restore health under all circumstances.[77]

In the 1856 edition of *Leaves of Grass*, addressed to "the workingmen and workingwomen of These States," the persona proclaims the gospel of health more convincingly than in any other version of the poems. Taking to the streets like a latter-day Epicurus, he tells anyone who will listen to him: "All comes by the body, only health puts you in rapport with the universe." Declaring that "a sick man, or an obedient man" is unfit to write his nation's poems, and denouncing timidity, obesity, and softness as inconsistent with poetic merit, this "stalwart and well-shaped heir" of all the poet-prophets of the past, who is skilled in "the physiology, phrenology . . . of the land," stops the young men to tell them the truth about themselves. He asserts his identity with "Christ, brother of rejected persons—brother of slaves, felons, idiots, and of insane and diseas'd persons"; predicts a new healthy race of "complete women and men, their pose brawny and supple, their drink water, their blood clean and clear"; and contrasts the pitiful urban masses who surround him to the "full-sized" and "untamed" heroes of the future, including his "ample-limbed" self.[78]

Three of the 1856 poems—"This Compost," "Song of the

Open Road," and "I Sing the Body Electric"—are singularly rich in physiological implications, but the observation of the sick and the dying constitutes an absorbing theme throughout this edition. The hauntingly lovely "Miracles" pictures "the sick in hospitals, or the dead carried to burial." "By Blue Ontario's Shore" glimpses "the corpse slowly borne from the eating and sleeping rooms of the house." (In later editions, this corpse becomes more specifically the carcass of outmoded tradition, and the line loses its poignancy.)[79] "Song of the Broad-Axe" reveals the observer of alcoholism and venereal disease—ailments which the poet had witnessed in the hospital wards and which took their toll in the Whitman family. The poem's excited descriptions of a great fire, of the "bloody" victim of Druidic rites, and of a battle illustrate the fascination with incidents of physical violence that drew Whitman to the accident wards of the New York hospitals:

> The uplifted arm, the clatter of blows on the helmeted head,
> The death-howl, the limpsey tumbling body, the rush of friend
>   and foe thither * * * *

"A Song of Joys" shows how closely the allure of violence and pain is linked to Whitman's sense of compassion. The poet who would one day express grief because "my enemy is dead, a man divine as myself is dead," sounds exultant as he imagines the thrill of killing:

> To taste the savage taste of blood! to be so devilish!
> To gloat so over the wounds and deaths of the enemy.

In the same poem, he cries out:

> I hear the alarm at dead of night,
> I hear bells—shouts!—I pass the crowd—I run!
> The sight of the flames maddens me with pleasure.[80]

Indeed, the poet developed a compulsive interest in firemen and confessed his love of fires because, as he admitted, "there is a kind of hideous pleasure about them."[81] His concern for injured firemen, like his compassion for wounded soldiers, fed on the psychological-sexual interplay of violence and suffering. By 1858, if not much earlier, he often visited injured firemen at the New York Hospital and at other institutions. And during an eight-week period in 1874, he sat at the bedside of William Alcott, a Camden fireman, observing the latter's sweet demeanor as his body slowly succumbed to the ravages of consumption. But he asked Dr. Bucke to eliminate from the 1883 biography a revealing reference to his attraction to fires and firemen.[82]

An ambiguity of motive also marks "This Compost," which transforms the theme of foul and deadly putrefaction (the "compost" of the title) into an affecting metaphor of immortality, artistic inspiration, and spiritual renewal. To be sure, Whitman's preoccupation with decay may betray a streak of gothic morbidity. But the inspiration for this lovely lyric on the theme of mutability derives in part from his interest in chemistry and the discovery that the processes of decay and the processes which support life are interdependent—the sort of reconciliation of opposites that matched Whitman's dialectic view of nature and his belief in the cyclic renewal of life. The poem derives, in part, from the poet's belief in the long-lived theory that infectious diseases are caused by miasma—the poisonous effluvia of decaying matter. In the *Brooklyn Daily Times* he quoted Dr. Dixon's explanation of miasma, with its implication that the process of decay is balanced against the "mysterious principle of life"—an explanation which may serve as a rough gloss of some of the physiological ideas inherent in "This Compost":

> . . . the subtle poison, called miasm . . . is a gas thrown off from decaying living creatures . . . the disorganized and decayed and decaying *elements* of all plants and animals, mosses and infusoria, so minute that the most powerful microscope can not detect their ultimate atoms. The whole animated world is made of these; every creature that lives . . . is evolved from the gases and the earths, and only resists decay by the mysterious principle of life; take this away, and decomposition at once commences the mysterious process of evolving the gases and restoring them to the air and earth, whence they derived their being. In some stages of this decomposition, it is known, that in sufficient quantities they are deadly poisons, and exert so depressing an influence upon the human body, that, when breathed into the lungs, they at once inoculate and poison the whole body, and so depress the life power that it sinks into typhus and yellow fevers.[83]

The chemist Justus Liebig (one of whose books was published in this country in the same publisher's series as Whitman's *Franklin Evans*) defined "fermentation, or putrefaction . . . as a process of transformations—that is, the arrangement of elementary particles, or atoms, of a compound, yielding two or more groups, or compounds, and caused by the contact with other substances, the elementary particles of which are themselves in a state of transformation or decomposition."[84] Reviewing Liebig's *Chemistry, in Its Application to Agriculture and Physiology* (1846), Whitman paid little heed to the book's technical complexities but seemed to relish its imaginative descriptions of what the German scientist had called "metamorphosis"—the simultaneous breaking down and re-creation of matter. Excited by the explanations of chemical processes, the poet exclaimed: "Chemistry—that involves the essences of creation, and the changes, and the growths, and formations and decays of so large a constituent part of the earth, and the things thereof! We can well imagine how a man whose judgment leaps over the mere artificial, can be an enthusiastic, life-devoted, student of this noble science."[85] Not surprisingly, he thought about composing a "Poem of Chemistry."[86]

Poe, who was sufficiently respectful toward the miasma theory to make it a crucial element in "The Fall of the House of Usher," had also called attention to the analogy between "atomic" physical chemistry and "the chemistry of the intellect," or Pure Imagination, which combines disparate elements to create Beauty. "Thus, the range of Imagination is unlimited," said Poe. "Its materials extend throughout the universe. Even out of deformities it fabricates that *Beauty* which is at once its sole object and its inevitable test. But, in general, the richness or force of the matters combined; the facility of discovering combinable novelties worth combining; and, especially the absolute 'chemical combination' of the completed mass—are particulars to be regarded in our estimate of Imagination."[87] For Whitman, too, the interlinked processes of decay and creation were analogous to the creative-artistic process.

Whitman's artistically finished treatment of this theme is "This Compost," whose underlying concept, as Henry Binns observed, may well be the simile "as the earth transforms morbidity into wholesomeness, so also does the spirit of man." Its theme may indeed derive from St. Paul's explanation of immortality: "that which thou sowest is not quickened, except it die; . . . thou sowest not that body that shall be, but bare grain, it may chance of *wheat*, or of some other grain: But God giveth it a body as it hath pleased him, and to every seed his own body."[88] The poem celebrates the fact that although "distemper'd corpses" and the "car-

Walt Whitman and the Body Beautiful

casses" of the "drunkards and gluttons of so many generations" are sown in the ground, the earth has miraculously "drawn off all the foul liquid and meat," and from this unsavory compost arises the miracle of birth: "The resurrection of the *wheat* appears with pale visage out of its graves * * * *"

"What chemistry!" exclaims the enraptured persona, that the ocean is clean despite all the "fevers" that have been deposited there, that the winds are not "infectious," that vegetation is pure:

> That when I recline on the grass I do not catch any disease,
> Though probably every spear of grass rises out of what was once a
>   catching disease.
>
> Now I am terrified at the Earth, it is that calm and patient,
> It grows such sweet things out of such corruptions,
> It turns harmless and stainless on its axis, with such endless
>   successions of diseas'd corpses,
> It distills such exquisite winds out of such infused fetor,
> It renews with such unwitting looks its prodigal, annual,
>   sumptuous crops,
> It gives such divine materials to men, and accepts such leavings
>   from them at last.[89]

Whitman's physical and spiritual worlds also intersect in "Song of the Open Road." The poem's air-atmosphere imagery is rich in transcendental implications. The "air that serves" the persona "with breath to speak" inspires him to noble thoughts; it is the "music falling in where it is wanted, and stopping where it is not wanted"—the mystic accompaniment to which he marches down the road of life. In the "open air" his miracles can be performed. The "great draughts of space" which he inhales signify his escape from personal limitations and furnish him with a vital clue to "the secret of the making of the best persons."[90] It is this same airy essence, the "show of summer softness," that rallies the despairing young man in "The Sleepers"; the inspirational "wind of the mountains" that whispers the secret of "Poems bridging the way from Life to Death" in "Proud Music of the Storm"; the "odorless" air that inspires the persona in "Song of Myself," section 2—the air whose vitalizing-curative properties enable him to inspire and heal others and to "filter and fibre" their blood in "Song of Myself," section 52.[91]

But the air-atmosphere imagery in "Song of the Open Road"

is also a challenge to the consumptive city folk to restore their health in the great outdoors. In a book which Whitman had read, Dr. Samuel S. Fitch described the lungs as pumps that fill the body with vital energy and, in logic resembling the poet's own, said that consumption is "a child of civilization; [it] results chiefly from the loss of symmetry, and from effeminacy, induced by too much clothing, too luxurious living, dissipation, too little exercise, and debilitating diseases and occupations."[92] In a noble appeal to the inhabitants of Manhattan, Dr. Trall declared:

> As long as human beings are permitted, and *compelled*, to congregate and breed and rot in *dank cellars, stifling garrets*, or in those pestilential structures called tenement houses, where every particle of air is loaded with miasm; where sickening stenches are ever present; where cleanliness and decency are as impossible as they were at the murderous prison house called Andersonville; and where scrofula, and venereal disease, and typhoid fevers, and consumption are never absent; all of the people of the great city must partake, more or less, of the poisonous materials and demoralizing influences which emanate therefrom.[93]

Long before "Song of the Open Road" was published, the Swiss physician Samuel Tissot had inculcated in two generations of doctors the principle that "elastic and pure air emancipates the system from torpor" (a recognizable theme in the poem) and had prescribed clean outdoor air to "revitalize" the blood, strengthen the body, and overcome scrofulous tuberculosis. Dr. Trall advocated the curative qualities of the "air-bath" (exposing the body to clean country air), reasoning that when a jaded citizen contracts a fever the result is typhus, but that when an outdoorsman gets a fever the result is a mere inflammation. Similarly, Dr. Dixon proposed an air cure which he half-jokingly labeled "ventupathy," alleging that a supply of pure air is needed to cure consumption, scrofula, menstrual malfunctions, and other complaints.[94] And another physician, in a medical volume which the poet read, declared that ailments of the eyes and ears are caused by city life but cured by the wholesome living and fresh air of the countryside.[95]

In "Arrow-Tip," one of his early tales, Whitman implied that one week of deer hunting in the Western forests "would do more good to our enervated city gentry than a hundred gymnasiums, or all the medicines in the drug-shops." As a journalist, he steadily pointed up the urbanite's desperate need for fresh air, arguing that healthy persons breathing fresh air can resist infection. Discussing his own partial recovery from paralysis in *Specimen Days*, he credited his "much-restored health" to being "two years, off and on, without drugs and medicines, and daily in the open air"; he waxed enthusiastic about Stafford Farm, where on warm, breezy days he walked in the mud and took his "Adamic air-bath and flesh-brushing from head to foot." He prescribed this same regimen of ventupathy (this "invisible physician" with its "silent delicious medicine") to his brethren, declaring, "Sweet, sane, still nakedness in Nature!—ah if poor, sick, prurient humanity in cities might really know you once more!"[96] It should be obvious, then, that a profound physiological faith underlies "Song of the Open Road": its healthy persona who is "done with indoor complaints," in both senses of that phrase; its Adamic vision of the "thousand beautiful forms" of men and women who will one day appear in the Western lands of America; and its solemn declaration:

> Now I see the secret of the making of the best persons,
> It is to grow in the open air and eat and sleep with the earth.

The 1856 edition also contained Whitman's greatest tribute to the human physique, the complete version of "Poem of the Body," subsequently titled "I Sing the Body Electric." To appreciate his achievement, one must understand that Victorian America rejected guiltless physical attraction and sexual exhilaration as suitable literary subjects. In literature as in the drawing room, the body had to be decorously garbed. Hawthorne, keenly sensitive to the physiology of sexuality, utilized head, heart, and spleen as moral metaphors rather than physiological forces. Thoreau, the consumptive naturalist whose prose writings reveal a deep concern with health and the bodily processes and a brilliant use of the symbology of the body, conceded that John Donne's poetry sprang from a knowledge of "the cerebral cortex, the nervous system, and the digestive tracts,"[97] but Thoreau's own poetry shows no such inspiration. Melville prodded Victorian ladies and gentlemen with the taunt that he could form no proper estimate of them without feeling their backbones,[98] and he composed opaque parables about the degradation of sexuality in an industrial society, but his flights of physiological frankness were launched over the heads of his readers and muffled in clouds of protective rhetoric. Oliver Wendell Holmes did, in fact, compose "The Living Temple" (which he called "The Anatomist's Hymn"), a lyrical tribute to the human body—the bloodstream, the nerves, the eyes, the ears, the brain. The poem's sometimes quizzical but generally prayerful praise of the body's divinity is presented decorously in stanzas of iambic tetrameter.[99] But Whitman alone wrote passionately, so that all may read, of the miracle of the human body without slighting the vital parts that lie between the shoulders and the shin bones.

"I Sing the Body Electric" (the portion of the poem corresponding to sections 1 through 8 had appeared in the 1855 edition) develops the metaphor of the body as an electrical attractor, energizer, and sublime mystery. Asserting the nobility of all physical attributes, it glorifies the body as the repository of generations yet unborn and as the domicile and complement of the soul:

> If any thing is sacred the human body is sacred,
> And the glory and sweet of a man is the token of manhood untainted,
> And in man or woman a clean, strong, firm-fibred body, is more beautiful than the most beautiful face.

The poem idealizes the hearty old man and his "massive clean bearded tanfaced and handsome" sons. It praises the sanctity of the mother and her sexual urge and the sanctity of the father and his urge for sexual union, demanding, "Where else does he strike soundings except here?"[100]

About the time he was preparing the 1856 edition, Whitman jotted down a notebook reminder to "Read the latest and best medical works / talk with physicians / study the anatomical plates / also casts and figures in the collections of design." The same notebook page also contains this entry: "A poem in which is minutely described the whole particulars and ensemble of a *first-rate healthy Human Body*—it looks into and through, as if it were transparent and of fine glass—and now reported in a poem." Further promise of such a poem, based on the concept of illustrated anatomy plates, appeared in the first version (the present section 7) of "I Sing the Body Electric":

> Examine these limbs, red, black, or white, they are cunning in tendon and nerve,
> They shall be stript away that you may see them.

Exquisite senses, life–lit eyes, pluck, volition,
Flakes of breast-muscle, pliant backbone and neck, flesh not
    flabby, good–sized arms and legs,
And wonders within there yet.[101]

The fulfillment of this promise is section 9 of "I Sing the Body Electric," whose thirty–six lines seem indeed to be inspired by Whitman's examination of the plates of an anatomy book and by his interest in pathognomy, the pseudo–science of body language. The passage glorifies "All attitudes, all the shapeliness, all the belongings of my or your body, or of any one's body, male or female * * * *" Section 9 is essentially a sonorous catalogue of the human anatomy, beginning with "Head, neck, hair, ears, drop and tympan of the ears" and extending to "Ankles, instep, football, toes, toe-joints, the heel." It scants nothing as it descends along the body, neither "the bowels sweet and clean" nor the male and female genital organs. It is careless of scientific distinctions and terminology, its anatomical designations mingling with references to "Sympathies," "love-perturbations," and "thin red jellies within you," but its effect is dazzling. After declaring that all physical attributes are beautiful and spiritual, the poem concludes by reaffirming the bond between body and soul and the correspondence between physical health and spirituality:

The exquisite realization of health;
O I say now these are not the parts and poems of the body only,
    but of the soul,
O I say now these are the soul!

The new poems in the 1860 edition of *Leaves of Grass* soften the emphasis on the theme of health and disclose Whitman's difficulty in shaping the persona as a eugenic paragon. "Starting from Paumanok" does propose a "programme of chants," including "Health chants—joy chants—robust chants of young men," and the "Messenger Leaves" poems show the healer-persona bestowing his electric touch or his "significant look" to invigorate the sick and despairing. Thus, in "To One Shortly to Die," sitting beside the deathbed and offering salvation: "I am more than nurse, more than parent or neighbor." In "To You," demanding: "Tell me what you would not tell your brother, wife, husband, or physician." In a related "Debris" poem, listening to the voices of the dying and interpreting their anguish.[102] However, the "Children of Adam" and the "Calamus" poems highlight the Whitman persona's crisis as a physical culture hero. In "Children of Adam" this model of eugenic fatherhood "deliriate with sex" also appears to be a self-stimulated lover dreaming about transient love affairs with humble and dependent young men. In "Calamus" his emotions range from ecstasy over real or imagined love affairs to frustration, hysteria, and despair over secret guilt. The very symbolism is ambiguous. The coarse wild calamus grass, his phallic token of masculine comradeship, is known in American folk medicine as an aphrodisiac; hence it may imply either healthy masculinity or jaded sensuality. "As if I were not puzzled at myself!" cries the persona, who seems ready to abandon his stated ambition "to strike up the songs of the New World" in order to "go with him I love." In this context, his poetic allegation that "affection shall solve every one of the problems of freedom" does not resolve the contradictions between individualism and equality, nor does it support his eugenic-evolutionary ideology.[103]

But circumstances helped Whitman to refashion a stellar role for the Whitman–Adam persona. Stirred by the hospital milieu, by its daily struggles with death, and by the opportunities it afforded him to observe agonies and to bestow personal affection, the poet became intimately acquainted with New York and Brooklyn hospitals, their management, their medical personnel, and with hundreds of their patients. Thus, at the beginning of the Civil War, when New York's civilian hospitals were filling up with injured and ailing soldiers, brought in from the war front on a contract basis, it was only natural that these young men should absorb his attention as the injured firemen and horsecar drivers had done. It seemed to him as if an entire generation of Americans was being hospitalized, and here, at last, was ample room for the full play of his sympathies, for his attraction to helpless young men, and for relating the activities of his own life to the role of the healer-persona.

Whitman observed local medical facilities and sometimes passed judgment on them and their doctors. He visited the two-hundred-bed Brooklyn City Hospital when its new building was opened in 1852, remarking that "it was entirely unprovided with any means of ventilation, one of the first requisites of a good hospital." The facility was the subject of an article in his local history

Walt Whitman and the Body Beautiful

series ("Brooklyniana," March, 1862), which described its heating and ventilation systems and the treatments of its patients. But when he returned there in the fall of 1864, he called it the worst-managed hospital he had ever seen.[104] As editor of the *Daily Times*, he showed a strong interest in the Kings County Hospital, especially in its smallpox cases, and in the Kings County Lunatic Asylum, praising both institutions for their professional excellence and their "right vital" humane spirit.[105]

The best glimpse of Whitman as an observer of hospitalized patients and their doctors prior to his Washington years is his "City Photographs" series (*New York Leader*, March and April, 1862), published under the pseudonym of Van Velsor Brush.[106] These four sketches describe the New York Hospital—the first hospital in America to operate essentially as a clinical school. Dr. D. B. St. John Roosa, who served there, called the institution, with its sizable library and its parklike grounds, "the medical and surgical center of the city." Its south building, in particular, he termed "a model in hospital architecture," an opinion in which Whitman concurred. Dr. Roosa believed that the New York Hospital was, at the time Whitman frequented it, "the greatest school of surgery in the whole country." Dr. John Watson, an eminent surgeon, declared that no hospital in the world at that time presented "a greater variety of acute and important diseases," had so dedicated a teaching staff or such opportunities for "autopsic examinations," or (because of its large bequests) was so well designed to serve the poor—particularly the workingmen and the accident victims to whom the poet was so strongly drawn until the sick and injured soldier boys exerted a greater appeal. Except on Tuesdays and Fridays, the hospital admitted only dignitaries, friends of the staff, or those with special passes, but Whitman was free to come and go whenever he wished. His fascination with violent accidents attracted him to this hospital, which, as Dr. Roosa explained, was located near "the wharves and piers, where the mighty engines of commerce are constantly crushing so many in their revolutions, and in the very heart of lower Broadway, with its countless sources of accidents, in fact very accessible to the places where half the casualties and crimes of the metropolis occur."[107]

Whitman's "City Photographs" are filled with statistics and excited descriptions of the New York Hospital's facilities, patients, and staff, the ailments and the injuries that were treated there, and, in his own words, the "tragic and thrilling associations, full of the romance of reality that is ten-fold deeper than anything born of literature." Gazing reverently in Governors Hall of the hospital at the portraits of the illustrious physicians whose names he recorded in these articles, he declared: "For my part, as I stand in the presence of these fine and eloquent faces, I acknowledge without demur that none of the world's many avenues of fame or heroism affords any higher field for the most courageous soul than the one represented by the doctors."

He names many of these doctors with awe. Dr. Valentine Mott, cofounder with Dr. Francis of the New York Academy of Medicine, is singled out as the first surgeon to operate on the *arteria innominata*. Drs. C. Wright Post and Kearney Rodgers are cited among the luminaries of surgery who have been associated with the hospital.[108] From Dr. Robert Roberts, the hospital's elderly urbane clerk ("a rare gentleman of the old school," Dr. Roosa called him), Whitman heard anecdotes of the hospital's glories told in an "Elia-like" style.[109] Whitman apparently made use of Dr. John Watson's report, "Thermal Ventilation and Other Sanitary Improvements Applicable to Public Buildings . . ." (1851) in describing the hospital's system for supplying heated air and removing stale air through a system of ventilating ducts.[110] He was also helped by the distinguished epidemiologist Dr. Joseph M. Smith, a "senior physician, whose records and lectures have been of service to me."[111]

Whitman frequented the hospital's wards, its surgery room, its supply rooms, and its offices. He appears to have gone to the hospital in September, 1857, to report on the stabbing committed by a patient in the delirium tremens ward. In December, 1858, he interviewed the staff doctors about an injured Brooklyn fireman.[112] He systematically visited hospitalized stage drivers: "Yes, I knew all the drivers [on the Broadway stages] then," recalled the poet who had pictured the death of a stage driver in "To Think of Time" and who had reportedly substituted for sick drivers on the job.[113] Dr. Roosa estimated that by the spring of 1862 Whitman—whom he described as a large, bearded man, dressed in the familiar proletarian costume and displaying deep sympathy for stage drivers—had visited there about fifty times. The poet was also drawn to the staff doctors—the nine men in their twenties who served there at any period—whom Dr. Roosa depicted as "solemn young men, so young in appearance." The latter reportedly found Whitman's presence restful and helpful." [114] One of them recollected that Whitman talked to the staffers mainly about books and poetry, but "never said much about the class whom he visited in our wards" beyond concerning himself with "the nature of the injury and the prospect of recovery." [115]

Whitman's retrospective impression of these visits reveals his attraction to the young doctors and their puzzlement over his unusual devotion to the hospitalized men:

> I used to go there frequently to see my injured stage-driver friends, and was always well received. The house doctors or surgeons were, as a rule, young men, and were kindly and sympathetic. We used to chat at odd times. They used to let me sit beside my injured friends, on the beds or cots, and gave me information at all times. I would travel about at times with some of these young surgeons, and take them to Pfaff's or some other convenient place for mild refreshment. They were a jolly set, and used to try to pump me as to why I liked stage drivers. I suppose the real reason was that the poor devils had such a hard life of it in all weathers that my heart went out to them, and besides I learned much from them. . . .
>
> I suppose that I learned to nurse suffering humanity and not to be afraid of blood, wounds, or manifestations of pain by nursing the sick or injured stage drivers. Yes, I can recall the names of some of the doctors about the New York Hospital. One was Flint, one McDonald—may be Dunlap. I am not sure as to this one. "Doc" was the usual name for them. There were a good many different ones in the years I used to go there. They were learning their trade then. There was also a sprightly young doctor about there, a sort of a wheel horse—he was always in demand. St. John or St. James Roosa; the other doctors used to say, "Where's the saint?" He was an awfully clever and handy man. I guess that they are all dead now. Some of them reached eminence and were useful to their fellow men. [116]

In the first of the "City Photographs," Whitman described the twenty-four-year-old "saint" as a gentlemanly house surgeon of "hearty and professional excellence." Like so many physicians to whom the poet was attracted, Dr. Roosa was broadly cultured and possessed a literary flair. He had served as a junior walker and senior walker at the hospital and had volunteered for a brief tour of duty as an assistant surgeon with the Fifth Regiment of the New

York National Guard before returning to the hospital as house surgeon. In 1862, Dr. Roosa left for Europe to pursue the study of otiology, served in the field once again, then settled in New York to practice ophthalmology and otiology with great distinction and to promote the graduate study of medicine.[117] However, Whitman was apparently unaware of these later phases of the physician's life.

At the hospital, most of the patients fascinated Whitman. Although the "City Photographs" reveal little about the children or women patients, they are filled with details about the inmates in the alcoholic ward; the sufferers from contusions, fractures, and fevers; the suspected case of leprosy; the injured firemen; the stage drivers; the workman "who had his hand nipped in a steam engine, and two fingers so lacerated they had to be taken off by a surgeon"; the injured railroad man who had received "a frightful wound and fracture of the bones of the ankle" and whom the poet carefully observed as he sank toward death in his three weeks at the hospital; and the grocery boy dying of the starvation inflicted by his stingy boss. But he was especially intrigued by the injured and sick soldiers, noting that "at one time I would find 'Rebeola' on two-thirds of the little card-racks at the head of their beds." (In a later installment he spelled the word "rubeola.")

Whitman thanked the surgeons for letting him witness "several very fine operations, and for their interesting explanations of them to me, before and afterwards." As he was to do in Washington, he made notes of what he saw and heard. Dr. Alfred North, who succeeded Dr. Roosa as house surgeon, apparently permitted the poet to watch him perform, or assist in, the resetting of a woman's dislocated jaw. Whitman also observed the amputation of the foot of a soldier who had been wounded in the first battle of Bull Run. The surgeon was Dr. Thomas Masters Markoe, adjunct professor of surgery at the College of Physicians and Surgeons of New York City (Columbia University). In the operating theatre, Whitman saw Dr. Markoe sever the soldier's leg just above the foot. "Under the old dispensations," Whitman explained to his readers, "the operation would have taken off the leg nearly up to the knee (at what is called the upper third), but in this case it was done by Dr. Markoe after what is known as the Symes' [sic] operation. The bones of the foot forward were all amputated, and then a flap of heel brought around and left to make a cushion to walk upon, so that the crippled leg will be only a trifle shorter than the other."[118] The poet's enthusiasm was warranted, for he had witnessed one of the earliest instances of the Syme's procedure performed anywhere in the world.

Another surgical operation that he attended was performed by Dr. George Absalom Peters, a consulting surgeon at the hospital, whom a biographer described as a skillful and painstaking man of "alert intelligence and quaint humor, united with a repugnance for showy methods." Whitman was admitted, along with a swarm of others, to Dr. Peters's operating theatre (little attention was paid to asepsis) to observe the removal of a gallstone. To the poet's delight, the patient remembered having seen the poet among the onlookers before he had drowsed into his chloroform-induced sleep. Whitman's little disquisition on ailments caused by calculus ("stones") indicates that Dr. Peters or a colleague had explained the operation to him and that he had taken notes.[119]

The "City Photographs" foretell the man who, within a year, would serve in the wards of the military hospitals in Washington. Praising an unnamed benefactress who brought gifts to the sick and injured young men, Whitman subtly drew attention to his own charitable efforts: "There are other good, benevolent women who come or send here—*and men too*." And watching the wards fill up with soldiers, he offered a foretaste of the magnetic poet who would soon broadcast his electric currents through the wards of the military hospitals in the Washington area: "One Sunday night, in a ward in the South Building [of the New York Hospital], I spent one of the most agreeable evenings of my life amid such a group of seven convalescent young soldiers of a Maine regiment. We drew around together, on our chairs, in the dimly-lighted room, and after interchanging a few magnetic remarks that show people it is well for them to be together, they told me stories of country life and adventures, &c., away up there in the Northeast. . . ."[120] In America's ailing and wounded soldier "boys" and in the tales of heroism and carnage that they brought back from the war front, Whitman had discovered the satisfying passion that enabled him to transform the Whitman-Adam persona into the figure of the beloved wound-dresser and to create America's greatest wartime poetry.

"I Pacify With Soothing Hand"

3

BEFORE LEAVING NEW YORK, Whitman was caught up in the wartime excitement:

> All the mutter of preparation, all the determin'd arming,
> The hospital service, the lint, bandages and medicines,
> The women volunteering for nurses, the work begun in earnest,
> no mere parade now * * * *[1]

His departure for Washington was spurred by a desire to find his brother George, a captain of the Fifty-first New York Volunteers, who had been reported missing in action; by a need for greater economic stability than he was afforded in his impermanent associations with New York and Brooklyn newspapers; by an urge to be near the heady atmosphere of hospitals, physicians, the sick, and the dying; and by the realization that he must relate the war to his poetic career if he was to be taken seriously as the "national" poet. One medical historian declares that Whitman had "realized that a self-acquired knowledge of the body and an understanding leaning toward those in distress fitted him aptly for the task" of hospital volunteer.[2] Though Whitman was to serve essentially as an observer or a bedside companion to the injured and dying, rather than in a strictly medical capacity, his understanding of the hospital milieu and his adaptation to the needs of the soldiers were indeed impressive.

He arrived in Washington in December, 1862. Late that month, near Falmouth, Virginia, he located his brother George, who was recuperating from a minor wound. There he observed, perhaps for the first time, the mounds of severed arms and legs which were a common sight on the grounds of the military hospitals. There, too, he commenced his systematic practice of bestowing small gifts and personal affection on the sick and wounded soldiers. After a few days, he returned by hospital train to Washington, where he found part-time employment as a copyist in the Army Paymaster's Office—a job which required only a few hours of his day and which he kept until being appointed to a clerkship in the Bureau of Indian Affairs and subsequently in the Attorney General's Office. At the end of December, he went to Campbell Hospital to visit two injured soldiers who had asked for him.[3] Soon afterwards, he related, "beginning at first with casual visits to see some of the Brooklyn men, I became by degrees more and more drawn in, until I now have been for many weeks quite a devotee to the business—a regular self-appointed missionary to these thousands and tens of thousands of wounded and sick young men here, left upon government hands, many of them languishing, many of them dying." He declared: "Upon a few of these hospitals I have been almost daily calling as a missionary, on my own account. . . ."[4] Appealing to his friends for help in meeting the out-of-pocket costs of gifts to the soldiers, he observed: "A benevolent person, with the right qualities and tact, cannot, perhaps, make a better investment of himself at present anywhere upon the varied surface of the whole of this big world than in these military hospitals, among such thousands of most interesting young men."[5]

The lure of the suffering soldiers drew him to visit all, or most, of the hospital installations in the Washington area. "Here," he declared, "I will egotistically confess, I like to flourish. Even in a medical point of view it is one of the greatest things and in a surgical point of view the same. I can testify that friendship has literally cured a fever, and the medicine of daily affection, a bad wound." He acknowledged "that simple first sympathy of man for man which drove me as it drove others into hospital work during the war. . . . The hospitals put our feet right on the ground—put us into immediate association with the bottom facts of virtue."[6] Here, too, he could bestow his compassion precisely on the native-born young men whom he had celebrated in the "Calamus" poems. As he said, "these government hospitals are not filled as with human debris like the old established city hospitals, New York, &c, but mostly with these good-born American young men, appealing to me most profoundly, good stock, often mere boys, full

Walt Whitman and the Body Beautiful

of sweetness and heroism—often they seem very near to me, even as my own children or younger brothers. I make no bones of petting them, just as if they were—having long given up formalities and reserves in my treatment of them." To his mother he wrote in June, 1863: "You can have no idea how these sick & dying youngsters cling to a fellow, & how fascinating it is, with all the hospital surroundings of sadness & scenes of repulsion and death. . . ." Of tending the sick and despondent boys, he wrote that same month that the work "grows upon me and fascinates me—it is the most affecting thing you ever see. . . ." These wounded, diarrhetic, feverish, and dying young soldiers, he confessed, "open a new world somehow to me. . . . I sometimes put myself in fancy in the cot, with typhoid, or under the knife. . . ."[7]

Whatever his motives may have been, his ministrations were efficacious. Going on his rounds, carrying the familiar leather knapsack filled with gifts and with items the soldiers had asked for—jams and jellies, fruit, tobacco, and coins—writing letters, chatting, sitting beside the sick and dying, changing the dressing on a wound, or reading poetry to the "boys"—white and black, soldier and teamster—he soothed them by his very presence.[8]

A dozen years after the fact, the journalist and historian John Swinton described a tour of the hospital wards on which he had accompanied the poet. Swinton mentioned no medical or quasi-medical services on the poet's part during the nocturnal visit. But (perhaps under the spell of the Whitman aura) he told of the curative effect of the hero-healer's contact upon the men. Whitman's personality, he declared, seemed to light up the wards as though he were "the Son of Love." He handed out comfits and oranges, wrote letters, and delivered messages; he conferred touches, words of cheer, or "a manly farewell kiss. He seemed to leave a benediction for everyone as he passed along." When he left late at night, the voices of the stricken men called after him: "Walt! Walt! Walt! come again; come again." Whitman had emptied his haversack and given "more than other men," concluded Swinton.[9]

Whitman's notebooks and diaries, as Glicksberg observes, offer many a "poignant glimpse" of the poet's tragic experiences and of the selfless manner in which he "adapted himself to each case, giving what was called for from the fullness of his heart." He visited the "worst fevers," the wounded, and the smallpox cases "without apprehension," as he said at the time, because someone had to go.[10] He took justifiable pride in his efforts to rouse the natural recuperative powers—the *vis medicatrix naturae*—of the soldiers:

> Nothing is of any avail among the soldiers except conscientious personal investigation of cases, each for itself; with sharp, critical facilities, but boundless love. The men feel such love more than anything else. I have met very few persons who realize the importance of humoring the yearnings for love and friendship of these American young men, prostrated by sickness and wounds . . . that does, in its way, more good than all the medicine in the world. . . . I have the consciousness of saving quite a number of lives by saving them from giving up—and being a good deal with them; the men say it is so, and doctors say it is so.[11]

The physicians did, in fact, agree. Dr. Bucke cited an (unnamed) surgeon in charge of one of the larger army hospitals in Washington who had observed Whitman's hospital labors during a period of several months and "was satisfied that he saved many lives."[12] Thus a fundamental truth adorns the lines in "By Blue Ontario's Shore":

> Upon this breast has many a dying soldier lean'd to breathe his
>   last,
> This arm, this hand, this voice, have nourish'd, rais'd, restored,
> To life recalling many a prostrate form.[13]

Whitman regularly visited the hospital complexes "dotting the landscape and environs" within sight of the Capitol—those veritable little towns "of wounds, sickness, and death," as he called them. In most of these hospitals he watched the soldiers among whom death stalked "by day and night along the narrow aisles between the rows of cots, or by the blankets on the ground, and touch'd lightly many a poor sufferer, often with blessed, welcome touch." He saw them endure, without crying out, the torments of "the wound, the amputation, the shatter'd face or limb, the slow hot fever, long impatient anchorage in bed, and all the forms of maiming, operation, and disease."[14] Afterwards, looking back over three years of service in hospitals and camps, he asserted that he had made "over 600 visits or tours" and had gone, "as I estimate, among 80,000 to 100,000 of the wounded and sick, as sustainer of spirit and body in some degree, in time of need." Some-

Walt Whitman and the Body Beautiful

times, he said, he had watched over the sick or dying soldiers "several nights in succession" and at times had tended the black troops or the escaped slaves in "the contraband camps." [15]

As an amateur critic of medical care, Whitman recorded his impressions of doctors and hospitals, excoriating some army physicians as dandies, butchers, tyrants, or "shysters" but praising the vast majority of attending surgeons for their devotion to the soldiers. As long as a "prospect" of survival remained for the afflicted, he affirmed, the doctors "strive hard—at least most of the surgeons do; but death certain and evident, they yield the field." [16] *Memoranda During the War* presents Whitman's "most emphatic testimony to the zeal, manliness, and professional spirit and capacity, generally prevailing among the Surgeons, many of them young men, in the Hospitals and the army. I will not say much about the exceptions, for they are few; (but I have seen some of those few, and very incompetent and airish they were.) I never ceas'd to find the best young men, and the hardest and most disinterested workers, among these Surgeons, in the Hospitals. They are full of genius, too. I have seen many hundreds of them, and this is my testimony." [17] Long after the war he confessed that he had given insufficient credit in *Specimen Days* to the labors of the military physicians, adding that if he were to prepare a revised edition of that autobiographical work it would more fully reflect the compassion and bravery of the doctors. [18]

Whitman expected, and claimed to have received, "general cordiality and deference among the doctors and officers, nurses, etc.," in most hospitals. He boldly advised some doctors about the performance of their duties. He alerted one of them, he said, to the fact that a Connecticut soldier could keep no food in his stomach, that the lad needed palatable food, and with the physician's permission brought him one of Mrs. O'Connor's rice puddings. He tried to warn a Dr. F. of the grave condition of a soldier, and when the doctor paid no heed, he told the head surgeon and got results. He informed another doctor that a soldier, Erastus Haskell, was in danger of dying from a fever. The doctor rewarded his anxiety by remarking, "I know more about these fever cases than you do—he looks very sick to you, but I shall bring him out all right." But by the time the doctor became properly alarmed by the soldier's condition, according to Whitman, it was too late. He spoke out against the personnel of Judiciary Square Hospital, whose reputation was not always favorable, because they had shown him "more impudence and dandy doctorism and needless airs . . . than all the two score other establishments in and around Washington."[19]

From the beginning of his service, he was most often at Armory Square Hospital, built in 1862 in accordance with a plan devised by the United States Sanitary Commission. According to volunteer nurse Louisa May Alcott, the hospital's "neatness, comfort, and convenience" made it "an honor to its presiding genius" and aroused "all the covetous propensities of such nurses as came from other hospitals to visit it."[20] Although its exposed wooden beams and its barnlike wards would seem primitive today, Whitman approvingly called it a model hospital, commending its wooden floors and plastered walls and, rather chauvinistically, the fact that nine-tenths of its patients were native-born American boys. By April, 1863, he was visiting there regularly. "I devote myself much to Armory Square Hospital," he told his mother, "because it contains by far the worst cases, most repulsive wounds, has the most suffering and need of consolation. I go every day without fail, and often at night—sometimes stay very late—no one interferes with me, guards, doctors, nurses, nor any one—I am let to take my own course." The soldiers there, he observed, "know how to love when the right love [is] afforded them . . . this is my element. . . ." In June, 1863, he noted that he had "fifteen or twenty" particular cases whom he visited regularly, and in August he claimed that "I seldom miss a day or evening" in an effort to do something for each of the hospital's seven hundred inmates. "So I go round—Some of the boys die, some get well. . . . I pet them, some of them it does much good, they are so faint & lonesome—at parting at night sometimes I kiss them right & left.—The doctors tell me I supply the patients with a medicine which all their drugs & bottles & powders are helpless to yield." Besides giving the "boys" affection, the poet doled out tobacco and occasionally brought wine or brandy to a sick soldier. He continued to visit this hospital most often, keeping in touch with his "boys" and with some of the physicians even after June, 1864, when he admitted to his mother than he had suffered "spells of deathly faintness." He was still visiting there in August, 1865, several months after the war had ended.[21]

In February, 1863, he witnessed an operation at Armory Square Hospital to remove some splintered bone from the wound of an injured New York soldier, apparently performed while the lad was propped up in bed. He admired the silence with which the soldier endured the pain and the expertise of the entire procedure: "There was an unusual cluster of surgeons, medical cadets, nurses, &c., around his bed—I thought the whole thing was done with tenderness, and done well." [22] He was also present at the same facility when his soldier friend Lewy Brown, wounded in battle the previous August, had his leg amputated in January, 1864. Lewy had asked the poet to remain at his side during the operation. The latter watched through a half-opened door a few days later when the surgeons reopened Lewy's bleeding wound, cut into the festering stump, and then stitched it up again after determining that the bleeding was superficial. He heard Lewy, still under the influence of ether, call his name and complain of pains in the amputated leg. Later he sat beside the soldier's bed, commenting on the pains that are "usual in such cases." After sharing so much of Lewy's anguish, he might guilelessly address him as "my darling son & comrade." [23]

Dr. D. Willard Bliss, a native of Auburn, New York, who had supervised the construction of Armory Square Hospital and served as its surgeon-in-chief, gave Whitman clearance to move freely among the hospitalized soldiers. In his letters to the families of men whom Dr. Bliss had attended, Whitman referred to him as "one of the best surgeons in the army." He related with pride that he was among those in attendance at a ceremony in August, 1863, when four cases of instruments were presented to Dr. Bliss. [24] Two decades later, when Whitman's friends tried to secure a pension for him from the House of Representatives, Dr. Bliss (who was said by a colleague to command "more influence in the halls of Congress than any score of other medical men") testified in the poet's behalf: "From my personal knowledge of Mr. Whitman's labors in Armory Square and other hospitals, I am of opinion that no one person who assisted in the hospitals during the war accomplished so much good to the soldier and for the Government as Mr. Whitman." [25] Dr. Bliss's sentiments ring true, but in urging Whitman's right to federal assistance, he was reminding Congress of his own suit for legislative redress, for the physician, who had attended President Garfield after the chief executive was shot in 1881, felt that the government had not properly compensated him for his professional services. However, Dr. Bliss had made implacable enemies in the District of Columbia Medical Society by championing the rights to membership of qualified blacks (including Whitman's wartime acquaintance, Dr. Augusta), women, and homeopaths. Ultimately, neither his petition nor Whitman's was approved by Congress.[26]

The medical historian Richard H. Shryock reminds us that if "we could recall the actual suffering of 1861–65, we might not so readily view the Civil War in terms of epic grandeur."[27] Indeed, Whitman consistently testified that he had found the war's innermost meaning in its dead and maimed, and he integrated this grim lesson into his portraits of war-torn America. *Specimen Days* makes the war the central reality of his own life and of his nation's destiny. *Memoranda During the War*, arranged from what he called his "pencillings on the spot," attests to the hectic spirit, the nausea, and the imminence of death in the years when the whole land seemed to him to be "one vast central Hospital." The war, he cautioned, "was not a quadrille in a ball-room. Its interior history will . . . never be even suggested. The actual Soldier of 1862–'65, North and South . . . and a hundred unnamed lights and shadows of camp—I say, will never be written—perhaps must not and should not be." The poet's friend and physician William Osler declared that by centering "the marrow of the tragedy . . . in the hospitals," Whitman's *Memoranda* had approached as closely as any other written work to the grim reality of the war.[28] His desire to publish the memoranda of his wartime experiences may have been spurred by the success of Louisa May Alcott's *Hospital Sketches* in 1863. Bronson Alcott's thirty-year-old daughter had volunteered as a nurse, arriving in Washington the same month as Whitman. Although she boasted (as Whitman did about himself) that she had never been sick a day in her life prior to her hospital service, she left after six weeks, claiming to have contracted typhoid pneumonia but apparently suffering (as Whitman later did) from nervous prostration induced by her terrifying experiences in the hospital wards. (After she returned home, she was quickly relieved of her "typhoid pneumonia" by a lady mesmerist.) The charming and evocative narrative of her nursing duties portrays her as a tormented but outwardly calm heroine of the military wards. Her tight-lipped stories about the deaths of soldiers, toward

Walt Whitman and the Body Beautiful

whom she felt a deep commitment, invite comparison with some of the passages in Whitman's *Memoranda* and in the *Drum-Taps* poems.[29]

In January, 1863, when the poet had barely established his routine of hospital visits in Washington, he wrote to Emerson about his exciting discovery of a new literary territory (whose outskirts he had tentatively explored among the disabled soldiers in the New York hospitals):

> The first shudder has long passed over, and I must say I find deep things, unreckoned by current print or speech. The Hospital, I do not find it, the repulsive place of sores and fevers, not the place of querulousness, nor the bad results of morbid years which one avoids like bad s[mell]s—at least [not] so is it under the circumstances here—other hospitals may be, but not here.
>
> I desire and intend to write a little book out of this phase of America, her masculine young manhood, its conduct under most trying of and highest of all exigency, which she, as if by lifting a corner in a curtain, has vouchsafed me to see America, already brought to Hospital in her fair youth—brought and deposited here in this great, whited sepulchre of Washington itself. . . .[30]

The report, written in moving but unvarnished prose and based on his on-the-spot observations, took form in *Memoranda of a Year* which he tried unsuccessfully to have published in the fall of 1863 and which he brought out, somewhat revised, more than a decade later, as *Memoranda During the War*.

For most readers, the poems in *Drum-Taps* (1865), tempered in the bloody holocaust, best evoke the truth of these terrible years. As if to symbolize the central reality of the war, the poet presents a bouquet of wounds and dirges to his muse, and triumphant goddess of liberty, in "Lo, Victress on the Peaks":

> No poem proud, I chanting bring to thee, nor mastery's rapturous
> verse,
> But a cluster containing night's darkness and blood-dripping
> wounds,
> And psalms of the dead.[31]

Next only to the war itself, the element that unifies *Drum-Taps* is the persona of the poet-healer, whose agonies are recollected in tranquility and filtered through the poems. Outwardly impassive, like the poet himself, the persona burns with suppressed emotions, for he has projected himself into each man's struggle with death. But he perseveres in his labors of mercy and of interpreting the wartime experience in terms of the democratic spirit "that, in all its diversities, at all times, under all circumstances . . . promulges liberty, justice, the cause of the people as against infidels and tyrants."[32] A self-portrait of this rough-hewn hero appears as the closing lyric of *Drum-Taps*:

> Not youth pertains to me,
> Nor delicatesse, I cannot beguile the time with talk,
> Awkward in the parlor, neither a dancer nor elegant,
> In the learn'd coterie sitting constrain'd and still, for learning
>   inures not to me,
> Beauty, knowledge, inure not to me—yet there are two or three
>   things inure to me,
> I have nourish'd the wounded and sooth'd many a dying soldier,
> And at intervals waiting or in the midst of camp,
> Composed these songs.[33]

Years later, after looking through William Ernest Henley's *In Hospital: Rhymes and Rhythms* (1888), with its embittered patient's-eye-view of the private hospital, Whitman labeled it a "curio," not without power "yet not all-powerful." Henley's persona is much too involved in the drama of his own suffering and in the dispassionate observation of the hospital milieu to suit Whitman's taste. By way of contrast, the wound-dresser hero of *Drum-Taps* articulates an entire nation's grief and thus achieves immense poetic power. This tragic hero, and not Lincoln, is the focal figure in "When Lilacs Last in the Dooryard Bloom'd," the greatest poem of the war years. Just as the death of Lincoln gives the nation its most vital unifying myth, as the poet wisely observed in his prose tribute to the fallen president, so the compassionate and conciliatory persona of the war poems objectifies the most enduring truths of the war and its aftermath.[34]

A handful of *Drum-Taps* poems reflect Whitman's experiences in campground and hospital. "The Wound-Dresser," a memento of his labors among the sick and dying soldiers, and "Come Up from the Fields Father," the evocation of his letter writing to the families of these soldiers, stem from his service in the Washington area hospitals. Two poems appear to have been inspired by his visit to Falmouth, Virginia, in the closing days of 1862, when he

Walt Whitman and the Body Beautiful

lived in his brother George's army tent and apparently joined a military party that went out to bury the dead who were left on the field after the disastrous Battle of Fredericksburg. "A Sight in Camp in the Daybreak Gray and Dim," with its trinity of dead soldiers—"the elderly man so gaunt and grim, with well-gray'd hair, and flesh all sunken about the eyes," the youth with still-blooming cheeks, and the man with "the face of the Christ himself"—is one such poem. The other is "As Toilsome I Wander'd Virginia's Woods," in which the persona beholds the haunting inscription on a soldier's grave—an autumnal vision which he compulsively recalls "at times through changeful season and scene." Four short poems—"Cavalry Crossing a Ford," "An Army Corps on the March," "Bivouac on a Mountain Side," and "By the Bivouac's Fitful Flame"—afford imagistic glimpses of army life.[35]

Two outstanding *Drum-Taps* poems apparently germinated, before Whitman's departure for Washington, during his visits to the injured soldiers at the New York Hospital, where he made notebook "pencillings" of their tales of heroism and carnage. The inspiration for "Vigil Strange I Kept on the Field One Night" may have been an account of the death of William Giggee on September 18, 1862, told to Whitman by a hospitalized soldier. The poet's prose transcription of the event reads in part: "I heard of poor Bill's death—he was shot on Pope's retreat—Arthur took him in his arms, and he died in about an hour and a half—Arthur buried him himself—he dug his grave." The poem makes use of these details, but it does not simply retell them. In its magnificently cadenced litany, "Arthur" disappears into the compassionate Whitman persona, who, in the transfiguring moonlight, watches over the beautiful dead youth.[36] "The Artilleryman's Vision," a soldier's staccato, hysterical account of a day on the bloody battlefield, was also apparently begun before Whitman's departure for the war zones. Although the final version of the poem has a single reference to the crippled and to "the wounded dripping and red," a draft version of the poem pictures the battle's aftermath in greater detail:

> Then after the battle, what a scene! O my sick soul! how the dead
> lie,
> The wounded—the surgeons and ambulances * * * *
> O what is here? O my beautiful young men! O the beautiful hair,
> clotted! the faces!
> Some lie on their backs with faces up & arms extended![37]

"A March in the Ranks Hard-Prest, and the Road Unknown" appears to be based on stories told to Whitman concerning two battles of the Civil War and on his own observations of traumas and death. It is a dramatic monologue whose tragic point of view is focused in the never-flagging memory of the Whitman persona, who once again becomes the hero of the terrifying episode. Some of the poem's details and phrasing derive from the poet's transcription, in New York, of a soldier's reminiscences of the Battle of White Oak Church. Narrated in the soldierly "we," this prose account describes a nighttime halt by a country church,

> used impromptu for a hospital for the wounded . . . all varieties, horrible beyond description—the darkness dimly lit with candles, lamps, torches, moving about, but plenty of darkness & half darkness—the crowds of wounded, bloated, and pale, the surgeons operating—the yards outside also filled—they lay on the ground, some on blankets, some on stray planks, or—the despairing screams & curses of some—the murky darkness, the gleaming of the torches, the smoke from them too—out of their senses, the doctors operating, the scent of chloroform, the glistening of the steel instruments as the flash of lamps fell upon them.[38]

Some of the poem's details and phrasing appear to be drawn from Whitman's record of soldiers' stories of the Battle of Chancellorsville, which occurred six months after his arrival in Washington:

> . . . the camp of the wounded . . . in an open space in the woods, from 500 to 600 poor fellows—the groans and the screams—the odor of blood, mixed with the fresh scent of the night, the grass, the trees—that Slaughter-house! . . . Some have their legs blown off—some bullets through the breast—some indescribably horrid wounds in the face or head, all mutilated, sickening, torn, gouged out—some in the abdomen—some mere boys—here is one his face colorless as chalk, lying perfectly still, a bullet has perforated the abdomen—life is ebbing fast, there is no help for him. . . .[39]

The twenty-five lines of "A March in the Ranks Hard-Prest, and the Road Unknown" into which these ideas are miraculously compressed are divisible into four sections. In the first six lines, "Our army foil'd with loss severe, and the sullen remnant retreating," emerges by night from the woods near a country church that has been converted to a makeshift hospital. In the second six-line

Walt Whitman and the Body Beautiful

segment, the persona enters the church, wherein the smoking red torches create a hellish glow. (Whitman was, in fact, reading Dante's *Inferno* during the period of his intensive hospital visitations.) [40] After scanning the carnage, the persona looks down and beholds many injured soldiers:

> At my feet more distinctly a soldier, a mere lad, in danger of
>   bleeding to death, (he is shot in the abdomen,)
> I stanch the blood temporarily, (the youngster's face is white as a
>   lily) * * * *

In the third segment, the persona imprints the scene upon his memory for future use and compresses it into a sensuous catalogue:

> Then before I depart I sweep my eye o'er the scene fain to absorb
>   it all,
> Faces, varieties, postures beyond description, most in obscurity,
>   some of them dead,
> Surgeons operating, attendants holding lights, the smell of ether,
>   the odor of blood,
> The crowd, O the crowd of the bloody forms, the yard outside
>   also fill'd,
> Some on the bare ground, some on planks or stretchers, some in
>   the death-spasm sweating,
> An occasional scream or cry, the doctor's shouted orders or calls,
> The glisten of the little steel instruments catching the glint of the
>   torches * * * *

In the fourth segment, the persona resumes his march into the dark unknown:

> But first I bend to the dying lad, his eyes open, a half-smile gives
>   he me,
> Then the eyes close, calmly close, and I speed forth to the
>   darkness * * * *

The soldier whom the persona has singled out—that lily-white face against the hellish red background—represents the thousands that he (like the historic Whitman) has tended, touching them with a presence like that of a living savior, stanching their bleeding wounds or easing their death spasms.

The finest evocation of Whitman's hospital service is "The Wound-Dresser," a somber self-portrait rendered in the same tones as "Prayer of Columbus." In this retrospective view by an old man, fated to relive his grim tours of hospital duty in "the rows of the hospital tent, or under the roof'd hospital," the persona's courage and equanimity never give out, it appears. But beneath the calm surface a tide of compassion wells up and nearly destroys his sanity, just as the physical and psychic strains of Whitman's hospital experiences had repeatedly prostrated *him*. The persona's compulsive and timeless journey, "with hinged knees returning" to the hospital corridors, is conveyed in the repeated statements, "I go," "I onward go," and "On, on I go." The central action in the poem—his dressing of wounds—is framed by the phrase "in dreams' projections," repeated in lines 20 and 59.[41]

The activities of the fictive wound dresser in the poem bear some resemblance to Whitman's hospital labors and to those of the army nurses and the military surgeons. Like Whitman, the wound dresser persona exhibits profound compassion and an electric presence. Like the army nurses, the persona attends the sick soldiers. Indeed, the poet testified to his own occasional washing and dressing of wounds, declaring that "I have some cases where the patient is unwilling anyone should do this but me."[42] But most of the nurses were poorly trained women who, besides changing surgical dressings, performed menial chores and were assigned to a particular group of invalids in a single ward. Like the surgeons, the persona walks from ward to ward, performing his errands of mercy. Thus, "in dreams' projections" the healer-persona pursues what the poet, in his New York Hospital reportage, had called the noblest career "of the world's many avenues of fame or heroism," that of a physician. It would appear that Whitman (whom O'Connor described as walking the hospitals) modeled the ambulatory wound dresser, in part, on a "walker" (the term commonly used to designate the young house surgeons, or interns, to whom he felt attracted).[43]

In order to achieve dramatic unity, the poem concentrates on the wound dresser and his patients rather than on any representative military surgeon and a cross-section of hospitalized soldiers. Whitman elsewhere acknowledged that "the prevailing maladies" which he had observed in the military hospitals were "typhoid fever, and the camp fevers generally, diarrhoea, catarrhal affections and bronchitis, rheumatism and pneumonia. These forms of sickness lead, all the rest follow." Diarrhea, he said near the war's end,

Walt Whitman and the Body Beautiful

was "the great disease of the army."[44] Many victims of serious injuries to the internal organs died before reaching the army hospitals, and those who were treated there often perished because the relatively primitive medical science of the era could avail them little. Nevertheless, the poem does describe those *wounds* which were most often treated in the military hospitals, essentially, as the poet remarked, injuries to the arms and legs.

The first section of "The Wound-Dresser" is a preamble in which the persona is "witness again" to the agonies of the hospitals. In lines added in the 1870's, he pictures his transformation into the role of wound dresser:

> Arous'd and angry, I'd thought to beat the alarum, and urge
>   relentless war,
> But soon my fingers fail'd me, my face droop'd and I resign'd
>   myself,
> To sit by the wounded and soothe them, or silently watch the
>   dead * * * *

The second section (lines 13 to 38) begins with a tribute to the joys of the archetypal soldier, but its mood quickly saddens as the poem focuses on the wound dresser, who relives his tours of hospital duty before the reader's eyes. His words seem to be spoken, as if from the grave, by the spirit of the dead poet to the generations of living Americans, for the mythic wound dresser has been charged with a solemn duty: forever to rekindle these grim memories in the hearts of his countrymen.

> But in silence, in dreams' projections,
> While the world of gain and appearance and mirth goes on,
> So soon what is over forgotten, and waves wash the imprints off
>   the sand,
> With hinged knees returning I enter the doors (while for you up
>   there,
> Whoever you are, follow without noise and be of strong heart.)

The alliterative and driving rhythmic lines which follow are an incantation to the godlike healer—a dream ritual in which the wound dresser is reincarnated through an act of memory. "Bearing the bandages," supplied in vast quantities by the ladies of the Sanitary Commission, and followed by an attendant who carries a refuse pail, he tends each soldier in a manner that seems superior to life:

Bearing the bandages, water and sponge,
Straight and swift to my wounded I go,
Where they lie on the ground after the battle brought in,
Where their priceless blood reddens the grass the ground,
Or to the rows of the hospital tent, or under the roof'd hospital,
To the long rows of cots up and down each side I return,
To each and all one after another I draw near, not one do I miss,
An attendant follows holding a tray, he carries a refuse pail,
Soon to be fill'd with clotted rags and blood, emptied, and fill'd
    again.

Just as he does in "A March in the Ranks Hard-Prest, and the Road
Unknown," the persona singles out from the mass of the wounded
one soldier, who thus becomes universalized into all those whom
he has tended:

I onward go, I stop,
With hinged knees and steady hand to dress wounds,
I am firm with each, the pangs are sharp yet unavoidable,
One turns to me his appealing eyes—poor boy! I never knew you,
Yet I think I could not refuse this moment to die for you, if that
    would save you.

In the poem's third section (lines 39 to 58), the persona attends
to the amputees, the soldier wounded in the neck, and the dying
soldier with the deep side-wound and "the yellow-blue countenance" symptomatic of the pyaemia and septicemia which were
chiefly responsible for the fact that 62 percent of the chest wounds
and 87 percent of the abdominal wounds proved fatal to the boys
in blue.[45] He also cleanses the wound "with a gnawing and putrid
gangrene, so sickening, so offensive." Indeed, "in dreams' projections" he visualizes that gangrenous wound, with its gray edge of
offensive slough, its flesh eaten away to lay bare artery and nerve;
he sees himself, like a walker or surgeon, etherizing the soldier,
cauterizing the wound with nitric acid or bromine, and dressing it
with powdered charcoal.[46] Throughout the passage, the merciful
and agonized persona is the center of the remembered drama:

On, on, I go, (open doors of time! open hospital doors!)
The crush'd head I dress, (poor crazed hand tear not the bandage
    away,)
The neck of the cavalry-man with the bullet through and through
    I examine,

Walt Whitman and the Body Beautiful

Hard the breathing rattles, quite glazed already the eye, yet life
    struggles hard,
(Come sweet death! be persuaded O beautiful death!
In mercy come quickly.)

From the stump of the arm, the amputated hand,
I undo the clotted lint, remove the slough, wash off the matter and
    blood,
Back on his pillow the soldier bends with curv'd neck and side-
    falling head,
His eyes are closed, his face is pale, he dares not look on the
    bloody stump,
And has not yet look'd on it.

I dress a wound in the side, deep, deep,
But a day or two more, for see the frame all wasted and sinking,
And the yellow-blue countenance see.

I dress the perforated shoulder, the foot with the bullet-wound,
Cleanse the one with a gnawing and putrid gangrene, so
    sickening, so offensive,
While the attendant stands behind aside me holding the tray and
    pail.

I am faithful, I do not give out,
The fractur'd thigh, the knee, the wound in the abdomen,
These and more I dress with impassive hand, (yet deep in my
    breast a fire, a burning flame.)

In the coda (lines 59 to 65) the image of the Christ-like healer
and the persona of Walt Whitman the hospital attendant converge
into a composite and timeless figure:

Thus in silence in dreams' projections,
Returning, resuming, I thread my way through the hospitals,
The hurt and wounded I pacify with soothing hand,
I sit by the restless all the dark night, some are so young,
Some suffer so much, I recall the experience sweet and sad,
(Many a soldier's loving arms about this neck have cross'd and
    rested,
Many a soldier's kiss dwells on these bearded lips.)

The very note of the empathy-wracked wound dresser who
cries out, "I am faithful, I do not give out," can be heard in Whitman's letters to his mother. In October, 1863, he confessed to her
that the stress of the "sympathy and anguish here in the hospital"

would be unbearable except for his outside interests—his job, his walks, his friends, and his poetry. "It is curious," he said, "when I am present at the most appalling things, deaths, operations, sickening wounds (perhaps full of maggots), I do not fail, although my sympathies are very much excited, but keep singularly cool— but often hours afterward, perhaps when I am home or out walking alone, I feel sick and actually tremble, when I recall the thing & have it in my mind again before me. . . ."[47] Painfully haunted by these nightmare visions, the poet was fated to "recall the thing" repeatedly. Witnessing the festive ball in honor of Lincoln's second inaugural, he found the merriment suddenly crowded from his mind by the tormenting vision of the hospital wards: "To-night, beautiful women, perfumes, the violins' sweetness, the polka and the waltz; but then, the amputation, the blue face, the groan, the glassy eye of the dying, the clotted rag, the odor of wounds and blood, and many a mother's son amid strangers, passing away untended there, (for the crowd of the badly hurt was great, and much for nurse to do, and much for surgeon.)" And in "Old War-Dreams" he paid an awesome tribute to the terror of "the thing":

> In midnight sleep of many a face of anguish,
> Of the look at first of the mortally wounded, (of that indescribable
>   look,)
> Of the dead on their backs with arms extended wide,
>   I dream, I dream, I dream.
>
> Of scenes of Nature, fields and mountains,
> Of skies so beauteous after a storm, and at night the moon so
>   unearthly bright,
> Shining sweetly, shining down, where we dig the trenches and
>   gather the heaps,
>   I dream, I dream, I dream.
>
> Long have they pass'd, faces and trenches and fields,
> Where through the carnage I moved with a callous composure, or
>   away from the fallen,
> Onward I sped at the time—but now of their forms at night,
>   I dream, I dream, I dream.[48]

The nightmare world of wartime suffering undermined the poet's health and his easy confidence as the spokesman of physical perfection. He never wholly abdicated his role as the poet of the body, but his postwar writings stress the spiritual and ethical elements of human experience rather than the physical ones. The later poems allude to the body only to furnish an occasional metaphor or illustrate a moral lesson. Thus, exclusive of the *Drum-Taps* lyrics, only three of the seven new poems added to the 1867 edition—"One's Self I Sing," "The City Dead-House," and "Return of the Heroes"—relate to the body. And the poet began, with this edition, his systematic deletion from the earlier poems of many allusions to science, medicine, and physical exuberance.

In *Democratic Vistas* (1871) he posed comfortably as his nation's benign moral diagnostician—"like a physician diagnosing some deep disease"—and seasoned his diagnosis of America's ethical health with such medicated figures of speech as "life's gymnasium," "freedom's athletes," and the "hectic glow" of apparent national health, and the miasmal image (fully developed in "This Compost") of nature's chemistry distilling human corpses and diseased matter into life-giving and spiritual food. Just as the "kosmical, antiseptic power" of "Nature's stomach," he declared, "is fully strong enough not only to digest the horrible matter always presented, not to be turn'd aside, and perhaps, indeed, intuitively gravitating thither—but even to change such contributions into the nutriment for the highest use and life—so American democracy's." He translated his wartime experiences in the hospitals and camps into a moral lesson and metaphor: the blood of the dead and wounded soldiers was destined to become the cement of national unity.[49]

"Song of the Exposition" (1871) seeks to replace the departed glories of war with the glories of labor and personal health. Stressing a point of view he had long advocated, Whitman asks the nation to dispense with its emphasis on

> The unhealthy pleasures, extravagant dissipations of the few,
> With perfumes, heat and wine, beneath the dazzling chandeliers.

Instead he proposes "superber themes for poets and for art": a work ethic ("healthy toil and sweat, endless, without cessation"), a modest life-style characterized by simple living and a wholesome diet, and a race of "longeve" (long-lived) and "sweet-blooded" persons to be the ideal breeders and citizens of the future. He exhorts the artists:

To exalt the present and the real,
To teach the average man the glory of his daily walk and trade,
To sing in songs how exercise and chemical life are never to be
    baffled,
To manual work for each and all * * * *
Whatever forms the average, strong, complete, sweet-blooded
    man or woman, the perfect longeve personality,
And helps its present life and health and happiness, and shapes its
    soul,
For the eternal life to come.[50]

Aside from this great public poem, the new poems of the 1872 edition of *Leaves of Grass* rarely touch on physiological themes. "Thou Mother with Thy Equal Brood" does describe a sweltering and diseased Mother America, symbolically afflicted with the "hideous claws" of breast cancer and flushed with the "hectic" of "moral consumption." But "Passage to India," the noblest poem introduced in this edition, typifies the poet's abandonment of physical themes.[51] Whereas "Song of the Open Road" (1856) had celebrated the joyous union of body and soul in their sensuous quest for self-discovery and comradeship, "Passage to India" concludes with a bittersweet canticle to the solitary soul launching its final journey after it has apparently divested itself of what the poet had formerly called the "excrementitious" body.[52] And for two decades thereafter, Whitman occasionally composed valedictory and introspective old-age poems and a scattering of bittersweet verses in which the once-vigorous hero diagnoses his own physical condition as if he were both doctor and patient.

The postwar years demonstrate the poet's unflagging interest in health and medical matters, faith in the healthy body as the crucial element in the development of a sound personality, and loyalty to those physiological values which had once enabled him to shape the idealized healer-persona. His interest in the curative sciences was sustained during these years by his chronic invalidism and by his contacts with medical men in the nation's capital and, afterwards, in Philadelphia and Camden. Although he charged the doctors with unjustifiable reliance on drugs, he declared that they were best qualified to appreciate his poetry. Dr. Bucke records his "speaking with more than usual deliberation to a group of medical men, friends of his, in answer to their inquiries," explaining to them that the intent of *Leaves of Grass* is to sing out "the ecstasy of simply physiological Being."[53] Years later, showing Horace Traubel a flattering letter from a Scottish ship's surgeon, Whitman remarked: "He's a surgeon, Horace, you notice; you remember what I've always said: surgeons, mothers, nurses—they should understand me best of all: they do not always do so, but they should. . . ." Those readers, he felt, could judge his poetry best "who know the physiological man—the physiologic-spiritual man."[54] His conversations with Anne Gilchrist's daughter Beatrice, who was attending the Women's Medical College in Philadelphia in 1877–78, often focused on the attributes of the ideal physician and the creative possibilities of medicine.[55]

Whitman measured the doctors who attended him not by medical expertise alone but by the extent to which they aided in his physical survival, by their willingness to dispense with the medicines that he hated and distrusted, by their reliance on the healing powers of nature, and by their personal qualities. His judgments show that he was not untouched by the emergence, after mid-century, of the doctor as a culture hero. These criteria are evident, for example, in his assessment of the thirty-one-year-old Dr. William Beverly Drinkard, who attended him following his stroke in 1873 and whom he called a "red-hot" Rebel but a "first-rate physician" who had been "very kind" to him. Dr. Drinkard, the first ophthalmologist in the City of Washington, was devoted to his patient's survival, erudite, meticulous, gentlemanly, and capable of perceiving that Whitman was an extraordinary man. The poet's esteem for him may be measured by his declaration that Dr. Drinkard meant almost as much to him as did Dr. Bucke, whom he credited with saving his life in 1888.[56]

Whitman's initial response to Dr. Matthew Grier, the thirty-three-year-old Philadelphian who treated him (with electric shock, alcohol, and pills) when he first settled in Camden, was also enthusiastic. The poet was impressed by Dr. Grier as "rather a curious fellow—a great bully, vehement, loud words & plenty of them (the very reverse of my valued Dr. Drinkard)—& yet I value what *he* says and does for me. . . ."[57] But because of his worsening physical condition, Whitman changed his mind and sought other medical aid. A similar shift of attitude characterized his relations with Dr. Dowling Benjamin (the protégé of Dr. James M. Ridge, at whose Camden drugstore–office at Third and Mickle streets the poet often stopped to chat about literature and who, in his professional career, was closely associated with all three Camden-based physicians who are known to have attended Whitman).[58] To William O'Connor the invalid wrote at first: "The doctor comes every day—(old school, but receptive & progressive—believes more in drugs and medicines than I do, but so far his diagnosis seems thorough, & his doses are justified by results). . . ." But because he could not long accept any doctor with a predilection for prescribing medicines and possibly because he objected to the doctor's rather erratic personality, he became disenchanted. Six years later, when Dr. Bucke recommended that Whitman again avail himself of Dr. Benjamin's services (for by then the Camden physician had become a medical educator and was prominent in state medical groups), Whitman dismissed the suggestion, alleging that Dr. Benjamin was a "drugger"—a bitter allusion to his proclivity for prescribing drugs and a probable slur at his training as a pharmacist and his proprietorship of a drugstore.[59]

A different sequence of events characterized Whitman's relations with two other attending physicians. The young and scholarly Camden physician Dr. James Francis Walsh visited the poet almost daily—sometimes in company with Dr. Osler—during his critical illness of 1888–89. (The doctor's brother was William S. Walsh, associated with J. B. Lippincott Publishers, whom Whitman called "a friend personally and literarily.") Initially, Whitman informed Dr. Bucke that he liked Dr. Walsh even though the latter gave him too much medicine; but after a while, having persuaded the doctor of his own distaste for medications, he approvingly wrote: "Dr. Walsh comes every day, seems to watch carefully but gives no medicine—I like him & his ways."[60] Whitman reacted similarly to Dr. John K. Mitchell, the son of Dr. S. Weir Mitchell, and himself the author of popular medical treatises. The young Philadelphia doctor, who would one day become a distinguished neurologist and therapeutist, attended the poet intermittently between 1888 and the end of 1890. Following a visit during which he prescribed calomel and other medicines that Whitman refused to take, the poet complained that the physician had "tried to fill me with doctor poisons." But after a subsequent visit by the doctor, the poet characteristically relented, declaring him to be "a fine young fellow," largely because Dr. Mitchell, acceding to his dislike of medicines, was prescribing few, if any, drugs.[61]

Walt Whitman and the Body Beautiful

Three of the physicians who attended Walt Whitman in Camden were the sort of intuitional and high-principled men of science who came close to his concept of the ideal physician. Richard Maurice Bucke, S. Weir Mitchell, and William Osler were medical innovators, successful practitioners, and men of letters. In varying degrees they sympathized with the poet's literary career and were moved by his personality and presence. In their professional ministrations, all three demonstrated a wholesome respect for the total organism and personality of their patients and a skepticism toward drugs.

From Whitman's first meeting with Dr. Bucke in 1877, the Canadian physician became his intimate friend and principal medical adviser. Eighteen years younger than the poet, this erudite and determined man had experienced a full and adventuresome life. An honor graduate of McGill University, Dr. Bucke began his quarter-of-a-century tenure as the superintendent of the asylum at London, Ontario, just before he met Whitman. The doctor seemed to possess some of the qualities of the intuitive healer that the poet had idealized. One of Bucke's associates observed that he had assumed the post at the asylum "with no special knowledge of psychiatry but with high intelligence and ideals, a rich background of experience and a keen interest in all things pertaining to the mind." The series of reforms that he initiated at the institution, based primarily on his shrewd observations of human nature, included the rejection of alcohol as a therapeutic, the establishment of a cottage system of residences, the relaxation of physical restraints upon his patients, and the assignment of the able-bodied inmates to regular chores. "Work," he declared, "is the most valuable curative agent we possess." His attitude toward the mentally ill was in accord with Whitman's belief that a physician should treat the whole person rather than some localized aspects of his illness. "It comes to this," said Dr. Bucke, who attained international honors for his work with the mentally ill, "that the treatment of the mind resolves itself into an endeavor to place the whole physical system on the best possible basis of health and efficiency."[62]

Dr. Bucke was predisposed to serve Whitman. A decade before their first encounter, he had read *Leaves of Grass*; the result, he declared, was "instantaneous and lasting." In 1872, following an evening devoted to reading poems by Whitman and certain English Romantic poets, he claimed to have experienced a psychic "illumination." Following his first visit to the poet, the mystic doctor asserted, "a sort of spiritual intoxication set in that did not reach its culmination for some weeks," and the subsequent contacts between the pair allegedly helped him to achieve "a spiritual existence on a higher plane." Bucke was convinced that Whitman was the best living proof that mankind could evolve a superior intuitive-spiritual sense of the sort exemplified by the persona in "Song of Myself." Two years after meeting him, Bucke dedicated *Man's Moral Nature*, in which this principle was expounded, "to the man of all men past and present that I have known has the most exalted moral nature—Walt Whitman." In 1883 he authored *Walt Whitman*; it was originally intended to promote the poet as an avatar of the godlike moral nature into which humanity must one day evolve, but under Whitman's strong editorial hand the book was transformed into a depiction of Whitman as a great personality and artist.[63]

In the summer of 1880, after much urging, Whitman went to Canada to visit Dr. Bucke and his family, whose home was located on the grounds of the large sanitarium which he superintended. The veteran critic of hospital facilities commented that Dr. Bucke's institution "is among the most advanced, perfected, and kindly and rationally carried on, of all its kind in America." He was fascinated by the inmates at the Sunday services in the newly completed chapel and the "hundreds and hundreds of Bucke's insane." But in his seventh decade, after having visited sick omnibus drivers and firemen, sat by the bedsides of thousands of soldiers, and committed his own brother to the Kings County Lunatic Asylum, he felt no exhilaration in watching the hapless patients: "It became a too-near fact—too poignant—too sharply painful—too ghastly true," he explained. To the old paralytic, the uses of adversity were seldom sweet.[64]

Bucke was Whitman's financial benefactor, confidant, self-anointed literary explicator, and medical supervisor. (He even aped the poet's appearance, sporting a linen shirt, a slouch hat, and a flowing beard.) His professional activities took him frequently to Philadelphia; his concern with Whitman's well-being brought him to Camden. He made sure that Whitman was attended by the best available medical talent, and he frequently sent medical advice through the mails. For his part, Whitman understood the importance of Dr. Bucke's devotion; neither his tempestuous enthusiasms nor his shortcomings as a literary critic could dampen Whitman's affection. In a letter to Tennyson, he introduced Dr. Bucke as "my good friend and physician." Always captious about his physicians, Whitman admitted that he was "as afraid of Bucke's [medical] advice as anybody's." But this "free, simple, manly man" was the brightest star in the poet's medical galaxy: "Doctor is the kingpin." He is "swift of execution—lucid, sane, decisive." "He is on top of the heap. He has such a clear head, such a fund of common sense—such steady eyes—such a steady hand. As you say, Bucke is a scientist, not a doctor; he has had severe personal experiences—is an expert in questions involving the mind—is in every sort of way a large man—liberal, devoted, farseeing. I especially owe him so much—Oh, so much!" And he inscribed a copy of his *Complete Poetry & Prose—1855–1888*, "To Dr. R. M. Bucke of Canada from his friend the author of this Volume—with best love—memories of many seasons, jaunts, talks, enjoyments, physician's help & steady faithfulness thro' thick & thin—May God bless you in y'r comings in & goings out Maurice—you & yours—is my prayer."[65]

Dr. Silas Weir Mitchell also served as Whitman's medical counselor during some of Whitman's Camden years. The pioneer psychiatrist and expert on the injuries of the nerves, who has been called "the father of neurology in America," was a distinguished medical educator as well as the author of novels, poems, and best-selling books of common-sense medical advice. He also invented the "rest cure"—a course of treatment based on a graduated program of "physical upbuilding" and mental "suggestion," fattening diet, exercise, electrical stimulation, and massage.[66] As if to confirm Whitman's belief (dramatized in the character of the healer persona and confirmed in occasional remarks) that a doctor's chief asset is his magnetic personality, an associate of Dr. Mitchell observed that his success as a therapist was "more largely the result of a personal factor—the deep faith the people had in his power to cure"—than of any medical secret he possessed.[67] Dr. Mitchell, who began attending the poet in the 1870's, may still have been caring for his medical needs in 1884 when he wrote to Dr. Oliver Wendell Holmes that "that queer creature" Whitman had entranced him with an account of his stroll with Emerson on the Boston Common a quarter of a century earlier. Mitchell was one of two benefactors who paid one hundred dollars apiece, in 1886, to attend the poet's Lincoln lecture in Philadelphia. An advocate of fresh-air therapy and the inventor of the camp cure, he demonstrated his esteem for Whitman in a volume of essays by including him—alongside Thoreau, Wordsworth, and Shakespeare—as one of the great poets of the outdoors.[68] "I did a great many things for him of which I have never talked, and some of those things involving pretty large expenditures," said Dr. Mitchell. "15$ a month I paid for more than 2 years to keep him alive."[69]

The aristocratic Mitchell "could help support Whitman," says his biographer, "but he could never forget that Walt was no gentleman." Whitman may have been sensitive to this condescension, but he concluded that Dr. Mitchell was "a man of the old school; he is well worth knowing. . . ." The poet opined, "I can't say he's a world-author, but he's a world-doctor for sure. . . ." Many of the neurologist's popular medical works and novels stemmed from his care and observation of Civil War casualties and therefore should have interested Whitman, but of these he left no opinion. He termed the physician's several volumes of poetry "nonvital," "stiff in the knees," and "very bad, too awful in their inadequacy— but personally he is a man to meet, to know. . . ."[70]

In 1884 (the year Whitman purchased his little house at 328 Mickle Street), Dr. Mitchell lured Dr. William Osler from Canada to be professor of clinical medicine at the University of Pennsylvania. In June, 1886, when the poet was suffering from what Dr. Osler diagnosed as "a transient indisposition," Osler responded to Dr. Bucke's request to visit the ailing Whitman, with whose person and poetry he was then unacquainted. Osler, who had graduated from McGill University and studied in the clinics of London, Berlin, and Vienna, was (like his patient) skeptical of drugs and reflected the renewed esteem in the medical world for the *vis medicatrix naturae*—what has been called "the defensive and prophylactic apparatus and the healing powers of nature."[71] In evaluating Dr. Osler as "very 'cute, a natural physician," the poet was paying him the supreme compliment by comparing him favorably to the born healer who is instinctively aware of the curative powers of nature—the prototype of the healer-persona in *Leaves of Grass*. Although Whitman was sometimes piqued by Osler's "pooh-poohs" of his pessimistic self-diagnoses and by his "professional air of the doctor," he vowed that Dr. Osler was "at the head of the band [of physicians]." At another time he called him "a great man—one of the rare men . . . he has the air of the thing about him—of achievement." [72] As a virtuoso scholar, expert in many branches of knowledge, Dr. Osler did attain international eminence as a clinician and medical educator and as a classicist. He served as Regius professor of medicine at Oxford and was knighted in 1921. Two decades after leaving Philadelphia, he defined Whitman's role as a teacher and prophet to the readers of the *Times* of London and asserted that the poet's teachings had molded his own outlook: "Possessed in rare degree of the Greek combination of the love of humanity with the love of craft—philanthropia and philotechnia," he declared, Whitman had been both practical and philosophical. [73]

Ever since Whitman's newspaper days, the poet had cherished the Hippocratic principle that the innate natural powers are the principal healers of disease. Like the homeopathic and eclectic doctors of an earlier era, he still denied that disease is usually a distinctive condition affecting a specific organ but held that it most often is a derangement of the *vis medicatrix naturae*. According to an authority, this principle means that "the final decision" between sickness and recovery "depends in most cases on the healing powers of nature, and . . . even the most ideal activity of the physician must find its fulcrum and measure in this regulative-compensatory reaction of the organism, in the natural defensive and protective apparatus." [74] To Horace Traubel, Whitman declared: "By nature, by observation, by the doctors, I have learned that the thing to do when I am really down is to rely upon the *vis*, as it is called—the inherited forces." The *vis*, he alleged, either comes to the sufferer's rescue or "all may as well be given up at once." His medical intuitions were sound. Progressive medical practice, as Richard H. Shryock points out, has learned to respect the "concern about complete physiological reactions to disease and injury." Whitman esteemed Dr. Osler because the Canadian physician treated the whole man rather than his localized ailments, because he applied the principle that a doctor must know the natural course of a disease before he can know his patient's reaction to any medication used in its cure, and because he was skeptical of drugs. He would have cheered Dr. Osler's advice to his medical students "to cultivate a keenly sceptical attitude toward the pharmacopoeia as a whole, remembering the shrewd remark of Benjamin Franklin, that 'he is the best doctor who knows the worthlessness of most medicines.'"[75]

The elderly Whitman was sometimes irked and sometimes amused by the doctors' air of self-confidence. Reacting to the medical care he had received, he asserted that he had "no great faith in or fear of doctors—they don't seem to do much good or much harm." On another occasion, he exclaimed: "Ah! those doctors: after all, Horace, do they know much? I love doctors and hate their medicine." Petulantly, he denounced

> the drug theory: there's something wrong about it: it's a poisonous viperous notion: it does not seem to fit with what we know of the human body—with the physical something or other and the mental something or other going together: they doctor a man as a disease not as a man: a part of him—doctor a part of him: a leg, a belly, an eye: they ignore the rest: as if it wasn't true that the seat of the trouble in most cases is not at the point of demonstration but way below somewhere: oh! I am impatient about it: it riles me—makes me say ugly things.[76]

During his wartime service, he claimed, he had observed that the doctors in the military hospitals prescribed too much medicine, thus "oftener making things worse." Because most drugs disagreed with him, he sometimes refused to take any medication. The quinine prescribed by Dr. Drinkard had made him dizzy; so did a medicine given him by Dr. Bucke to counteract his feeling of "caving-in-ness." Yet, in contrite moments, realizing that his criticism of the doctors may have been intemperate, he acknowledged that as long as patients insist on getting "a powder or two" from the doctors, the latter will feel obliged to prescribe medicines.[77]

He continued to insist that the body requires "saner correctives" than drugs and, like the practitioners of an earlier era, to equate good health with a well-functioning stomach. In this period, Dr. Austin Flint pointed to the lingering popularity of "the notion that very many diseases originated in, or were perpetuated by, causes acting within the alimentary canal."[78] The dyspeptic old poet observed, "Indigestion accounts for fully nine-tenths of all our ailments"; but like the Walt Whitman of four decades earlier who had sketched out a manual of health, he denounced abstinence and self-denial, arguing that "a fair allowance of victuals and drink" is needed to build the blood and that "behind the tally of genius and morals stands the stomach, and gives a sort of casting vote."[79] One of the "physical lessons" he claimed to have learned in the Civil War hospitals was "how much physical trouble is traceable to stomachic derangement." He insisted on "some sort of intimate association between a man's belly and his soul that no amount of spirituality can get rid of." Like Melville, who alleged that "Robustness and Health are great trencher-men," he maintained that health is the basis of artistic excellence.[80] Extolling the "grit of the body first of all—as the original guarantee of the rest" and implying that his own salubrious poetry stemmed from his original bodily vigor, he pointed out that Carlyle's dyspepsia "is to be traced in every page" of his writings.[81] Throughout his career, he claimed that sound animal functions and a smoothly operating organism are the primary endowments of the Adamic man, unspoiled by the corruptive powers of civilization, and of the heroic artist. Even after he was physically shattered, he longed to bestow upon his beloved countrymen and countrywomen the sort of perfect health that he had attributed to the hero-persona of *Leaves of Grass* and to inspire and hasten the creation of a new race of hardy men and women.

The Medical Pseudo-Sciences

"The Ultimate Brain"

4

PHRENOLOGY HELPED WHITMAN TO DEFINE personal greatness, the nature of poetry, and the role of the ideal poet.[1] "Through the fertile years of Whitman's productive life," declared Edward Hungerford, "he clung firmly to three ideas related to phrenology. The poet who should represent and interpret American life should be well developed in all the phrenological organs of his head. He himself was so developed, and his poetry corroborated his phrenology. The structure of poetry itself should have a solid base in the science of phrenology."[2] Additionally, phrenology served as a major source of Whitman's ideas about physiological and moral evolution, and furnished him not only with language and ornamentation for *Leaves of Grass* but also with metre-making arguments for some of the poems.

Phrenology emerged, at the end of the eighteenth century, as an attempt to formulate a medically based faculty psychology that could explain why individuals were characterized by particular traits. Its inventor, Dr. Franz Joseph Gall, a pioneer in scientific brain surgery and the investigation of the spinal cortex, assumed that all talents are innate, that they depend on organic structures within the brain, and that the brain is "the organ of all faculties, tendencies, and feelings."[3] His investigations of patients in European asylums had convinced him that all human traits (faculties) are situated in specific areas of each of the brain's hemispheres and that their shape and dimensions influence the shape and size of the skull. Each phrenological faculty (or "organ") from Veneration to Destructiveness was said by him to have a positive function and, when properly exercised, to be the source of physical and moral gratification. These faculties—the control centers of specific activities—were supposed to be grouped within the skull in the following manner: "The animal propensities at the side of the head, between and around the ears; the social affections in the back and lower portion; the aspiring faculties in its crown; the moral on its top; and the intellectual on the forehead; the perceptives . . . over the eyes; and the reflectives, in the upper part of the forehead."[4] In order to see the plausibility of this arrangement, we need only to compare the low-browed and flat-topped head of a beast to the ovular head of a nobly civilized human—his forehead elevated by his intellectual and imaginative faculties and the top of his skull rounded upward by his reverential and moral faculties.

Applying Lamarck's famed law of exercise (the more an organ is used, the larger and stronger it becomes), Dr. Gall decided that the volume and strength of each phrenological organ can be known by plotting and calibrating the contours of the head. Measuring the size, and hence the strength, of the forty or more of these organs, which assertedly control all animal and mental functions as well as such "instincts" as the love of family, orderliness, and the worship of God, provides the basic phrenological data. The relative sizes or the combinations formed by the organs were also believed to be important. According to this concept, for instance, a large phrenological organ of Combativeness matched with a large organ of Inhabitiveness denotes a defender of his country, whereas a large organ of Combativeness paired with a large organ of Acquisitiveness merely denotes a greedy person. The size, the contours, and the bearing of the head were all said to vary according to sex, race, and temperament and to reveal individual differences in stamina, involuntary behavior, sentiment, and the reasoning powers.

Character was defined by phrenologists as the total interaction of the phrenological organs with one another and with the rest of the body. A perfect phrenological endowment, they maintained (just as Whitman did) can exist only in "the complete man" who possesses a full complement of "physical, intellectual, social, and spiritual" qualities. Thus, for example, they attributed the success of Henry Ward Beecher to a combination of excellent phrenological endowments and to the fact that he was, as they said, "a splendid animal."[5] And Whitman, as we know, claimed outstanding bodily and phrenological qualities for himself.

Each child, phrenologists said, is born with a distinctive per-

Walt Whitman and the Body Beautiful

sonality pattern and a measurable potential for greatness, but it is eligible to become more than the sum of its inherited characteristics. For according to a principle popularized by Dr. Gall's collaborator Dr. Johann Gaspar Spurzheim and the Scottish phrenologist Dr. George Combe, men and women may alter their inborn faculties and their physical traits during their lifetimes and then transmit an improved organic constitution to their children. By selective mating and by carefully training their children, parents may endow their offspring with desirable qualities or temper the undesirable ones in their genetic makeup, thus breeding out hereditary defects in successive generations and strengthening socially desirable qualities. Like the Transcendentalists and the Whitman persona, phrenologists claimed that everyone can learn to sense whether his behavior harmonizes with nature's laws. By obeying these laws and the teachings of phrenology, they said, each normal child, *"from the day of birth,"* may aspire to grow up "to be a gentle, a benevolent, and a pious adult."[6] In this manner they envisioned an end to criminal traits, to crime, and to unhappiness. And the concept that America is destined to be the setting of this moral and physiological Eden was stressed in the writings of the American phrenologists no less than in Whitman's poems.

Because the Whitman-Adam persona sometimes speaks in terms not far removed from the countless "laws" promulgated by the phrenologists—a congeries of semiscientific generalizations about health, society, and genetic renewal—these "laws" are relevant to an understanding of the poet's outlook. Perhaps the most useful codification was that made by Orson S. Fowler, the movement's chief theoretician in America and a guiding spirit in the phrenological enterprises of Fowler and Wells, a company closely involved in Whitman's poetic fortunes. The "laws" declared that a nation's future depends on a race of wholesome mothers who *"take all possible means to cultivate their physical energies"* and that "domestic life furnishes a proper and healthy stimulus for the virtuous exercise of all our mental faculties, as well as the faculties of the body." They held that "the aristocracy of family, or birth, is superior to that of wealth" and that one should trace his ancestry in order to discover what traits he has inherited. They proclaimed the need to preserve or restore the physical powers through diet, exercise, and an obedience to hereditary principles. Only in this manner will mankind enjoy well-being, become the parents of superior children, and "obviate, in part, the virulence of the original sin," which is identified as "transmitted depravity" or the violation of these same genetic principles.[7]

Phrenology was bitterly ridiculed. Admitting that its teachings may have "a certain truth," Emerson called phrenologists "theoretic kidnappers and slave-drivers" who "esteem each man the victim of another" because they attribute personality solely to inheritance and thus destroy free will. He accused them of pretending to read each man's character "by such cheap signboards as the color of his beard or the slope of his occiput," of affecting an "impudent knowingness," and, worst of all, of trying to explain spiritual truths in naively mechanistic terms.[8] Although Dr. Holmes credited the phrenologists with helping to overcome medical supernaturalism and pioneering in the study of "anthropology" and "congenital tendencies," he, too, declared that the attempt to analyze the brain by observing the shape of the skull was "founded on a delusion." He labeled phrenology a pseudo-science because it "consists of a *nomenclature*, with a self-adjusting arrangement, by which all positive evidence, or such as favors its doctrines, is admitted, and all negative evidence, or such as tells against it, is excluded." Phrenologists, he said, have foisted their lucrative and specious diagnoses on "women of both sexes, feeble-minded inquirers, poetical optimists, people who always get cheated in buying horses, philanthropists who insist on hurrying up the millennium, and others of this class. . . ." Toward phrenology Holmes grew increasingly hostile. And toward Whitman, some of whose poems he classified "among the most cynical instances of indecent exposure I recollect outside of what is sold as obscene literature," he was even more resentful. The invasion of the inviolable precincts of science by this "poetical optimist" was to Holmes as reprehensible as what he deemed to be Whitman's profanation of the muse.[9]

Despite such opposition, phrenology's bracing doctrines appealed to a reformist era and inspired sallies of the romantic imagination. They won the enthusiastic acceptance of many American intellectuals, including Walt Whitman. When Dr. Spurzheim lectured in Boston in 1832 (he died there the same year), he converted many eminent persons to his cause. Dr. Charles Knowlton revised his *Fruits of Philosophy* (1832), the first book on birth control published in the United States, to incorporate Spurzheim's doctrines.

Equally influential was the extensive American tour, less than a decade later, of George Combe, whose phrenological discourse *The Constitution of Man* was alleged by an enthusiast to have sold more than one hundred thousand copies, for a while rivaling the sales of the Bible in the English-speaking world.[10] Combe's ardent convert Horace Mann, the most prominent educator of the day, endorsed phrenology as the great empiric science of the brain, a branch of knowledge that could eliminate falsehood and serve as "the guide to philosophy and the handmaid of Christianity. Whoever disseminates true Phrenology is a public benefactor," he proclaimed.[11] Henry Ward Beecher, who preached phrenology from the pulpit, called it the best "system of natural philosophy," the philosophy of the common people, "which has underlaid [*sic*] my whole ministry."[12] To an era which longed for amelioration, Orson Fowler proposed a phrenological-physiological formula for attaining salvation and predicted that "a new order of beings" will "people the earth—a race endowed by nature with all that is noble, great, and good in man, and all that is virtuous, lovely, and exquisitely perfect in woman, marred with few defects, enfeebled with few if any diseases, defaced by few moral blemishes, and corrupted by no vices"—a day of "millennial glory" when the earth shall "become a perfect paradise!"[13]

In 1888, Whitman told a story about a drunken phrenologist who wandered into ancient Athens. The amused Athenians blindfolded the man and had him read the head "bumps" of Socrates. After the phrenologist had analyzed his subject as a lecher, a glutton, and a rascal, the crowd mocked him, but Socrates admonished them that these traits were indeed elements of his character which he had managed to suppress.[14] Whitman may have recalled the story from William Godwin's *Lives of the Necromancers*, which he had reviewed four decades earlier in the *Brooklyn Daily Eagle*, or from Johann Kaspar Lavater's *Essays on Physiognomy*, which was Godwin's probable source. In neither of these earlier versions, however, is Socrates examined by a phrenologist.[15] The aged Whitman had subconsciously modified the tale, thus showing that phrenology was still meaningful to him. In fact, his writings and conversations had long been laced with proud references to his own phrenological endowment, and many of his aesthetic judgments had been colored by phrenological values.[16]

Whitman's contacts with phrenology began in the mid-1840's, when the vogue of cranial analysis reached its crest. During the decade preceding the publication of *Leaves of Grass*, the poet read widely in phrenological publications, visited the Fowler and Wells phrenological parlors to view their famous "Golgotha of skulls" and to have himself analyzed one or more times, and absorbed the physiological and poetic teachings associated with phrenology. Although he never mastered some of the phrenologists' special techniques, he generally shared their attitudes toward the human body and their faith in improving the breed. Beginning in March, 1846, he apparently wrote several notices in the *Daily Eagle* reflecting an interest in phrenological lectures and publications. Initially, he found phrenology to be a "conglomeration of pretension and absurdity," but before the year had passed he had become favorably disposed to its doctrines. On November 16, in a review of Spurzheim's authoritative *Phrenology, or the Doctrine of Mental Phenomena*, he called the author "the most cautious, skeptical and careful of the Phrenologists" and declared that phrenologists were scientific and "philosophic revolutionizers." [17] On March 8, 1847, he wrote a favorable notice of Spurzheim's *Education: Its Elementary Principles*—a book that supplied him with ideas about the gifted child and the natural ways to ripen its innate faculties. Two days later, he advised his readers that "there can be no harm, but probably much good, in pursuing the study of phrenology." After objecting to the ridicule heaped on phrenology merely because of its novelty, he declared: "Among the most persevering workers in phrenology in this country, must certainly be reckoned the two Fowlers and Mr. Wells. . . ." Then he referred favorably to two books by Orson S. Fowler, apparently having read both of them: *Physiology, Animal and Mental, Applied to the Preservation and Restoration of Health of Body and Power of Mind*, which he called an "opportune" treatise "on health, and the means of preserving or retrieving it," and *Memory and Intellectual Improvement, Applied to Self-Education and Juvenile Instruction*, which explained the phrenological formula for developing the latent talents of children by permitting them the sort of leisurely self-discovery that is immortalized in "There Was a Child Went Forth" and "Out of the Cradle Endlessly Rocking." And for the next dozen years or so, Whitman made extensive use of phrenological writings. [18]

Whitman continued on good terms with Fowler and Wells for

many years. He regularly read their *American Phrenological Journal*, quoting from it in his newspaper columns, cutting out articles for his scrapbooks, underlining passages that interested him, and quite possibly contributing to its pages as early as 1853.[19] Apparently he was less attracted by the phrenologists' distinctive methods of character analysis than by their "other interests—education, moral instruction, and health."[20] In all likelihood he read in one issue of the periodical that, like the Franklins, the Adamses, *and* the Whitmans, "all great men are from long-lived parentage."[21] When Lorenzo Niles Fowler examined the poet in 1849 (possibly aware of his subject's preoccupation with longevity), he commented that Walt was descended from a long-lived race and may have presented him with a genealogy of the descendants of John Whitman, a putative ancestor who lived about 1640. "A Memoir of John Whitman," prepared by a Judge Mitchell and incorporated as a lengthy footnote in Orson S. Fowler's *Hereditary Descent*, alleges that piety and longevity had been the outstanding characteristics of John Whitman and four generations of his New England descendants, an impressive number of whom were clergymen and deacons. Whitman could not have faulted Fowler's flattering conclusion that "the original Whitman stock, predominated over all those that intermarried with it, not in imparting age merely, but also, in rendering all the descendants conspicuous for high moral and religious feelings, as well as for strong common sense."[22] Fowler and Wells, which may have had a hand in Whitman's abortive lecture plans, supplied some of the publications which he sold—and presumably read—in the printing office–bookstore that he operated in 1850–51. These included various periodicals; Orson S. Fowler's *Love and Parentage, Applied to the Improvement of Offspring* (1844), perhaps the first marriage manual in the tradition of Marie Stopes and Abraham Stone; and George Combe's *Lectures on Phrenology* (1839), in a copy of which he made extensive notations.[23] In 1856 the firm published Whitman's sprightly "New York Dissected" articles in their successful *Life Illustrated* weekly. As editor of the *Brooklyn Daily Times*, 1857–59, he excerpted passages from *Life Illustrated* in his columns and reviewed favorably such Fowler and Wells books of household instruction as *The Farm* and *The Garden*; such pocket manuals as *How To Talk, How To Behave*, and *How To Do Business*; Daniel Harrison Jacques's simplistic *Hints Toward Physical Perfection: or, The Philosophy of Human*

Beauty (1859); and both Horace Mann's noble speech "Demands of the Age on Colleges" and Mrs. Mann's *Christianity in the Kitchen*, whose doctrinaire application of vegetarianism and pseudo-science to the problems of household management and morality amused him.[24] His satirical sketch, in the same newspaper, deriding phrenologists, trance mediums, and vegetarians for trying to short-circuit God's plan must be weighed against his many genial reviews of Fowler and Wells books, his declaration that "so much valuable information for so little money we venture to say can be found nowhere else," and his glowing praise of the firm "whose publications on almost every subject have become the recognized standard in the several departments of information of which they treat."[25]

By 1855, when Fowler and Wells became involved in the distribution of *Leaves of Grass*, the firm had moved to 308 Broadway, directly across from the New York Hospital. Its phrenological parlors, which featured "an immense variety of skulls, from the idiot up to the most brilliant intellect,"[26] attracted thousands of the curious and many celebrities who came there to have their craniums calibrated and their names publicized. The firm published several mass-circulation magazines, chiefly related to health fads, and about two hundred book titles, mostly about problems of health, but many of its books treated such "practical" matters as household management, manners, education, chemistry, botany, or shorthand, and a scant few were volumes of belles lettres. Its booklist included a reprint of Margaret Fuller's *Papers on Literature and Art* (a work said to have influenced the poet)[27] and Hannah Gardner Creamer's *Delia's Doctors; or, A Glance Behind the Scenes* (1852), a stilted but amusing novel that ends with an impassioned testimonial to health reforms. Mrs. Creamer's mockery of female delicacy and her insistence on fresh air and wholesome exercise were consistent with the attitudes of Whitman and the Fowlers, but her story is also a good-natured spoof of phrenology, hydropathy, mesmerism, and other fads to which the publishing house was committed.

When Fowler and Wells undertook to distribute the 1855 edition of *Leaves of Grass*, which the poet had apparently produced at his own expense, Whitman had been on good terms with the firm for at least eight years. He was sympathetic to its "causes," wrote favorable reviews of its publications, and knew its management and staff. Hence the firm stocked and advertised the edition and guardedly published his anonymous self-review (by "a correspondent") in the *American Phrenological Journal*. *Life Illustrated* carried the second known review of his poems, reprinted Fanny Fern's declaration that Whitman's poems were uplifting for female readers, plugged *Leaves of Grass* in issues of August and October, 1855, and heralded the second (1856) edition of the poems by declaring, rather deceptively: "The author is still his own publisher, and Messrs. Fowler and Wells will again be his agents for the sale of the work." But according to Madeleine B. Stern, the historian of the Fowlers, the book was in effect a "joint venture" between author and publisher; indeed, "Fowler and Wells were its publishers, not in name but in act," though they did not openly acknowledge the relationship. The firm covertly brought out this edition of about one thousand copies and, by way of advancing the volume's sales, printed a parody of Whitman in a June, 1857, issue of *Life Illustrated* and advertised the parody in the *New York Tribune*.[28]

Whether or not its author designed it that way, the second edition of *Leaves of Grass* harmonized to a remarkable degree with the Fowler and Wells style and with their spirit of republican reformism. Like many of their publications, it may be read as a guidebook to the secrets of health, social justice, and spiritual advancement. It resembles one of their octavo handbooks: its table of contents seemingly offers thirty-two prescriptive poems about the attainment of physical, spiritual, and national greatness, and, like most of the firm's popular volumes of health panaceas, it concludes with an extensive body of testimonials in the form of generally favorable reviews of the poet's writings. Its poems *could*, in fact, serve a perceptive reader as a manual of physical-moral self-discovery. Unlike the first edition, in which the untitled "Song of Myself" was preceded by a crabbed-looking prose preface and followed by several lesser poems, this edition can be read as a rounded presentation of the poet's inspirational gospel. And its expressions of faith are not undercut, as they are in subsequent editions, by such poignant cries of doubt and despair as "Tears" and "As I Ebb'd with the Ocean of Life."

The second edition counsels each reader to take heart and to acknowledge his own potential for fulfillment. Its lead poem, "Poem of Walt Whitman, an American" ("Song of Myself"), introduces the persona as the archetypal American hero, and its tenth poem, "Poem of You, Whoever You Are," challenges the reader to emulate the greatness of the persona. Situated between these two poems, "Poem of Women" ("Unfolded Out of the Folds") offers a sexual and genetic key to perfection (phrenology *was* a sexual-genetic science); "Poem of the Daily Work of the Workmen and Workwomen of These States" ("A Song for Occupations") brings to the laboring classes the counselor-persona's bracing gospel that all progress is "for you"—for the most "greasy or pimpled" among them; "Poem of Many in One" ("By Blue Ontario's Shore") salutes the "nonchalant breeds" of flawless Americans being ushered in by a race of poet-heroes:

> Of the idea of perfect individuals, the idea of These States, their
> bards walk in advance, leaders of leaders,
> The attitudes of them cheer up slaves and horrify despots.[29]

"Poem of Salutation" ("Salut au Monde!") hints at the persona's spiritual mediumship (spiritualism was another Fowler and Wells "cause"); and "Broad-Axe Poem" ("Song of the Broad-Axe") pictures the eugenically and phrenologically perfect Adam and Eve in the new Eden of America's western lands. Other new poems in this edition also contain a measure of phrenological relevance. "Poem of Remembrance for a Girl or a Boy of These States" charges the younger generation with the civic duty of begetting and conceiving a new breed of Americans, and "Poem of Procreation" ("A Woman Waits for Me") links the generative act to the process of physical and racial amelioration. The most magnificent poems introduced in this edition (later entitled "Crossing Brooklyn Ferry," "A Song of the Rolling Earth," "This Compost," and "Miracles") are all testimonials to the cosmic laws governing and perfecting mankind and to the delicate correspondences between these laws and human experience.

Whatever the affinities between the second edition of *Leaves of Grass* and the Fowler and Wells spirit, the company's decision in 1857 to abandon the book seems to have been a reasonable one. These "business men, who never slumber at the post of duty," as one supporter described them,[30] chiefly catered to the family trade, and Samuel R. Wells had already cautioned Whitman in mid-1856 that the firm could not continue to publish the book unless certain objectionable passages were deleted. Why should they be burdened with a volume containing "A Woman Waits for Me," whose celebration of sexual tumescence was the focus of their displeasure, or by "Bunch Poem" ("Spontaneous Me"), which mingles the praise of chaste parental love and sexual improvability with the glorification of all prurient urges? Why publish a work which deliberately flaunted, in its appendix, a scurrilous notice, reprinted from the *Boston Intelligencer*, attacking the poet as an indecent and lunatic babbler, "roaring in pitiable delirium"? Obviously, not all the dissatisfaction was on Whitman's side in mid-1857 when Wells discreetly suggested that the poet seek a new publisher and when the poet stated that "Fowler & Wells are bad persons for me."[31] The company was glad to be rid of a poor publishing venture. But any impression of animus on Whitman's part should be tempered by the warmth of his reviews in the *Brooklyn Daily Times* and by his continued enthusiasm for phrenology.

Had Whitman never been involved with Fowler and Wells, with their picturesque personalities and their many a quaint and curious volume of forgotten lore, it is fair to conclude that *Leaves of Grass* would have been a far different book.

Phrenology helped Whitman to present his poetic image to the world and to formulate a definition of poetry. It crystallized his belief that the poet must be a cynosure of manly vigor, whose perfect brain contains those powerful faculties—Ideality, Self-Esteem, and Individuality—which enable him to test the world of experience against his instinctive sense of an ideal world and to correlate material data with spiritual truths. It reinforced his concept that a poet must be a man of perception and feeling rather than a trained or eloquent writer. And it helped him to define the artist as one who beholds the similitudes of inner being in the physical appearances of men and women and to advertise himself as one whose body is an emblem of his own physical excellence, for, as one phrenologist declared, phrenology is the science of "the outward symbols of the mind, the study of the mind's language . . . the study of the mental language written in and on the outward man."[32]

A magazine essay that Whitman read also developed the theme that man's outward physical traits are the emblems of his inner being and (in words that Whitman underlined) that "no one [artist] can truly *express* a quality of the soul, unless he is in some degree endowed with that quality." To depict heroism the artist must be heroic; to portray character the artist must be able to reveal its "natural marks" in the body and the countenance. A mastery of phrenology, physiognomy, and pathognomy (treating the outward signs of character revealed in the head, the face, and the carriage, respectively) was said to be the mainstay of the true artist or poet, who must know perfectly "all the powers which govern the body of man" as well as "*the marks* of these powers" which are manifested in the physical appearance of the subject.[33] The ideal artist, it was argued, must be a sensitive observer who reveals his own splendid personality and the personalities of his fellows through the emblem-language of phrenology, physiognomy, and pathognomy. And the Whitman persona does just that.

Whitman's method of self-presentation in the 1855 edition was consistent with phrenological practice and theory. The *American Phrenological Journal* published dozens of articles about poets, from Shakespeare and Goldsmith to Lowell and Willis, each selection made up of three components: an engraving of the poet; a phrenological analysis, often based on the engraving; and a narrative sketch of the poet's person and writings. Each element of evidence—pictorial, phrenological, and biographical—was meant to corroborate the others. Thus, George Combe's essay on Sir Walter Scott, in the *Journal*'s first volume (1838–39), included Scott's portrait, a report on his phrenology, and a short biography. Combe's *ex post facto* analysis revealed that Scott possessed the large organ of Ideality essential to a poet and the well-developed organs of piety and historical memory needed by a writer of historical narratives.[34] At least one *Journal* biography of a poet—that of the long-lived Samuel Rogers—was preserved among Whitman's papers. On a larger scale, *The Life of Horace Greeley*, by James Parton, exemplified the same triple approach. Parton (who, like Greeley, was a friend of Whitman) presented his readers with engravings of Greeley, a formal report of Greeley's phrenological traits, taken from the pages of the *Journal*, and information about Greeley's walk, weight, skin color, and health habits.[35] This method of describing literary personages was justified by Orson S. Fowler, who alleged that the portraits of artists serve as "the mirror of the outer man. Nor should their biography, however interesting, in and of itself, be unaccompanied by either their physiognomical likeness or their phrenological development, because these, especially the latter, give *tangibleness and certainty* to the mental and moral picture." A man's physiognomy, Fowler maintained, reveals more certain truth than any verbal biography, and his phrenological diagnosis is more reliable than any portrait.[36]

The outsetting bard, who broadcast his mytho-biography and his mytho-phrenology to the world in various literary works, seemingly trusted to his photograph to authenticate the man behind the poems. His noble physiognomy, in its most rugged pose, is presented as the frontispiece of the 1855 edition. In an anonymous review of the book, he wrote: "Its author is Walt Whitman, and the book is a reproduction of the author. His name is not on the frontispiece, but his portrait, half-length, is. The contents of the book form a daguerreotype of his inner being, and the title page bears a representation of its physical tabernacle." And "Song of Myself" reiterates:

> Writing and talk do not prove me,
> I carry the plenum of proof and every thing else in my face,
> With the hush of my lips I wholly confound the skeptic.[37]

Whitman appropriated the phrenologists' definition of the poet to his own uses. Nelson Sizer, a Fowler and Wells staffer, had declared that "PHRENOLOGY . . . is the true touchstone of poetry, for it enables the reader to recognize precisely the faculty, or class of faculties, employed in the production of the faintest shade of fancy, or boldest flight of genius. . . ." Only "a fine and strong temperament, combined with a high endowment of the faculties," can produce a poet, such as Shakespeare, able to "touch with a master's hand every string in the mental harp, and breathe his strains in harmony with every emotion of the soul. . . ."[38] An often-cited example of such congruity between poetic skill and the poetic skull was William Cullen Bryant, whom phrenologists claimed as a friend and an advocate. Bryant's "peculiar poetry, character, talents, and disposition," Lorenzo N. Fowler declared in 1850, "all coincide with the shape and development of his brain; which indicates a predominance of affection, sentiment, refinement, and intelligence."[39] Similarly, Poe presented himself to the public with a pictorial likeness of himself, an autobiography that stressed his athletic prowess, and a summary of his phrenological traits that purportedly substantiated his poetic temperament and his genius.[40]

Because Whitman was not an academic like Longfellow or

Lowell, he welcomed the phrenological doctrine that true poets combine an innate poetic temperament; well-defined phrenological traits; an aptitude for observation, absorption, and growing up in harmony with nature; and the electric eloquence that derives from superb manhood. A mastery of poetry, according to the phrenologists, is not acquired but is "entailed" from the right sort of parents. Emerson's declaration that the birth of a true poet is the greatest event in the history of a people was not meant as a phrenological dictum. Nor, perhaps, was Whitman's poetic celebration of "the birth of the maker of poems" as an occasion seldom witnessed by "every century nor every five centuries." But in proclaiming that his own combination of physical and phrenological traits had been "called up of the float of the brain of the world to be parts of the greatest poet from his birth out of his mother's womb and from her birth out of her mother's" (1855 preface), Whitman was being doctrinaire.[41] For he certainly knew Orson S. Fowler's maxims, "that Poetry is INHERITED" and that "the 'poetic TEMPERAMENT'—the first great condition of the poetic talent—is transmitted." As proof of this hereditary thesis, Fowler had cited the parentage of Goethe, Schiller, and Burns, especially stressing the importance of the poets' splendid mothers.[42] Whitman's idealization of his own "perfect mother" and his emphasis on his own inherited poetic genius reflect the argument that great poets and lawgivers are always *born* with the requisite endowments. As Spurzheim said: "There are persons who may be called fortunate, if not elect, namely, those who, from the felicity of their natural constitution, desire only what is good, who act from love, and show pure morality in all their actions. In these happy beings, the superior feelings predominate over those common in men and animals." Educating these superior individuals, he added, is chiefly a matter of preserving their health and channeling their inborn qualities. The late-flowering poet of Manhattan could take comfort in Spurzheim's and Fowler's advice that children are best trained by letting them slowly assimilate the world about them.[43] Loafing, listening, observing nature and her laws—thus does the superbly endowed child become America's kosmos-poet.

Fundamental to the production of poetry, phrenologists claimed, is a well-developed faculty of Ideality (Gall had called it the organ of Poetry)—the faculty said by an American phrenologist to be "the prophet of universal perfection, the inspirer of a

Walt Whitman and the Body Beautiful

strong desire for a perfect life, a perfect mind, a perfect wisdom, and a perfect love." In combination with other well-developed faculties, a large Ideality is supposed to mark its possessor as a born poet. "This faculty and temperament," he said, "is the spring-source of all true poetry. It loves, writes, feels, thinks poetry. It is always poetical."[44] Spurzheim's *Phrenology*, which the poet had read, explained that "the poetic turn of mind results from a peculiar mode of feeling, a certain manner of viewing the world and events. . . . Vividness, glow, exaltation, imagination, inspiration, rapture, and warmth in the expressions, are required to constitute compositions worthy of the name [of poetry]; all is represented [by the poet] in exaggerated terms, in a state of perfection, as it ought to be. Poets picture forth a factitious and imaginary world. . . ." The degree of exaltation experienced by poets, Spurzheim concluded, varies according to the faculty of Ideality's "greater or smaller development."[45] Similarly, Poe boasted of his own powerful Ideality but called Joseph Rodman Drake an inferior poet because the latter had been endowed with a weak "Faculty of Ideality—which is the sentiment of Poesy."[46] Whitman, too, apparently showed off his large Ideality in the 1855 preface by presenting himself as one who could test everything by his intuitive sense of cosmic fitness. "Whatever satisfies the soul is truth," he declared. "The prudence [transcendental intuition] of the greatest poet answers at last the craving and glut of the soul."

In presenting his claim to be a born poet, Whitman exploited the phrenologists' dictum that great literary men are self-reliant and well-sexed paragons of health. A phrenologically inclined physician specified that a true poet should exemplify the greatness of America, speak the language of the senses, and express "complete manliness." And Fowler suggested that "no man can ever become extra great, or even good, without the aid of powerful sexuality. This alone so sexes his ideas and feelings that they impregnate the mentalities of his fellow men. Every intellectual genius on record," he continued, "evinces every sign of powerful manhood; while the ideas of the poorly sexed are tame, insipid, emasculated, and utterly fail to waken enthusiasm."[47] Whitman copied from Fowler's *Physiology, Animal and Mental*, the dictum: "Morality and talent are affected more by food, drink, physical habits, cheerfulness, exercise, regulated or irregulated amativeness than is supposed. . . ."[48] In similar terms, he explained the superiority of *Leaves of Grass* over Tennyson's polite productions by contrasting the effete salon poets who neglect their bodies and indulge in secret vices with his athletic, sane, defiant self. In a notebook that he kept prior to publishing *Leaves of Grass*, he wrote: "What is lacking in literature can only be generated from the seminal freshness and proportion of new masculine persons." He illustrated the concept in the first version of "By Blue Ontario's Shore":

> How dare a sick man, or an obedient man, write poems?
> Which is the theory or book that is not diseased? [49]

And as late as 1881 he mockingly contrasted his own masculine genius with "the accepted notion of a poet" as "a sort of male odalisque, singing or piano-playing a kind of spiced ideas, second-hand reminiscences, or toying late hours at entertainments, in rooms stifling with fashionable scent." [50] Whitman insisted upon his own physiological excellence, as Arthur Wrobel explains, because "a complete vision of the similitude that interlocks all living things is available only to those who realize good health and exquisitely developed senses, who are sensuously equipped to collaborate with nature and duplicate its spiritual and moral rectitude." [51]

Such reductive reasoning by Whitman and the phrenologists may seem incompatible with serious literary criticism, implying as it does that the debility of Pope, Keats, Swinburne, Poe, and Lanier had unfitted them for artistic greatness. And in fact Whitman did exclude all of them from his poetic pantheon, alleging for example that Keats's poetry "does not come home to the direct wants of the bodies and souls of this century." [52] But picking among the eclectic hash of phrenological theory for the succulent tidbits that could nourish his own physiological-poetic ideal, he was able to find sustenance for the myth of the Whitman persona and language to articulate the persona's vision of the world.

In formulating the images of himself as the inspired poet and teacher, Whitman drew upon a broad range of phrenological sources. He relied especially upon his 1849 phrenological examination (and possibly upon other such examinations of himself) in shaping the autobiographical elements of publicity releases, the 1855 preface, and the several poetic spillovers of the preface. He utilized divers aspects of the pseudo-science as vital components in

"A Song of Joys"; in "Unfolded Out of the Folds" and "There Was a Child Went Forth," lyric evocations of his poetic self-discovery; and in "Faces," a prophetic vision of his flawed countrymen evolving toward perfection.

Much of Whitman's mytho-phrenology is rooted in his phrenological examination of July 16, 1849, which he exploited as a prophetic revelation of his true self and as proof that the fates had happily converged in the person of the graying Brooklyn Boy to produce at last the great American poet. But a close reading of the phrenological diagnosis discloses that the importance of the "Phrenological Description of W. (Age 29 / Occupation Printer) Whitman" does not depend chiefly upon what the equivocating document states, but on Whitman's subsequent, and constantly retouched, fiction that he is revealed therein to possess the characteristics indicative of a poet.[53] Whether he was lured to have his cranial configurations interpreted at the phrenological parlors of Fowler and Wells, corner of Beekman and Nassau Streets, by the company's flattery, by a desire for publicity, or by a curiosity about the secrets of his inner being, we cannot tell. Nor do we really know how he reacted to the experience.[54]

Lorenzo Niles Fowler, who evaluated the "bumps" which supposedly indicated the development of Whitman's organs or faculties, probably entered each measurement in the printed chart of a copy of Orson S. Fowler's *Self-Instructor in Phrenology*. His narrative report, following the company formula, was taken down in Pitman shorthand and then transcribed in a handsome script. The report evaluated Whitman's physical organization and then interpreted the secrets supposedly revealed by his phrenological faculties, starting with those located at the lower back of the head, moving forward faculty by faculty, and ending with the areas over the eyes. Rather ambiguously, the examiner told Whitman that he could stay well if he watched his health habits, and complimented him on his phrenological indicators of longevity and on his being a feminist and a gregarious, adaptable, and friendly man who "would be or *are* a kind husband—an affectionate father." (What an unfortunate guess concerning a man allegedly never "bothered up" by women!) He was told that he minded his own business (a dubious compliment to a newspaperman), in guarded terms that he was a physical coward and a glutton, that he was too plain-spoken, and that he was "what you appear to be at all times." (If Whitman was fully revealed by his appearance and the pseudo-scientific indicators of his bearing, his face, and his cranium, why did Fowler fail to remark upon his client's aptitude for poetry?) He was praised for his fine "social feelings," his inventiveness, and his justness. But he was cautioned that he was too "little inclined to the spiritual or devotional and have but little regard for creeds and ceremonies," that he was not "any too sanguine" (a shrewd hit), and that he generally realized "as much as you hope for." (Typically ambiguous, that last statement could mean that Whitman got whatever he set out to get or that he was a stoic who had learned to curb his desires.) He was flattered on his perceptive skills and his orderliness, but never once on his sense of beauty or the shaping spirit of his imagination that underlay his poetic genius. "By practice might make a good accountant," the equivocating document declared.

In addition to this well-known examination, probably conducted without an audience in the inner rooms of the phrenological parlors, it is possible that Whitman was analyzed at least once again when he and his poetic ambitions were better known to the phrenologists. Admitting in 1888 that "I probably have not got by the phrenology state yet," he alluded to such an occasion "[t]hirty years ago or more [when] a circle of *célèbres* in phrenology gave my head a public dissection in a hall—for one point, marked my caution [the phrenological organ whose supposedly large development pleased him] very high—seven and over." [55] Other related recollections imply that the chief examiner at the "public dissection" was Nelson Sizer. [56] The inconsistent capsule reports of his phrenological endowments that Whitman included in his self-reviews between 1855 and 1860 are ostensibly based on a short-form summary of his 1849 examination by Lorenzo N. Fowler, but they may have been derived from a later reading, such as the one he seemingly recalled in 1888. The details in the capsule versions do not tally with those contained in the lengthy transcript of the 1849 report; they are generally closer to the poet's mytho-phrenology. And as a recent study has pointed out, the 1849 document is a discursive second-person narrative, whereas the terse summaries used in the reviews are phrased in the third person. [57]

Typical of Whitman's short-form reports is one included in his anonymous self-review in the *Brooklyn Daily Times* (1855), in

Walt Whitman and the Body Beautiful

which he exults in "his physiology corroborating a rugged phrenology" and appends a summary to document his boast:

Phrenological Notes on W. Whitman, by L. N. Fowler July 1849.— Size of head large, 23 inches. Leading traits appear to be Friendship, Sympathy, Sublimity, and Self-Esteem, and markedly among his combinations the dangerous faults of Indolence, a tendency to the pleasures of Voluptuousness and Alimentiveness, and a certain reckless swing of animal will.

This phrenological capsule, reprinted several times with minor variations, shows the touch of a brilliant publicist trying to intrigue his readers by presenting a more romantic and sensuous figure than the one depicted in the discursive 1849 analysis. A variant version of this summary includes a reference to the poet's large head, his splendid vitality, his "power to live to a good old age," and the allegation that he is "too unmindful, probably, of the convictions of others." [58]

Whitman adapted these phrenological data very resourcefully in presenting his poetic credentials in the preface to the 1855 edition of *Leaves of Grass*. [59] The document specifies that the gift of poetry is innate—not learned in schools. "Who troubles himself about his ornaments or fluency is lost." It characterizes Whitman · as the "greatest poet," whose splendid ancestry has endowed him with unexampled health, flawless phrenology, and superb generative and creative powers. "All beauty comes from beautiful blood and a beautiful brain. If the greatnesses are in conjunction in a man or woman it is enough," it declares. It repeats the familiar boast that great poets are descended from great mothers. (The issue of great *fathers* is blurred in the vague comment that the poet learns from and surpasses the intellectuals and scientists whose "father-stuff" has begotten him.) It asserts the poet's claim to powerful organs of Ideality, Self-Esteem, and Individuality, and presents a cryptic roster of his astonishing phrenology: "Extreme caution or prudence, the soundest organic health, large hope and comparison and fondness for women and children, large alimentiveness and destructiveness and causality, with a perfect sense of the oneness of nature and the propriety of the same spirit applied to human affairs. . . ."

The foregoing phrenological capsule singles out no fewer

than ten of the poet's superb faculties.[60] The organ of Caution, in the combination cited, tempers and directs his judgment and energy. Hope, the organ of optimism, imparts, in the combination given, a tenacious drive toward perfection. Comparison, an "analysing, criticising, and inductive faculty [which can] illustrate with great clearness and facility from the known to the unknown, discover deeper analogies which pervade nature, and have an extraordinary power of discovering new truths," enables the poet to understand the transcendental emblems in the world. Alimentiveness, the faculty of healthy appetite, characterizes the man with the strong *vis*. Destructiveness confers rudeness and forcefulness. Causality helps its possessor to perceive fundamental causes and principles. Moreover, the poet's "fondness for women and children" alludes to his faculties of Amativeness and Parental Love. And his boast of "a perfect sense of the oneness of nature and the propriety of the same spirit applied to human affairs" constitutes (in the first part of the phrase) a fair definition of the poetic-perfectionist organ of Ideality and (in the second part of the phrase) a definition of Eventuality—the faculty of history and the observation of human behavior.

The specification of phrenological traits in the 1855 preface is calculated to exploit Whitman's innate poetic qualifications, especially the creative sense associated with Ideality, the faculty that enables him to test the extant world against the ideal world and to point out to his fellows "the path between reality and their souls." By exercising his Individuality (an individuating, creative faculty), he can behold humanity not as "dreams or dots" but as spiritually worthy beings. By exercising his Eventuality, he "forms the consistency of what is to be from what has been and is."[61] The combination of powerful Ideality and powerful Causality guarantees mental and emotional strength, as George Combe had said, and the joining of these two well-developed faculties with Eventuality constitutes the very foundation of the poetic personality.[62] By way of suggesting that he possesses all of these attributes, Whitman says: "Sanity and ensemble characterize the great master." He invents terms as he needs them, using "Prudence" to denote a faculty attuned to Emersonian Compensation, or the law of the universal balance in nature, and arbitrarily making Prudence the most important poetic trait, as if to say, He who would be a true poet must be a transcendentalist. In sum, the 1855 preface is an improvisation that shows the poet to advantage, exploiting some of the readings in the 1849 analysis and distorting others. Lorenzo N. Fowler had indeed found that Whitman's organ of Suavitiveness, or polite amiability, was underdeveloped, as befits one of the "roughs," but he had classified the poet's organ of Hope only as "average" (not "large," as stated in the preface), and his organs of Color, Time, Secretiveness, and Marvellousness (the faculty of spirituality or the "inner light," of which he might be expected to boast) as only "moderate" (weak).

Whitman reworked the self-portrait of the 1855 preface to produce a miniature likeness of his mytho-phrenological self in "Song of the Broad-Axe" (1856). The poem contains a distinctive sketch in which no fewer than sixteen of his phrenological traits are specified; but once again the faculties he shows off do not precisely match those he has stressed in any other phrenological statement:

> Never offering others, always offering himself, corroborating his
> phrenology,
> Voluptuous, inhabitive, combative, conscientious, alimentive,
> intuitive, of copious friendship, sublimity, firmness, self-
> esteem, comparison, individuality, form, locality,
> eventuality * * * *63

Probably because the poem features the persona as the idealized constructor and eugenic hero—the perfect Western breeder—this portrait stresses his well-developed sexuality, domestic virtues, and perceptive traits and plays down the romantic or satanic streak that is apparent in other phrenological sketches.

"By Blue Ontario's Shore," in which large parts of the preface were incorporated, illustrates two phrenological ideas. Like the preface, it defines human perfectibility largely in phrenological and physiological terms. And it demands that American poets learn to judge their countrymen by their physiognomy, phrenology, and pathognomy:

> The freshness and candor of their physiognomy, the copiousness
> and decision of their phrenology,
> The picturesque looseness of their carriage * * * *
> Who are you, indeed, who would talk or sing in America? * * *
> Have you learned the physiology, phrenology, politics,
> geography * * * of my land? * * *

"Unnamed Lands" implies that the phrenology of a people reveals them as surely as do their speech, manners, or institutions. (Had not George Combe declared that the American character is best judged by its phrenology?)[64] Not surprisingly, superb phrenologies are assigned to the trial figures of the Whitman persona, Epicurus and Sesostris, and to the breed of perfect poets whose advent is foretold in several poems.[65]

"A Song of Joys" also articulates certain phrenological ideas. It glorifies the physical exuberance of outdoor men—firemen, fishermen, and laborers. In describing the pleasures of warfare and violence, it illustrates the operation of Destructiveness, the faculty whose large development, phrenologists said, imparts "that determination, energy, and force which remove and destroy whatever impedes progression . . . that iron will which adheres till the very last. . . ." A moving passage in the poem alludes to the perceptive, moral, and intellectual faculties, and particularly to Ideality, Comparison, Eventuality, and Language:

> O the joy of my Soul leaning poised on itself—receiving identity
>   through materials, and loving them—observing characters,
>   and absorbing them;
> O my Soul, vibrated back to me, from them—from facts, sight,
>   hearing, touch, my phrenology, reason, articulation,
>   comparison, memory, and the like;
> O the real life of my senses and flesh, transcending my senses and
>   flesh * * * *[66]

And another passage translates the persona's delight in his Self-Esteem, a faculty which the *Self-Instructor* defined as "self-respect and reliance; magnanimity; nobleness; independence; dignity; self-satisfaction and complacency; love of liberty and power . . . manliness; lofty-mindedness . . . ; the highest respect for *self*"; a "stress on the personal pronouns"; a "boundless ambition to be and do some great thing"; and so erect a carriage "as to lean backward."

> O the joy of manly self-hood!
> Personality—to be servile to none—to defer to none—not to any
>   tyrant, known or unknown,
> To walk with erect carriage, a step springy and elastic,
> To look with calm gaze, or with a flashing eye,
> To speak with a full and sonorous voice, out of a broad chest,

Walt Whitman and the Body Beautiful

To confront with your personality all the other personalities of the earth.[67]

"There Was a Child Went Forth" is a poetic *tour de force* which idealizes the poet-hero's unfolding from childhood to manhood in terms of Whitman's systematic application of the phrenological theories of education. Exercising his native faculties without constraint, the poem's child passes through a series of developmental stages before he launches himself into the adult world. His growth, as described in the poem, generally parallels the three phases of prepubertal development outlined by Dr. Spurzheim: "infancy" (from birth to two years), "childhood" (two to seven years), and "adolescence" (seven to twelve years). Because genius is inborn, not cultivated, Orson S. Fowler had pointed out, education can only "polish the marble" or "DEVELOP AND DIRECT" one's innate talents. Hence, if the poem's child is truly a superior being, reared in harmony with the laws of nature and phrenology, he must instinctively mature into an outstanding, self-reliant adult.[68]

In children, Fowler said, "observation must always *precede* reasoning"; they are best educated by "*observing facts*, and ascending through *analogous* facts up to the laws that govern them." To stimulate children's learning and to arouse their powers of observation during "infancy," he urged parents to "crowd OBJECTS" upon their notice even before they are three months old. The first section of "There Was a Child Went Forth"—the child's "curious" beholding of the "curious" growth of plants and animals and his observation of children and adults—exemplifies the stimulation of its Perceptive Faculties (Individuality, Eventuality, Comparison, and Causality), which according to Fowler should be exercised by the child during its "infancy." These faculties are not merely perceptual organs; they also govern the highest intellectual functions. Individuality, for example, is the "looking faculty." Eventuality, controlling memory and the inferences drawn from observation, is best stimulated, according to Fowler, by showing small children "the whole process of vegetation, from planting the seed in the ground, up through all its changes of swelling, sprouting, taking root, shooting forth out of the ground, becoming a thriving plant or vegetable, budding, blossoming, shedding its blossoms, and producing seeds like that from which it sprung."

Demonstrably, Whitman's "infant" hero is trained according to this phrenological formula:

> The field-sprouts of the Fourth-month and Fifth-month became
>   part of him,
> Winter-grain sprouts, and those of the light-yellow corn, and the
>   esculent roots of the garden,
> And the apple-trees cover'd with blossoms and the fruit afterward,
>   and wood-berries, and the commonest weeds by the
>   road * * * *

Similarly, the boy's "childhood"—his nascent awareness of the social world—illustrates the proper nurture of his organ of Causality (*l'ésprit métaphysique*, Dr. Gall had called it), which will prevent him from drawing false inferences from his environment, and, by implication, from slipping into skepticism or evil.[69]

The central section of "There Was a Child Went Forth" (lines 19 to 27 of the final version) depicts the relation between the child and his parents and the child's troublesome doubts concerning the quality of his parentage. The phrenological principle of tracing back one's inheritance, particularly by diagnosing the personalities of one's parents, is essential to an understanding of the poem's famous description of the child's home life:

> The mother at home quietly placing the dishes on the supper-
>   table,
> The mother with mild words, clean her cap and gown, a
>   wholesome odor falling off her person and clothes as she
>   walks by,
> The father, strong, self-sufficient, manly, mean, anger'd, unjust,
> The blow, the quick loud word, the tight bargain, the crafty
>   lure * * * *

The mother seems to be the sort of ideal woman whom Whitman and the phrenologists would choose to give birth to a poetic hero. But the father's apparently overwrought selfish propensities—his organs of Combativeness, Secretiveness, and Destructiveness (which Gall had originally called Murder)—are also beneficial to the child, whose superb personality is shaped and tempered by the blending of his father's and his mother's genetic patterns. The mother's gentle qualities make him curious and affectionate; the father's aggressive qualities endow him with the self-reliance he needs to persevere in a difficult world. This fortunate blending of phrenological faculties confirms our favorable impression of the superior child "who now goes, and will always go forth every day."

Whitman could have found a suitable literary precedent for this sort of ideal parentage in Carlyle's *Life of John Sterling* (1851). In terms that suggest Whitman's genetic formula in "There Was a Child Went Forth," Carlyle credits Sterling's poetic nature largely to his "beautiful, much-suffering, much-loving house-mother. From her chiefly . . . John Sterling had derived the delicate aroma of his nature, its piety, clearness, sincerity; as from his Father, the ready practical gifts, the impetuosities and the audacities, were also (though in strange new form) visibly inherited. A man was lucky to have such Mother; to have such Parents as both his were." [70]

Pathognomy and physiognomy, two lesser pseudo-sciences, also influenced Whitman's poetry. Pathognomy, the revelation of the personality through the body's characteristic movement and bearing, was defined by Dr. Gall as "the pantomime by which men and animals express their sentiments and their ideas" in accordance with natural laws, and by Whitman in his manuscript "Notes for an Intended Dictionary" as "the expression of the passions—the science of the signs by which a state of a person is indicated by the soft or mobile part of the body." [71] Like many semi-scientific insights that could not be tested in a laboratory, this one (formulated by the American phrenological theorist Dr. Joseph Rodes Buchanan) was based on pragmatic observations. [72] In our own time, Wilhelm Reich and his followers in psychoanalysis have studied the body's structure and mobility as vital indicators of bio-energetic patterns and clues to psychic harmony or disharmony. [73] The first published version of "I Sing the Body Electric" demonstrates that pathognomy (as Whitman understood it) is an important component of *Leaves of Grass*:

> The *expression of the body* of man or woman balks account,
> The male is perfect and that of the female is perfect.
>
> The expression of a wellmade man appears not only in his face,
> It is in his limbs and joints also . . . . it is curiously in the joints of
>   his hips and wrists,

> It is in his walk . . the carriage of his neck . . the flex of his waist
>   and knees . . . . dress does not hide him,
> The strong sweet supple quality he has strikes through the cotton
>   and flannel;
> To see him pass conveys as much as the best poem . . perhaps
>   more,
> You linger to see his back and the back of his neck and
>   shoulderside.[74]

Whitman also applied the concepts of physiognomy in his prose writings and made striking and subtle use of them in his poetry. He boasted of his own "Hollandisk physiognomy," and he referred to the frontispiece portrait of the 1876 edition as

> This heart's geography's map, this limitless small continent, this
>   soundless sea * * *
> This condensation of the universe, (nay here the only universe,
> Here the idea of all in this mystic handful wrapt.)[75]

The faces of the young men who caught his fancy are sometimes described in his notebooks with a degree of physiognomic precision. Observing a group of Tennessee veterans in Washington, he praised their "pleasant, even handsome physiognomy; no refinement, nor blanch'd with intellect, but as my eye pick'd them, moving along, rank by rank, there did not seem to be a single, repulsive, brutal or markedly stupid face among them."[76]

The pseudo-science of physiognomy had been formulated in Lavater's *Essays on Physiognomy* (1778), which combined the theory that human nature is readable in the features of the face with the venerable theory of the "humors." Contending that "in every human countenance, however debased, humanity still is visible, that is the image of the Deity," Lavater generalized that the nobler the countenance, the nobler the being. He asserted that humanity is steadily evolving toward a greater roundness of skull, a more prominent forehead, wider eyes, and a less bestial protuberance of the mouth—indicators of mankind's universal progress toward virtue and intelligence. Perhaps without conscious intent, he equated perfect human features with the Germanic ideal of beauty. Reasoning that "universal shape corresponds with universal character," the phrenologists appropriated physiognomy's theories and terminology to supplement their own.[77] And inspired by physiognomy's method of character reading, such writers as Balzac, Poe, Hawthorne, and Whitman (whom Lorenzo Fowler's analysis had called "a good physiognomist") utilized the details of physiognomy in their literary works.[78]

"Faces," a masterpiece of the first edition of *Leaves of Grass*, employs physiognomy, phrenology, and a faith in evolutionary-genetic perfection to develop one of Whitman's most remarkable poetic dream visions. Its theme derives from Lavater's motto, "Though the wicked man constrain his countenance, the wise can distinctly discern his purpose." Its inspired persona, who descries the advancement of his flawed fellow citizens in time's unending scheme, demands rhetorically: "Do you suppose I could be content with all if I thought them their own finalè?" He sees the latent greatness in the most shattered and unfulfilled of them. "The Lord advances" all mankind, he proclaims: "always the reached hand bringing up the laggards." Sounding the very tone of Lavater, he describes the faces of the choicest humans:

> These faces bear testimony slumbering or awake,
> They show their descent from the Master himself.[79]

The lines suggest Bronson Alcott's precept that "all heads are portraits, more or less exact, of the typical Godhead. But the features elude stiffening in the brittle clay." And they parallel a similar sentiment in "Song of Myself":

> I see something of God each hour of the twenty-four, and each
>   moment then,
> In the faces of men and women I see God, and in my own face in
>   the glass * * * *[80]

Whitman divided the poem of "Faces" into five rather arbitrary sections. The first section (lines 1 to 15)—an impressionistic parade of a score of human types—demonstrates his virtuoso command of phreno-physiognomic lore:

> Sauntering the pavement or riding the country by-road, lo, such
>   faces!
> Faces of friendship, precision, caution, suavity, ideality,
> The spiritual-prescient face, the always welcome common
>   benevolent face,

The face of the singing of music, the grand faces of natural lawyers
and judges broad at the back-top,
The faces of hunters and fishers bulged at the brows, the shaved
blanch'd faces of orthodox citizens,
The pure, extravagant, yearning, questioning artist's face,
The ugly face of some beautiful soul, the handsome detested or
despised face,
The sacred faces of infants, the illuminated face of the mother of
many children,
The face of an amour, the face of veneration,
The face as of a dream, the face of an immobile rock,
The face withdrawn of its good and bad, a castrated face,
A wild hawk, his wings clipp'd by the clipper,
A stallion that yielded at last to the thongs and knife of the gelder.

Sauntering the pavement thus, or crossing the ceaseless ferry, faces
and faces and faces,
I see them and complain not, and am content with all.

Each figure in the preceding passage is clothed with a visual presence and a set of attributes that may be recognized by specific verbal clues derived from the pseudo-sciences. Whitman apparently expected the reader to translate these clues into the appropriate phrenological or physiognomic archetypes and then to conjure up the appearance and bearing appropriate to each. (The technique of furnishing fragmentary hints which the reader must flesh out in his own imagination is the usual method in Whitman's verse catalogs.) "Faces of friendship," for example, recalls Whitman's lusty camerados, for Friendship, or Adhesiveness, is the phrenological organ of comradely love. The physiognomic quality of Precision characterizes an artist, whose "delicacy and elegance employed in minute things" is obvious in the whole visage, and particularly in his aquiline nose. Caution denotes both an emotional trait and its phrenological organ, whose ample presence bulges the "upper-side head outward from the crown, a little further back than the ears." The phrenological organ of Suavity bestows "grace or urbanity" on the character and bulges the side forehead. The organ of Ideality—the quintessential faculty of the imagination—is evident in the high artistic brows that characterize the portraits of nineteenth-century artists. The long, delicate-featured "spiritual-prescient face," said by phrenologists to be "elevated at the top-head," marks the person who is governed by "Faith" and "the 'light within'"—possibly a clairvoyant who communes with the spirits. The "benevolent" face, bulged above the forehead and associated with the "Motive-Vital" temperament, belongs to the hard-working farmer or laborer—hence the aptness of Whitman's expression, "the always welcome common benevolent face."

"The face of the singing of music" exhibits the "pathos and intensity" conferred by the "Mental-Vital" temperament as well as the large head, prominent mid-forehead, puffed-out eyes, and broad cheekbones associated with the well-developed phrenological organs of Tune, Language, Eventuality (or memory), and the social and moral faculties. The "grand faces of natural lawyers and judges" are, as the poet testifies, "broad at the backtop." Lawyers were said to require large organs of Combativeness, Self-Esteem, and Approbativeness (the "desire to excel and to be esteemed"); these, and specifically Approbativeness, are illustrated in phrenological manuals as broadening the backtop of the head. The natural lawyer's well-developed faculties of Language and Eventuality enlarge the middle of his brow and widen the area around his eyes—physical traits which George Bernard Shaw attributed to that great untrained advocate Joan of Arc.[81] "The faces of hunters and fishers" are "bulged at the brows" because Individuality (the organ charged with distinguishing objects) widens the distance between the eyes; the organ of Size bulges the "inner angle of the eyebrow"; and the organ of Weight, governing balance and dexterity, particularly in athletics and the outdoor life, conspicuously expands the mid-eyebrow. These outdoorsmen resemble Melville's Queequeg, whose brows are said to be "very projecting, like two long promontories thickly wooded on top."[82]

Other faces can be envisioned. The "shaved blanch'd faces of orthodox citizens" belong to the urbanites whom Whitman denounced as weaklings and "foofoos"; they lack the manly beard, and their pallor signifies weakness and the Nervous temperament. The "face of an amour" is illustrated by Lavater as depraved looking, flabby, weak-jawed, and dull-eyed, for perverted Amativeness, as Fowler stated, "occasions grossness and vulgarity in expression and action." The "face of veneration" reflects the presence of a strong phrenological faculty governing reverence to God; like the dome of a hypaethral temple, this organ is situated at the top of the head. The clipped hawk and the gelded stallion symbolize those who have lost their rightful masculinity. Finally, "The ugly face of some beautiful soul, the handsome detested or despised face," illustrates the principle that only the inspired observer can probe beneath the superficies to discover the emblematic meaning of a face. Lavater cited Socrates as an example of a homely man whose face could "offend the eye that searches only for beauty," and Whitman praised Lincoln's physiognomy despite its lack of "technical beauty." "He has the face like a hoosier Michael Angelo," he said, "so awful ugly it becomes beautiful, with its strange mouth, its deep cut, criss-cross lines, and its doughnut complexion." [83]

The second section of "Faces" (lines 16 to 33) parades the bestial dregs of humanity. The "abject louse," the "milk-nosed maggot," and the creatures without features illustrate Lavater's precept that "lower forms" of humanity closely resemble animals. "That certain men 'look like' one or another species of animal is an ancient observation," Fowler remarked. "And when in looks, also in character." By calling a face "a dog's snout sniffing for garbage," Whitman applies Lavater's observation that the snout denotes bestiality and that a projecting jaw represents "Stupidity, Rudeness, Malignity, [or] Avarice." By describing a murderer's face shaped like a knife (an apt synecdoche that suggests the head of a brutal fish) the poet illustrates Lavater's observation that a backward-sloping forehead denotes viciousness. [84] The face that "is a haze more chill than the arctic sea" suggests Lavater's description of Judas Iscariot ("Immovable icy coldness, without a spark of sensibility") and a similar description of him, in a passage on the bilious temperament, that is copied into one of Whitman's notebooks. The "face of bitter herbs" brings to mind the victims of unscrupulous apothecaries, of whom the poet had remarked: "How many wry faces they are the cause of—the ipecac and castor oil creatures!" [85]

As one who cannot be deluded by mere surfaces, the sharp-sighted persona perceives these vile, drugged, and moribund beings as the phallic-genetic emblems of an inevitable physical perfection: "Those are really men! . . . the bosses and tufts of the great round globe!" [86] The godlike qualities that exist beneath their "creas'd and cadaverous" features are affirmed in the poem's third section (lines 34 to 45 in the final version):

I see your rounded never-erased flow,
I see 'neath the rims of your haggard and mean disguises.

Splay and twist as you like, poke with the tangling fores of fishes
    or rats,
You'll be unmuzzled, you certainly will.

This "cadaverous march" of muzzled humanity suggests another of Lavater's axioms: "As are the mouth and lips, so is the character."[87] When mankind is unmuzzled and its animalistic features have disappeared "in a score or two of ages," Whitman implies, men will have become a race of gods.

The fourth section (lines 46–67) conjures up an evolutionary procession headed by the heroes of the future who will one day be created by parents endowed with perfect genitalia. All is procession, says the persona:

In each house is the ovum, it comes forth after a thousand years.

Spots or cracks at the windows do not disturb me,
Tall and sufficient stand behind and make signs to me,
I read the promise and patiently wait.

The operation of these sexual-genetic laws which will eventually eliminate human defects excludes no one: "Off the word I have spoken I except not one—red, white, black, are all deific * * * *"

This affirmation does not mean, however, that all races may march abreast in the evolutionary procession. Like most intellectuals in his day who believed in racial progress, Whitman assumed that the evolutionary vanguard was white-skinned. Physiognomy, with its Anglo-Saxon bias, was quite conventional in asserting the inferiority of red and black peoples. Typically, Lavater pictured an "African" with a short, flat nose, buck teeth, and a head broad at the base but narrow at the top (physiognomic signs of insensitivity, animal viciousness, powerful sexuality, and limited intelligence) and demanded sarcastically: "What care of education can arch this skull of a negro like that of the star-conversant [white] astronomer?" Sizer's *Heads and Faces* displayed a bestial caricature of an Indian with a narrow receding forehead and captioned it, "American Indian: Ideality Deficient."[88] And Whitman preserved among his papers an article from *Life Illustrated* ("The Standard Civilized Head") in which physiognomy, phrenology, and craniometry were used to prove the superiority of white Americans.

The article divided human skulls into three types: the prognathous, with its projecting jaw and its "top-head depressed or irregular," allegedly characteristic of savage peoples such as "Africans"; the pyramidal or cone-shaped, belonging to pastoral peoples such as American Indians; and the elliptical or oval, crowning all the highly civilized Indo-Germanic peoples who have "risen from the slough of savagism," from the ancient Greeks to the go-getting white Americans, whose sophisticated mental faculties allegedly round out the upper front end of their egg-shaped heads.[89] Such reasoning left an impress on Whitman. Thus, until he altered the line in 1881, "To Think of Time" alluded to a "zambo [Sambo] or a foreheadless Crowfoot or a Camanche" as pitiful objects at the bottom of the evolutionary scale.[90]

The perfected Caucasian visages in "Faces," crowned by their "high pioneer-caps," resemble the vigorous Westerners in "Pioneers! O Pioneers!," "Song of the Broad-Axe," and other sketches of the heroic persona:

> This face is a life-boat,
> This is the face commanding and bearded, it asks no odds of the
> rest,
> This face is flavor'd fruit ready for eating,
> This face of a healthy honest boy is the programme of all good.

The "face commanding and bearded" invites comparison with Whitman's phrenological description of himself as "full of animal blood, masterful, striding to the front rank, allowing none to walk before him, full of rudeness and recklessness. . . ."[91] The face of "flavor'd fruit ready for eating" (despite its homosexual innuendo) highlights the persona's pose, particularly in "Song of Myself" and the "Messenger Leaves" poems, as a savior—the bread of life incarnate.

The fourth section of the poem also introduces "a full-grown lily's face"—the fair, delicate features of a young, sexually aggressive woman. (Her description suggests the appearance of the blonde, handsome, and womanly Jenny Lind, whom Sizer described as the "ideal Woman" for phreno-physiognomists.)[92] This idealized woman reappears as the triumphant central figure in the fifth section of "Faces" (lines 68–84). With the passage of time she has become the contented grandmother of many full-grown grandchildren—farmers and farmers' wives. Unlike the genteel ladies glorified by conventional poets, she is beautiful in the un-affected simplicity of her old age: "the justified mother of men." Applying the physiognomists' dictum concerning women, that "the more beautifully formed the more exquisite and perfect the mentality," we may conclude that this grandmotherly figure is angelic or deific, for the poem says that "her face is clearer and more beautiful than the sky." This lovely and fulfilled matron symbolizes the triumph of the sexual-genetic prophecies that underlie the structure and ideology of "Faces" and of other important poems in *Leaves of Grass*.

"The Body Electric"

5

SOME OF THE MOST DAZZLING IMAGERY in *Leaves of Grass* derives
from the new science of electricity, which many of Whitman's
contemporaries believed would unlock the secrets of the universe
and bridge the chasm between materialism and the idealistic faith.
Orson S. Fowler termed electricity "the grand agent or instrumentality of life in all its forms, all varieties of human, animal, and
vegetable life included . . . the master workman, or grand executive, of every animal function and mental exercise."[1] D. H.
Jacques identified it as a "subtle fluid [which] seems to form the
connecting link between the soul and the body, and to be the in-
strument by means of which the former builds, rebuilds, or shapes
the latter. . . . The ancient Magians called it the living fire."
(Whitman's poems also refer to electricity as a subtle fluid, "the
subtle electric fire," or "the pulses of fire ceaseless to vivify all.")[2]
In words that appear to be echoed in "Song of Myself," a contemporary mystic pronounced electricity "the Jacob's ladder" between
the material world and the realm of the angels.[3] Ralph Waldo
Emerson was sufficiently intrigued by such speculations to describe the center of each man's universe, with its boundless cir-
cumference of concentric circles, as an electric generator and to
conjecture that there is some "principle of fixture or stability in the
soul" around which "the eternal generator abides."[4]

In the century preceding the appearance of Whitman's masterpiece, electrical science had made a quantum leap. The invention
of powerful batteries had led to the discovery of new elements in
the universe and to the development of new technologies. Instantaneous communication had become an established fact. Michael
Faraday had demonstrated electromagnetic induction when the

poet was twelve years old; Samuel F. B. Morse had built a telegraph line linking Baltimore and Boston a dozen years later. During an era in which American manufacturing relied chiefly on steam and water power, the telegraph represented a milestone of technical ingenuity that could be integrated, together with the locomotive and the factory, into the Edenic landscape of the American garden. Always inspired by inventions, Whitman refers several times to the telegraph in his poems and speaks metaphorically of *Leaves of Grass* as a telegraph—"the thread-voice, more or less audible, of an aggregated, inseparable, unprecedented, vast, composite, electric *Democratic Nationality*."[5]

Whitman's multifaceted metaphor of "the body electric" should be viewed in the context of many decades of scientific research into animal electricity. Faraday, Du Bois-Reymond, and a host of scientists had verified and measured the operation of electricity in the organs of animals and human beings. Conjectures about the possible functions of animal electricity—particularly the equation of animal electricity with the willpower and the life force—had stirred the literary imagination. An influential example of such literary-electrical convergence was Mary Shelley's hero Dr. Frankenstein, whom the author described as "a man of great research in natural philosophy" who had utilized "a theory on the subject of electricity and galvanism, which was at once new and astounding," and who had "collected the instruments of life round me that I might infuse a spark of being into the lifeless thing that lay at my feet."[6] Fictional characters in the writings of Hawthorne, Poe, Melville, and others also infuse electricity from electrical machines or from their own bodies into other persons in order to alter their physical or mental states. But the Whitman-Adam persona, whose electrical faculties empower him to invigorate his countrymen and to become spiritually transcendent, is the supreme culmination of this intriguing literary tradition.

Some of the books that Whitman read help us to understand his own interpretation of electricity as a vital force. Thus, the Reverend Chauncey Hare Townshend, in a volume on mesmerism that the poet perused a dozen years before publishing his masterpiece, defined the human body as "an electrical machine." "Facts prove," Townshend said, "that our bodies are electric and that the degree of electricity varies in different individuals."[7] George

Walt Whitman and the Body Beautiful

Moore, in *The Use of the Body in Relation to the Mind* (1847), which stressed the reverence for, and the happy coexistence of, the soul and the body, described the life-giving element in the blood as electric. Like Whitman, Moore assumed that the sperm is an electric nucleus, the sole source and transmitter of human and animal life; that the open air furnishes the electricity by which the blood is vitalized; that light, air, exercise, and a sane regimen are the great physical restoratives; and that through magnetism (or mind-expanding drugs) one can train oneself to receive the inspirational "divine afflatus." [8]

Notes on the Medical Application of Electricity (1849), by Whitman's friend Dr. William Francis Channing, illustrates the elusive line between the scientific and nonscientific approaches to physiology. The volume, intended as an objective summary of the medical evidence linking nervous energy to electricity, describes the various types of batteries used in medical therapy and documents the efficacy of electricity in shock treatment, in destroying diseased tissue, and in curing digestive ills, tetanus, pleurisy, epilepsy, and cholera. Although the relation of electricity to the nervous system had not yet been clearly established, Dr. Channing theorizes (like his contemporary "electricians") that the direct application of electricity can normalize the organism and stimulate the sexual drive. [9] In a somewhat similar context, the Whitman persona declares that he will "discorrupt" the bodies of those who "engirth" him "and charge them full with the charge of the soul." [10] His discorrupting "charge," like Dr. Channing's curative batteries, has complex physical and metaphysical implications.

Orson S. Fowler explained rather imaginatively that the anatomical system in both parents is paralleled by a "vital or magnetic" organization, controlled by the brain, which transmits a genetic code, or pattern, during conception. (In Fowler's time the German naturalist Lorenz Oken had defined the sperm as electric.) Fowler combined this idea with the antic theory of epigenesis, or preformation, which characterized the embryo as a fully formed but minute body which unfolds during pregnancy like a flower in the bud or the "Homunculus." of Tristram Shandy:

> This great magnetic constitution has two great central poles; the one, in the head—the other, in the chest. This *magnetic nature to the germ of parentage*, is imparted to the germ of life, imbodied in it, only that *it is yet folded up or concentrated in the great central pole of the chest*,

where embryo life commences, and then deposited, by that function which imparts being, in the place provided for its nutrition, where, also, nature has stationed a full supply of maternal vitality, to feed it till it can germinate, as does the egg when subject to incubation, or seeds supplied with terrestrial magnetism.[11]

The notion of the electrical origin of life—and of these electric "poles"—occurs also in *Leaves of Grass*. The preceding passage has remarkable affinities to "Unfolded Out of the Folds" (1856), a glorification of Whitman-Adam's coupling with his muscular Eve, which develops the metaphor of "unfolding" in ten parallel lines and, like Fowler's statement, implies that the electrical genetic codes transmitted to the child originate with the mother as well as the father. Although the poem is essentially a voyeuristic and vulval ritual celebrating the begetting of the hero-poet, its electrical and embryological implications give it richness and subtlety.

> Unfolded out of the folds of the woman man comes unfolded, and
>   is always to come unfolded,
> Unfolded only out of the superbest woman of the earth is to come
>   the superbest man of the earth * * *
> Unfolded out of the folds of the woman's brain come all the folds
>   of the man's brain, duly obedient * * *
> First the man is shaped in the woman, he can then be shaped in
>   himself.[12]

Dr. Edward H. Dixon, the cantankerous urologist, was another author whose theories about the electrical nature of life and sexuality help us to interpret the currents that flowed into the making of *Leaves of Grass*:

> Electricity is the MOTOR of the [nervous] system [said Dixon], the nerves only conduct it; all the organs are under its influence. . . . The sexual organs are electric, no part of the body is richer in nerves. . . . The male in health is positive; the female negative. All substances living or dead are either in a positive or negative condition of electricity. . . .
>
> There can be no doubt that *all adult male animals produce life by inherent electric power, without the aid of the female*; for the spermatozoids contained in healthy semen are undoubtedly alive; and as that fluid is continually reproduced from the blood by the testes, which are enclosed in dense sacs, there is evidently no possibility of union of the sexes in these creatures, preparatory to their emission in the sexual act. Indeed, no sexual organs or organization have

Walt Whitman and the Body Beautiful

been discovered by the microscope; *the life therefore must be purely electric. . . .*

Dixon contended that the positively charged system acts within the womb as an attractor and nucleus of all the elements needed for the development of the fetus. Like Whitman, he felt that the health and "electricity" of the parents determine the development of their child. Because he regarded the world as an electrical ambience, he maintained that health depends on the proper electrical balance within the body. And his assumptions—that electricity constitutes the "undiminished source of life," transmitted from one generation to another and withdrawn only by death or disease, and that "the sun is the source of light, electricity, and life"—are not unlike similar assumptions in Whitman's verses.[13] Thus, an 1876 poem expresses faith in "The sun there at the centre though conceal'd, / Electric life forever at the centre * * * *"[14]

To understand the Whitman persona, supercharged with the electric life-essence for self-realization and ideal fatherhood, one must recognize that the poet sometimes employs the premise (particularly in the early editions of *Leaves of Grass*) that the male is the sole transmitter of the electric spark of life and that the female is the source chiefly of the life-giving sustenance. Whitman's trope of a male "body electric" is more than a dazzling metaphor to exalt the masculine ego; it is distilled from the prevailing physiological faith and sanctioned by reputable scientific thought. As Lorenz Oken explained, the fetus is created when the semen, which alone contains "infusoria," or living matter, combines with the "vitellus," the yolk or female nutritive substance, "but in such a manner that the female substance gives it mass, while the male bestows the polarity," that is, the electric life-giving impulse. Dr. Trall expressed this idea simply: "The female furnishes the ovum or germ of future being, while the male communicates the vivifying principle [electricity]."[15] In the first edition of "A Song of Joys," the persona's phallic electricity is clearly identified:

> O love-branches! love-root! love-apples!
> O chaste and *electric* torrents! O mad-sweet drops!

And the original version of "A Woman Waits for Me" contains a virtual paraphrase of Oken's description of the male-female relationship:

O! I will fetch bully breeds of children yet!
They cannot be fetched, I say, on less terms than mine,
Electric growth from the male, and rich ripe fibre from the female are the
    terms. [16]

The deletion of these lines in 1860 when, perhaps, their physiological inaccuracy had become obvious to the poet, has served to blur the principle of electric maleness which animates the Adamic persona in *Leaves of Grass*.

The persona's astonishing phallic electricity is more than a physiological or genetic attribute, because it relates him to the sexual-creative force of the universe and to the cosmic drama of electrical intercourse. "Is not electricity the father and begetter of all Matter?" asked the author of an essay entitled "Electricity the Great Acting Part of Nature." [17] This concept had venerable antecedents. William Gilbert and Sir Thomas Browne, seventeenth-century physicists and physicians, had used the word "coition" to indicate the magnetic attraction and repulsion of celestial bodies; the mystic Robert Fludd had referred to the "Etheriall Sperm, or Astricall Influences, [which] are of a far subtiler condition than is the vehicle of visible light." [18] Updating these ideas in Whitman's time, Orson Fowler described how the positively charged sun attracts the negatively charged earth until she, too, becomes positive, and is repelled: "and this their oscillation, tantamount to their sexual intercourse, is perpetually generating that matter, which comets are everywhere gathering up, and embodying into newborn worlds, and wheeling into orbits, which this identical sexual element is peopling with all forms of life." Drawing an analogy between the operation of the celestial bodies and human sexuality, Fowler explained that the male's positive charge and the female's negative charge create the attraction necessary to bring semen into the womb. Electricity, he argued, is the central fact of love: "this male electricity and female magnetism is the soul of gender, and its interchange, in which loving consists, is Nature's creative instrumentality." [19]

In a manuscript fragment, possibly derived from Fowler, Whitman observed: "The analogy holds this way—that the Soul of the Universe is the Male and Lover, the impregnating and animating Spirit—Physical matter is the Female and Mother, and waits barren and bloomless till the jets of life from the masculine vigor, the undermost first cause of all that is not what Death

                                              Walt Whitman and the Body Beautiful

is. . . ."[20] He elaborated the analogy between human and celestial coupling in section 21 of "Song of Myself," wherein the cosmic persona, identifying with the masculine moon ("he that walks with the tender and growing night") embraces the "voluptuous" and "prodigal" earth and the "magnetic nourishing night" with "unspeakable passionate love" like "the bridegroom" embracing "the bride." Since female electricity was said to be magnetic, we may assume that the womb of the "nourishing night" is entrusted with the precious vitellus and that the cosmic sexual embraces of the persona, enacting the role of the electro-deific "Male and Lover," spark the creation of that matter of which the universe is formed.[21]

Soon after this interplanetary lovemaking, the persona waxes prophetic, as he invariably does after episodes of sexual arousal. In section 24, as an inspired healer and clairvoyant, and something of a human galvanometer (he is the "index" of the cosmic "current"), he develops a second, and more intriguing, analogy between his creative sexuality and the operation of the celestial spheres:

> Through me the afflatus surging and surging, through me the
> current and index * * * *
> Through me many long dumb voices,
> Voices of the interminable generations of prisoners and slaves,
> Voices of the diseas'd and despairing and of thieves and dwarfs,
> Voices of cycles of preparation and accretion,
> And of the *threads that connect the stars*, and of wombs and of *the
> father-stuff* * * * *

The electrical and spermatic "threads" connecting the stars seem to be a projection of the persona's sexual and visionary powers. Just as the "father-stuff" represents the electrical source of human life, so the stars represent the electrical sources of universal life. In apparent trial lines for the preceding passage, Whitman had associated these "threads" with the electric cores, located in various parts of the body, whose existence Fowler had postulated:

> I heat the cores within and fix the central part of the cores
> And I carry straight threads thence to the sun and to distant unseen
> suns

Metaphorically, the persona's electro-spermatic ejaculation becomes the ecstatic rainbow spanning the infinitude between his conscious self and the paradise of his desiring:

Something I cannot see puts upward libidinous prongs,
Seas of bright juice suffuse heaven.[22]

These "threads that connect the stars" in "Song of Myself" may be said to be made of "mettle," a term denoting sperm. Thus, the "mettlesome" young men in "A Song of Joys" are athletic, well-sexed youngsters; Manhattan itself is called "mettlesome" by the poet; and the American South ("O Magnet-South") is celebrated for its "quick mettle, rich blood, impulse, and love!" (This "quick," that is, life-giving, mettle is the spermatic life source.)[23] And if "the threads that connect the stars" are imagined to be strands of mettle reaching from the phallic persona to the very heavens, then Whitman has achieved the pinnacle of cosmic arrogance! Among his contemporaries, this wild fancy could be matched only by Melville, who contrasted the asexual Bartleby to "the mettlesome Lord Byron," constructed a monstrous three-hundred-foot stone and mortar "erection" in "The Bell Tower," and created literature's most irrepressible phallus in the form of Moby Dick, whose huge tun of sperm (*his* emblematic "father-stuff"), if stretched fine enough, might also "connect the stars."

Whitman's audacious hyperbole reminds us, of course, that neither his theories of male and female sexuality nor his many other adaptations of electrical lore display much regard for consistency or scientific accuracy. As with phrenology, Whitman seemed to value electricity chiefly for its metaphoric possibilities and its power to symbolize human and poetic transcendence. As electricity was a mysterious power grounded in the earthly, material world and yet a part of the celestial ambience; as it seemed to be the link between the physical, mental, and spiritual worlds; and as it seemed to constitute the very psychic essence, Whitman incorporated it into his poetic imagery and language.

Whitman used electrical concepts to illustrate the dynamism and intuition that qualified him to be his nation's poet. He admitted his personal attraction to those whom he found "physically and mentally magnetic," and he preserved a clipping on "Personal Magnetism" which stated that "the large magnetic power which every person may well covet is a *birthright*" and that those who lead unhealthful or dissipated lives "squander and exhaust this

Walt Whitman and the Body Beautiful

'capital stock' of power; they become as Samson when shorn of his locks" and impart no influence to others.[24] Many of the poems depict Whitman-Adam as a sexually magnetic superman whose body attracts "all I meet or I know." The equation of strong physical attraction with the mystic powers of the magnet had been familiar for many centuries. Paracelsus claimed that each human being has "a magnetic power by which he may attract certain effluvia of good or evil quality in the same manner as a magnet will attract iron." Before 1800, the German physician J. C. Reil described the "magnet" of the flesh—an uncanny power operating upon the senses through a volatile essence which vital and well-balanced persons may perceive flowing in and out of their bodies.[25]

Similar ideas underlie the celebration, in "A Song of Joys," of the "magnetic" drawing powers and "vast elemental sympathy which only the human soul is capable of generating and emitting in steady and limitless floods." "To A Pupil" (1860) challenges the reader to develop such a highly charged "body and soul that when you enter the crowd an atmosphere of desire and command enters with you", and it defines this attraction as "the *magnet!* the flesh over and over." The sexual forces that draw the persona "so close by tender directions and indirections" ("Myself and Mine") are magnetic. To the male lover who sits beside him, Whitman-Adam confesses: "Little you know the subtle electric fire that for your sake is playing within me." When his lover holds him by the hand, he says: "Then I am charged with untold and untellable wisdom * * * *" (The electrical "charge" is related to his magnetism; and the quasi-sexual act of hand-holding heightens his perceptual and prophetic powers.) With characteristic bravado, he exclaims:

> Know, I am a man, attracting, at any time, her I but look upon or
> touch with the tips of my fingers,
> Or that touches my face, or leans against me.

Equating electricity with fire, he boasts to his Eve of "My limbs and the quivering fire that ever plays through them, for reasons, most wondrous * * * *"[26]

Whitman implied that his own electromagnetism qualified him for oratory and poetry alike. Great orators, Dods remarked, have had "strong muscular powers" and have "electrified" their audiences to "bring them into a magnetic sympathy with the speaker." And, boasting of the "self-healing energies that are generated within his own physical being," the electrical healer J. R. Newton declared that he could transmit a "magnetic force and principle with the words I speak."[27] At one time, Whitman, too, had thoughts of becoming an orator who could enthrall his hearers through the instantaneous "electric spirit" which vibrates from soul to soul "by the lightning of eloquence," augmented by carefully studied "[s]weeping movements, electric and broad style of hands, and all the upper joints." He pictured himself on the lecture platform: "Suddenly the countenance illumined, the breast expanded, the nostrils and mouth electric and quivering, the attitude imperious and erect—a God stands before you."[28] But he rejected oratory in favor of becoming the nation's bard whose "electric voice" could infuse others with the vitalizing and inspirational currents that flowed through himself.

As a poet energized by "this electric self out of the pride of which I utter poems" (a phrase that recalls Tennyson's delight in "this electric force, that keeps a thousand pulses dancing"), his senses become attuned to the "clear electric base and baritone of the world."[29] His poems assure his countrymen that *Leaves of Grass* can put them in contact with the electric heart of nature— "Nature encompassing these, encompassing God—to the joyous, electric all." He promises to create "divine magnetic lands," "a freer, vast, electric world," and to make America's "cities electric," too. He broadcasts democratic chants, "shooting in pulses of [electric] fire ceaseless to vivify all." Like a mesmerist, "with a flowing mouth and indicative hand," he informs the nation of his electric, life-giving powers: "I cannot be discharged from you!" he puns. His poems, he claims, can unite the disparate elements in the American personality: they can "compact you, ye parted, diverse lives."[30] Following the "shock electric" of the Civil War, he invokes the electric spirit of that conflict to fill his poems with its "pulses of rage," so that he may proclaim the truth. He prays, in "Song of the Universal" (1874) that this therapeutic electric spirituality may purge America's future of corruption:

> Out of the bulk, the morbid and the shallow,
> Out of the bad majority, the varied countless frauds of men and
> 　　states,

Walt Whitman and the Body Beautiful

Electric, antiseptic yet, cleaving, suffusing all,
Only the good is universal.

He also pictures himself as Mother Columbia's lover, impregnating her with his electric and vivifying spirit:

Attracting it body and soul to himself, hanging on its neck with
    incomparable love,
Plunging his seminal muscle into its merits and demerits.

Europe with its feudal allure can never "magnetize" Mother Columbia, he asserts, but he boasts that as the nation's great poet he can indeed "fill the gross the torpid bulk with vital religious fire." Nor does he celebrate Columbia for her products or wealth alone: "it is for thee, the soul in thee, electric, spiritual."[31]

The belief that the force which moves the heavenly bodies is identical with the essence which animates and controls all life is a venerable one. In the 1770's, when Galvani and Hunter had fired the imagination by their scientific investigations into the electricity of living creatures, Franz Anton Mesmer, a German physician, codified the principles of animal magnetism, hypothesizing that the mysterious force is a superfine substance which can penetrate any surface at any distance. This force, he asserted, may be stored in the body and transferred from person to person through an act of the will. (The voluntary transfer of this force is the operative principle in the belief, which Whitman shared with the mesmerists, that superfluous "electricity" bestowed by healthy and strong-willed persons can restore their weaker brethren to health.) Like the Whitman persona, Mesmer claimed that he could convey this curative essence by touching his subjects or merely looking at them or thinking about them. In the alleged power of magnetism to heal bodily ills and to probe the subconscious, he saw a way to perfect the human race. Animal magnetism, he proclaimed, is "the GENERAL AGENT, whose existence . . . alone can restore the harmony of the natural state."[32]

The hypothesis that electricity is a transferable vitalizing force (mesmerism) intrigued scientists and visionaries. During the dozen years preceding *Leaves of Grass* (before the popularity of ether and chloroform had obscured the efficacy of mesmerism as an anesthetic), *The Zoist*, an influential English journal, chronicled the wonders of mesmerism as a medical cure-all and a medium for the truth-drawing powers of clairvoyance. Herbert Spencer contributed to its pages, and Harriet Martineau, who mesmerized Charlotte Brontë and converted Elizabeth Barrett Browning to mesmerism, published impassioned testimonials there. During this period, Charles Dickens demonstrated a flair for mesmeric therapy and introduced mesmeric details into his novels. Tennyson, Frances Trollope, W. H. Channing, Margaret Fuller, Poe, and numerous medical and literary figures endorsed the practice.[33] In 1821, Joseph-Claude Récamier, a celebrated physician and student of animal electricity (*la dynamométrie vitale*), had performed the first recorded surgery under mesmeric hypnosis. By mid-century, operations during mesmeric sleep had been performed by Dr. John Elliotson, the distinguished English physiologist and physician, and by Dr. James Esdaile in India.[34] Timothy Shay Arthur made dental extraction during mesmeric sleep the pivotal incident in a potboiler romance whose mesmerist villain takes advantage of a New England village girl's somnolent state to gain an evil dominance over her.[35]

During these years, Whitman had already accepted the teachings of mesmerism. In August, 1842, he informed the readers of the *New York Sunday Times* that "[s]ome seasons ago" he had ceased to be "a devout disbeliever in the science of Animal Magnetism," a few lectures and demonstrations having convinced him that "there is such a thing as Mesmeric sleep" and that the "strange things done by the subject at the will of the Magnetizer" are not the result of collusion or fraud, but that hypnotic manipulation and "Mesmeric somnambulism" are beneficial. He was excited by the artistic implications of mesmerism, declaring that it "reveals at once the existence of a whole new world of truth, grand, fearful, profound, relating to that great mystery, in the shadow of which we live and move and have our being, the mystery of our Humanity."[36] Thereafter he remained interested in this half-science, and he utilized it in his poems, particularly in characterizing the Whitman persona.

Mesmeric powers, such as those exercised by the Whitman persona, were described by John Bovee Dods in a book that Whitman apparently read. The millennium, Dods said, will arrive when each man has learned to mesmerize and to make use of "the whole power" within himself. Mesmerism, he declared,

. . . is the innate power of the living mind, executed through the agency of the will. It is that power which created worlds, for this was done by the will of God. It is that power by which worlds are governed, and creatures ruled, for this is also done by the will of God. It is this power by which we make impressions reciprocally upon each other, for that is done by the will of man. And lastly, it is "that power which shall awake the dead from dreamless slumber, into thoughts of heaven," for this will be done by the will of God, and there is no medium, only electricity, through which He can come into contact with his creatures.

Alleging that Christ had healed the leper and raised the dead through the exercise of this same electromagnetic power, Dods further insisted that mesmerism is a valid Christian doctrine.[37]

Dods's argument about the restorative powers of mesmerism recalls Whitman's claims about his own magnetic accomplishments. At the Boston printing office where he was seeing the 1860 edition of *Leaves of Grass* through the press, he reportedly claimed that he could "cheer up" and "strengthen" a sickly lad from his boarding house by charging him with some of his own "magnetism."[38] In a similar fashion, he attributed his success in healing the sick and affection-starved soldiers in the military hospitals to his freely bestowed "magnetic flood of sympathy and friendship," his "magnetic personality," and "the simple matter of [his own] personal presence, and emanating ordinary cheer and magnetism." It is "the most solid of facts," said he, that "even the moving around among the men, or through the ward, of a hearty, healthy, clean, strong, generous-souled person, man or woman, full of humanity and love, sending out invisible currents thereof, does immense good to the sick and wounded." Were these "currents" electrical? William Douglas O'Connor apparently thought so, for he claimed that Whitman's friendliness and goodness were "felt upon his approach like magnetism" and that his personality and "magnetic touch" had sustained the soldiers.[39]

The healing powers exercised by the poet-nurse and by the Whitman persona may be compared to those of J. R. Newton, who cured the eighteen-year-old Olivia Langdon, the future wife of Mark Twain, of the neurasthenic after-effects of a fall which had kept her bedridden for two years. To Mark Twain, Newton explained that "perhaps some subtle form of electricity proceeded from his body and wrought the cure." Dr. S. Weir Mitchell, who treated several patients who had fallen under the sway of the man whom he called "the charlatan Newton," found no instance of an organic improvement resulting from Newton's practice, but he admitted that a patient "who was merely idea sick—a class of patients we all know well," might be favorably influenced by this sort of faith healing.[40] As an efficacious healer, Whitman, too, bestowed his personal affection and magnetic presence to stimulate the will to live in soldiers whose injuries and despair may have rendered them what Dr. Mitchell called "idea sick." According to Whitman's reasoning, once the soldier has regained the will to survive, he activates his *vis*—the body's natural recuperative powers—and begins to regain his health.

According to the mesmerists, a magnetic healer needs a powerful will, physical vigor, and a plentiful supply of the electrical "nervo-vital fluid" that has not been dissipated by excessive sexuality or unwholesome living. By the action of his will, the healer transmits his electricity to the patient, reanimating and balancing the vital power throughout the patient's system or restoring the vital power to a weakened part of the body. Dods explained the healing process in a way that illuminates the behavior of the Whitman persona:

> Now let a person whose brain is fully charged, come in contact with one whose brain is greatly wanting in its due measure of this fluid, and let the person possessing the full brain gently and unchangeably hold his mind upon the other, and by the action of the WILL, the fluid will pass from the full brain to the other, until the equilibrium between the two brains is attained. The sudden change in the receiving brain produces a coolness and a singular state of insensibility. That is MAGNETISM; and it is in perfect accordance with the principles of philosophy in the known realms of nature.[41]

Many persons in high places, Whitman alleged, are "sad, hasty, unwaked somnambules," lacking the electric willpower. The politicians whom the poet beheld were said to be mostly "galvanized" old men, shocked into a little action but "having no vitality from the heart."[42] To these, and to all humanity, he offered hope. In trial lines for "Song of Myself," the persona undertakes to recharge the weakened electric "cores" of his fellow citizens with his own "jets of life"—jets of the subtle electric fluid:

Walt Whitman and the Body Beautiful

Strength
Where is one abortive, mangy, cold
Starved of his masculine lustiness?
Without *core* and loose in the knees?
Clutch fast to me, my ungrown brother,
That I *infuse* you with grit and *jets of life*
I am not to be scorned (?):—I Compel;
It is quite indifferent to me who [you] are.
I have stores plenty and to spare
And of whatsoever I have I bestow upon you.
And first I bestow my love.[43]

Through the force of his will, the vigorous healer-hero, prodigal of his electric fluid, disseminates curative electricity to vitalize the sick and despairing; they absorb it, and are benefited:

We effuse spirituality and immortality,
We put a second brain to the brain,
We put second eyes to the eyes and second ears to the ears,
Then the drudge in the kitchen—then the laborer in his stained
    clothes—then the black person, criminals, barbarians—are no
    more inferior to the rest,
The frivolous and the blunderer are not to be laughed at as before,
The cheat, the crazy enthusiast, the unsuccessful man, come under
    the same laws as any.—[44]

As the persona exercises his mesmeric powers in sections 39, 40, and 41 of "Song of Myself," he appears to become a primal energizer.[45] Electricity emanates from his body, his fingers, and his breath. The electricity of paternity charges his loins. His will is exerted to heal the souls and bodies of all sufferers. He turns "the knob of the door" and fills "every room of the house" (the human body) with "an armed force" or "grit" by bestowing his surplusage of life-giving electricity. As his healing powers merge with his electric love and his electric clairvoyance, he becomes the peer of all the gods:

The friendly and *flowing* savage . . . . Who is he?
Is he waiting for civilization or past it and mastering it? * * * *

Wherever he goes men and women accept and desire him,
They desire he should like them and *touch* them and speak to them
    and stay with them.

Behaviour lawless as snow-flakes . . . . words simple as grass
. . . . uncombed head and laughter and naivete;
Slowstepping feet and common features, and the common modes
and *emanations,*
They descend in new forms from the tips of his fingers,
They are wafted with the odor of his body or breath . . . . they fly out of
the glance of his eyes * * * *

You there, impotent, loose in the knees, open your scarfed chops
till I *blow grit within you,*
Spread your palms and lift the flaps of your pockets,
I am not to be denied . . . . I compel . . . . I have stores plenty
and to spare,
And any thing I have I bestow * * * *

On women fit for conception I start bigger and nimbler babies,
This day I am jetting the stuff of far more arrogant republics.

To any one dying . . . thither I speed and twist the knob of the
door,
Turn the bedclothes toward the foot of the bed,
Let the physician and the priest go home.

I seize the descending man . . . . I raise him with resistless *will.*

O despairer, here is my neck,
By God! you shall not go down! Hang your whole weight upon
me.

I dilate you with tremendous breath . . . . I buoy you up;
Every room in the house do I fill with an armed force . . . . lovers
of me, bafflers of graves:
Sleep! I and they keep guard all night;
Not doubt, not decease shall dare to lay finger upon you,
I have embraced you, and henceforth possess you to myself,
And when you rise in the morning you will find what I tell you is
so.

I am he bringing help for the sick as they pant on their backs,
And for strong upright men I bring yet more needed help.

In the foregoing passage, the persona appears to engage in a
sort of mesmeric breath therapy. His breath is no idle wind: it is a
charge of his own electrified energy or the operation, through
him, of the universal deific electricity. Long before Whitman
wrote this great poem, J. P. F. Deleuze, a pioneer mesmerist, had
instructed the practitioner who wished to revitalize his run-down
patient or to heal him of an injury to "place a piece of linen several

times folded, or a fragment of woolen or cotton cloth upon the suffering part; apply the mouth above it and breathe through it; it excites a lively sensation of heat, and the breath, which is charged with the nervous fluid, introduces it into the system. Then expel the pain by [mesmeric] passes." Deleuze also advised the practitioner to sit opposite the patient in a comfortable room, take the subject's hand thumb to thumb ("Spread your palms," commands the Whitman healer-persona), gaze steadily into the subject's eyes until the hands of the subject and the operator become equally warm, then pass his fingertips downward along shoulder and arm, shaking out electric currents until the subject is mesmerized. Deleuze specified that the operator who accomplishes beneficial results must be healthy and must *will* to help his subject.[46] In his alleged cures of severe organic diseases, J. R. Newton made use of a silver tube about three inches long: "I place it over the parts affected, *outside* the clothing, and with powerful exhalations I send the magnetism, which passes out with the breath, thereto, willing the disease to depart. The healing influence permeates the organ and affects [sic] a cure." The disciples of the Anglo-American mystic Thomas Lake Harris were said to be "open breathers," within whose bosoms heaved "the palpitating Breath of God" which "energized" them to perform good deeds and repel evil, to receive the visitations of "fairies" from the spiritual realm, and to heal others.[47] But the Whitman persona's display of breath therapy is as awesome as that of any mesmeric therapist or spiritual healer.

Because electrical healing does not necessarily involve hypnosis, readers of *Leaves of Grass* may fail to recognize those passages which represent the persona as a mesmeric healer. Phineas Parker Quimby, at one time a successful mesmerist, claimed that the formalities of mesmerism are unnecessary to effect electrical cures; accordingly, he abandoned mesmerism to become a "mental" healer. Quimby explained that his revised practice is "unlike all medical practice. I give no medicine and make no outward applications," he said. "I tell the patient his troubles and what he thinks is his disease; and my explanation is the cure. If I succeed in correcting his errors, I change the [electric] fluids in the system and establish the truth, or health. The truth is the cure."[48] Thus Quimby anticipated some aspects of psychosomatic medicine; his theory also resembles the sort of rationalization that the Whitman persona makes about his successful healing in "Song of Myself."

Although secular physicians had practiced electric shock therapy and induced electric currents to treat the sick for nearly a century, mesmerists in Whitman's day generally claimed that their healing powers were derived from the Deity and that they were acting as His agents. There is a strong resemblance between these mesmeric healers and the Christ-like persona of the "Messenger Leaves" poems who infuses others with his curative electricity. Placing his hand on the flawed man in "To You, Whoever You Are," like a typical mesmerist, the persona inspires him with a faith that he can be made whole and be crowned with a nimbus. In the startlingly sexual imagery of "To Him that Was Crucified," the persona compares himself to Christ because both are "transmitting the same charge and succession" and both will eventually "saturate time and eras, that men and women of races, ages to come, may prove brethren and lovers, as we are." In "To Rich Givers" he bestows "the entrance to all the gifts of the universe"; and in "To a Pupil" he defines these gifts in terms of magnetism.[49]

Through his touch and his breath, the healer-persona lavishes similar gifts upon his readers, infusing the very paper and ink of *Leaves of Grass* with a beneficial electric charge. Employing similar techniques, J. R. Newton practiced long-distance "treating by magnetized letters," and Isabel, the dark enchantress of Melville's *Pierre*, transmitted an electric impulse through the medium of the iron oxide in her ink, mesmerizing the hapless Pierre as soon as he received her fateful missive.[50] Whitman deleted from "A Song for Occupations" the statement, "I pass so poorly with paper and types," probably because it conflicted with his desired image as an immortal electrical personage who can convey his powers through the printed page. (The spirits of the dead, according to some mediums and spirit-rappers, could communicate with them by means of similar "electroplate" or "electrotype" impressions.) On a more positive note, "Calamus 5" offers the reader "The old breath of life, ever new, / Here! I pass it by contact to you, America"; and an 1872 dedicatory poem implies that Whitman has charged his book with the "leavening" electricity of his breath, so that the reader who holds the volume in his hand may feel the poet's "pulse" and his "heart's-blood."[51]

Electrical themes are superbly articulated in "Song of the Open Road."[52] Healthy and free-footed, but carrying his "old de-

Walt Whitman and the Body Beautiful

licious burdens" of human responsibilities, the persona takes to the road and absorbs its lessons. Invigorated and energized by the electrical and spiritual qualities of the open air, he feels that "the impassive surfaces" of the road will impart their secrets to him and that the "spirits" of those who have gone before will be "evident and amicable with me." He interchanges his own magnetism with that of others. On this public and cosmic road, he acknowledges the divine electricity operating within himself and becomes wonder-struck—a self-ordained seer. He is ready to behold miracles and to perform them. And his astounding assumptions are not unfounded. Before this poem was composed, Alcott and others had cited Faraday's discoveries concerning the electric properties of oxygen in order to show that fresh air imparts physical and psychic revitalization. Health, electrical biologists argued, is a condition characterized by abundant body electricity, properly balanced between positive and negative charges. In the open sunlit spaces, the persona's blood can become oxygenated and electrified by his deep breathing, and his body can be vitalized by the atmospheric currents. Moreover, as Dods said, this airborne electricity is "an atmospheric emanation from God." [53] No wonder the persona relaxes all inhibitions and declares: "I think I could stop here myself and do miracles"; "I inhale great draughts of air"; [54] "I am larger, better than I thought." Alluding to the magnetic bond between human beings, and possibly to the effect of photosynthesis on his dynamic self, he demands: "Why are there men and women that while they are nigh me the sunlight expands my blood?"

As a "fluid and attaching character," he displays his power to generate the electro-mesmeric fluid and his capacity for Adhesiveness (the personal and phrenological concept of comradeship):

> The efflux of the soul is happiness, here is happiness,
> I think it pervades the open air, waiting at all times,
> Now it flows unto us, *we are rightly charged*.
>
> Here rises the *fluid* and *attaching* character,
> The fluid and attaching character is the freshness and sweetness of
>   man and woman,
> (The herbs of the morning sprout no fresher and sweeter every
>   day out of the roots of themselves, than it sprouts fresh and
>   sweet continually out of itself.)

> Toward the fluid and attaching character exudes the sweat of the
>   love of young and old,
> From it falls distill'd the *charm* that mocks beauty and attainments,
> Toward it heaves the shuddering longing ache of contact.

Thus charged and exuding "charm" (the mesmeric force), the persona perceives "divine things more beautiful than words can tell" and becomes prophetic. In perfect health, he goes forth to recruit the conformist city-folk, calling on the "Forth-steppers from the latent unrealized baby-days" to shed their "duplicate" selves (the unfulfilled "other I am" of "Song of Myself") and to join his progress through life and the beyond.

There is a notable resemblance between the nineteenth-century trance mediums who experience a "superior state" of clairvoyance and the visionary persona of *Leaves of Grass* who appears, more or less clearly, as a medium or clairvoyant who can penetrate cloth, flesh, or the solid earth; make contact with the innermost consciousness of men and women; heal the sick; behold the future and the past; interact with the powers that animate the universe; and, with impassioned lyricism, reveal what he has experienced. His vaunted physical strength and personal excellence confirm that he is indeed serving as the medium of immense and benevolent inspirational forces. For, as the spiritualist John Humphrey Noyes observed, "an afflatus [an inspirational spirit or "control"] which is strong enough to make a strong man its medium *and keep him under*, will attain the greatest success; or in other words, that the greater the medium the better, other things being equal." And as J. R. Newton remarked, "Just as I live, in principle and truth, by just such powers shall I be controlled; the better life I live, day after day, the better the angels, from the celestial spheres can come and operate [through me] to heal the sick."[55] The substance and ideology of mystic visions generally conform to the value systems and personal anxieties of the visionary. "The phantoms formed in the human brain," it has been said, are in fact "sublimates of [the] material life-process."[56] Just as the purported trances of Andrew Jackson Davis were filled with his Swedenborgian, Fourierist, and Jacksonian prejudices,[57] so the content of Whitman's mystical-literary visions projects his outlook, his feelings, and his sublimated tensions. It is consistent with Whit-

Walt Whitman and the Body Beautiful

man's thought that his visionary poems should foretell the eventual triumph of the complete human personality whose bodily health complements his total spiritual development. And it is also consistent that he should proclaim the clairvoyant-mystic power, which he calls "the trance of the healthy brain," to be a democratic birthright:

> Who wills with his own brain, the sweet of the float of the world
>   descends and surrounds him,
> If you be a laborer or apprentice or solitary farmer, it is the same.

According to Whitman's version of popular mysticism, anyone may achieve self-induced inspiration. The persona instructs a pupil: "You are to grasp with your own mind vigorously"; in the exercise of his clairvoyance, the pupil can expand his capacities and "find a strange pleasure." [58]

Obviously, *Leaves of Grass* shares many traits common to the writings of Blake, Novalis, Emerson, and other Western literary mystics, and its resemblances to the utterances of Eastern mystics have been impressively argued. [59] Despite the volume's affinities to mysticism throughout the world, we should not overlook its ties to the most popular and accessible mystics of Whitman's day, the spiritualists. In 1853, Nathaniel Parker Willis had estimated "that the number of Spiritualists in New York City could not be less than forty thousand; the magnetic circles held at this time about three hundred; in Brooklyn and Williamsburgh at least twice that number; whilst several thousand mediumistic persons, over twenty public test mediums, and at least a hundred clairvoyant and medical mediums could be found in and around the city. . . ." [60] Many of the American seers claimed to initiate their own mystical experiences and preserved their revelations in impressive literary records.

The parapsychologist J. B. Rhine has defined spiritualism as a Christian doctrine which emphasizes that the spirits of the dead survive as personalities and communicate with the living through living mediums, generally with the assistance of "spirit guides or controls." With the help of these spirit entities, the mediums may act as healers, "give counsel dealing with a wide range of personal and practical affairs through their ability to draw upon the supposedly wider knowledge and insight of the spirit world," and display "clairvoyant knowledge of hidden and distant events" of the past, present, or future.[61] Within the broad limits of this definition, we may sometimes behold in the untrammeled Whitman persona the striking resemblance to a spiritualist medium who contacts the spirits of the dead, travels without hindrance through the world of dreams, comprehends the unvoiced yearnings of all beings, identifies with and "becomes" them, heals them, affirms their greatness and immortality, and reveals what he has experienced in the spirit world.

Observing that the Whitman persona "played the role of a poetic clairvoyant," Howard Kerr has commented: "Whitman's own self-dramatization as inspired bard unconstrained by barriers of space or time resembled in many ways the role of clairvoyant prophet played by Andrew Jackson Davis, Thomas Lake Harris, and others. But Whitman does not seem to have made much explicit use of spiritualism, which still awaited a Yeats for whom it could supply a unifying vision."[62] Whereas the epic visionary poems of Thomas Lake Harris (allegedly dictated to him during episodes of "magnetic sleep" by disembodied spirits, including those of Coleridge, Byron, Shelley, and Keats) abound in "spiritual cosmography" and specifications of the operation of the world of the spirits,[63] Whitman's mystic poems and his known comments on spiritualism espouse no specific spiritualist creed, politics, or technology. We may reasonably conclude that he held "creeds and schools in abeyance," preferring to integrate spiritualist elements into his own creative vision rather than to write in conformity with any known spiritualist system.

The affinities of *Leaves of Grass* to spiritualism were perceived by some of Whitman's contemporaries. Indeed, the poet reprinted a favorable review of the first edition of his poems from *The Christian Spiritualist* (1856), one of about twenty spiritualist periodicals then published in the United States. Although likening Whitman to "a drunken Hercules among the dainty dancers," the reviewer credited him, together with Emerson, with creating poems in response to an influx of the spirit and praised him as "an American medium destined to give new songs to the people." Observing that Whitman's "song is highly mediatorial," the reviewer speculated that "probably he is unacquainted with the Spiritual developments of the age." But a British spiritualist declared unambiguously in 1870 that *Leaves of Grass* is a work of "that advanced and

Walt Whitman and the Body Beautiful

transcendental kind that belongs only to writers who have been baptized into the true Jordan of Spiritualism, and have ascended from its banks into the borders of the Summer Land"—those who have "walked and talked with the angels." This critic asserted that Whitman is indeed "one of us" (spiritualists)—"the poet of the opened eye—the spiritual poet and seer" to whom "all worlds and ages are open"—in short, the poet of the modern era most genuinely inspired by the spirit world.[64]

Whitman admitted his link to the spiritualists in a statement that might be more convincing if it had not been planted in an anonymous self-review. Speaking of himself in the third person, the poet said: "His scope of life is the amplest yet in philosophy. He is the true spiritualist. He recognizes no annihilation, or death, or loss of identity. He is the largest lover and sympathizer that has appeared in literature."[65] Later, he penned "Mediums" (1860), a prophetic and self-congratulatory lyric steeped in spiritualism or, as it was sometimes called, "the invisible faith":

> They shall arise in the States—mediums shall,
> They shall report Nature, laws, physiology, and happiness,
> They shall illustrate Democracy and the kosmos,
> They shall be alimentive, amative, perceptive,
> They shall be complete women and men—their pose brawny and
>   supple, their drink water, their blood clean and clear * * *
> Strong and sweet shall their tongues be—poems and materials of
>   poems shall come from their lives—they shall be makers and
>   finders,
> Of them and of their works, shall emerge divine conveyers, to
>   convey gospels,
> Characters, events, retrospections, shall be conveyed in gospels—
>   Trees, animals waters, shall be conveyed,
> Death, the future, *the invisible faith*, shall all be conveyed.

In "Apostroph," the persona urges contemporary "mediums" to "journey through all The States" in order "to teach! to convey *the invisible faith!*" In "These Carols," he ascribes the inspiration of his own songs to "the Invisible World." In "As I Walk These Broad Majestic Days," he avers that the democratic principles of *Leaves of Grass* are in harmony with "the rapt promises and luminè of seers, the spiritual world." And in "Thoughts," wherein he hears "the earth at large, whispering through medium of me," and declares that "all I see and know, I believe to have purport in what will yet be supplied," there is at least a verbal suggestion of his own mediumship.[66] Whitman asked the readers of the *Brooklyn Daily Times* to distinguish between vulgar spirit-rapping and genuine spiritualism, which he deemed worthy of their respectful investigation, and he translated this advice into a poetic testimonial:

> I have the idea of all, and am all and believe in all,
> I believe materialism is true and spiritualism is true, I reject no
>   part.[67]

During the mystic experiences which are described in *Leaves of Grass*, the persona's clairvoyant faculty is heightened and "set free," according to F. O. Matthiessen, to follow "the natural bent of its own affinities." In a notebook jotting, Whitman recorded a similar definition: "a trance, yet with all the senses alert—only a state of high exalted musing—the tangible and material with all its shows, the objective world suspended or surmounted for a while, and the powers in exaltation, freedom, vision—yet the *senses* are not lost or counteracted."[68]

A comparison of the persona's mystic experiences to those of the Seeress of Prevost, an untutored German farm woman, is most instructive. During her trances, she reportedly entered into a somnambulistic state in which she saw herself "out of her body and sometimes double." At such times, she beheld her body from the outside through the eyes of her other self, the supersensory faculty which she called the "nerve-spirit"—the immortal companion of the soul in life and death and the guide on her dream-journeys to the dead. In "sleep-waking" or "clairvoyance," she said, "the inner-man steps forward and inspects the outer, which is not the case either in sleep or dreaming." During this "state of the most perfect vigilance . . . the inner spiritual man is disentangled and set free from the body." Hence, "sleep-waking" may be regarded as "the coming forward of the inner-man, or the spiritual growth of man." She reported that her episodes of "sleep-waking" had several successive stages: a wakeful state in which she entered the inner life; a magnetic dream in which she appeared (like many mesmeric subjects) to be out of her mind; at times, an intermediate state in which she became cataleptic and "lay torpid and cold"; a half-waking state in which she sometimes spoke in tongues and showed off an uncanny knowledge of ancient languages; and, finally, a "sleep-waking state, where she was clairvoyante and prescribed."[69]

In comparable fashion, the Whitman persona enters quickly into the dream state. During his visions, he often appears to become agitated, irrational, or overwhelmed. He does not speak in tongues, but he is able to "translate" the thoughts of other persons and of the spirits of the dead. He is sometimes brought to the nadir of despair—with its attendant terrors of death and hopelessness—and to a condition that is roughly analogous to the Seeress's torpid catalepsy, during which an array of miserable and perverse spirits kept her in a state of terror. Obviously, the persona's excursions into the dark regions of the soul are not exceptional components of the visionary experience. And when the persona is in the highest sleep-waking state, he, too, is clairvoyant and utters exalted truths.

Mesmerism explained such clairvoyance, or "true spiritual extasis," in terms of man's dual sensory organization. During clairvoyance, said the English mesmerist Joseph Haddock ordinary sensory faculties are augmented by the "internal consciousness," "the associate spirit," or the "inward *image-forming* faculty," which the Seeress had called her "nerve-spirit" and Whitman, in his poems, referred to as the "eidólon," the "I myself," the "journeymen divine," and so on. During a successful trance, Haddock observed, the clairvoyant's associate spirit is brought "into a *sensational* connection with the associate spirit of the person sought for . . . *this associate spirit appears to the clairvoyant to be the real individual sought*. . . ." Such experiences are "treasured up in the *internal* memory, while the *external* memory and all immediately connected with it is quiescent."[70] The German mystic Jung-Stilling maintained that the inner self leaves the body during a trance to contact the spirits of others and that it may be mistaken by living persons for its physical alter ego. Both the Seeress of Prevost and Elizabeth O'key, a popular juvenile medium whom Dickens witnessed, claimed to be served by associate spirits. And like the Whitman persona, both of them experienced trances which were characterized by schizophrenia, frenzy, and horrifying probings of their repressed desires.[71]

When the senses are exalted, Haddock said, a medium sees objects in a dazzling light that reveals both their separateness and their basic unity. Any part of the body may admit electricity and thus serve as an extrasensory organ of vision. Darkness is no hindrance, for the light by which the medium sees supposedly issues from his brain; it is not the light reflected from an object.[72] Hence the clairvoyant becomes like Emerson's "seeing eyeball": "I am nothing. I see all. The currents of the Universal Being circulate through me; I am part or particle of God." He becomes like the somnambulistic hero of "The Sleepers," whom darkness cannot deter from observing a brilliant universe, or like the persona in a poem related to section 27 of "Song of Myself," who can see with all parts of the body. The electrical nature of that visionary experience is accentuated by the poor pun on the "magnitude" ("magnetude") by which he threatens to raise the girder of the house and by his resemblance to those men who, reportedly, could lift great weights and perform prodigies of strength when they were mesmerized:

> I am cased with supple *conductors, all over,*
> They take every object by the hand, and lead it within me;
> They are thousands, each one with his entry to himself;
> They are always watching with their *little eyes*, from my head to
>   my feet;
> One no more than a point lets in and out of me such bliss and
>   *magnitude*,
> I think I could lift the girder of the house away if it lay between
>   me and whatever I wanted.

That this all-seeing, all-feeling state is achieved through the agency of an associate spirit and accompanied by the persona's schizophrenic behavior is confirmed in a related fragment:

> Yet I strike and dart through . . . . . .
> I think I could dash the girder of the earth away
> If it lay between me and what I wanted.
>
> Surely I am out of my head!
> I am lost to myself—and nature *in another form* has laid down in
>   my place * * * *[73]

During this mystic experience, the persona's spiritual self has apparently abandoned its physical habitat for a time ("I am lost to myself") and, exercising its supernatural image-forming faculties, has examined the earthly body in which it is housed during the body's lifetime.

The persona's exercise of his psychic powers may go unrecognized because of the widespread impression that a clairvoyant must be subject to the will of another person, and, with a possible exception noted below, *Leaves of Grass* does not reveal the persona as a mesmeric subject, obedient to the will of a human hypnotist. But clairvoyants were not always mesmerized by operators. Some of them were self-starters who could recall their visions in copious detail. For example, a Parisian mesmerist was reportedly a "spontaneous somnambulist" who wrote verses while in a trance. And the Seeress of Prevost, who sometimes told her visions in rhyme, could allegedly be mesmerized by the spirits of the dead or initiate her own clairvoyant sleep, letting out a sort of electric shock as she did so.[74] As the Whitman persona enters the sleep-waking state in section 5 of "Song of Myself," seemingly without mortal assistance, he evidently experiences the same sort of shock that "reach'd till you felt my beard, and reach'd till you held my feet." (The "you," in this context, appears to be his associate spirit or second self.)

The associate spirits of others are able to "address our interior and spiritual sense of hearing," said Davis, only when the electricity in the seer's brain is in a state of balance with external electricity. And Dods explained that "if our nervous system could be charged with the nervo-vital fluid [electricity], so as to render the brain positive, *and thus bring it into an exact equilibrium with external electricity*, then we should be clairvoyant." Surcharges of electric "fluid" in the nervous system, "passing in right lines from the mind, as a common centre, and in every direction, through the pores of the skull, render it transparent. Uniting with external electricity, which passes through these walls and all substances, which are also transparent, the image of the whole universe, as it were, in this transparent form, is thrown upon the mind, and is there seen, and seen, too, independent of the retina."[75] This same electrical equilibrium is an attribute of the "equable" and clairvoyant Whitman persona. Like the sun, the electro-deific heart of the universe, he, too, is a veritable godhead or creative force:

> Of these States the poet is the equable man,
> Not in him but off from him things are grotesque, eccentric, fail of
>   their full returns * * *
> He is the equalizer of his age and land * * * *

He judges not as the judge judges but as the sun falling round a
    helpless thing,
As he sees the farthest he has the most faith * * * *

The persona claims to be a spiritualistic superman ("Kosmos"),
who embodies what he himself calls the "equilibrium" of Nature
and "Who has not look'd forth from the windows the eyes for
nothing, or whose brain held audience with messengers for
nothing * * * *" 76

The electrical equilibrium required for communication with
the spirit world implies passivity and quiescence. A good medium
(or spirit-rapper), said Davis, is "surcharged . . . with a vital magnetism and vital electricity," and "at times generates a soft and
high quality of vital electricity, which renders him alternately *positive* and *negative*, and therefore a *good medium* through which spiritual intelligences could manifest their willingness and desire to approach and communicate with mankind." Besides retaining his
electrical equilibrium "on *all* occasions, the medium must remain
perfectly passive, as to the time and nature of the manifestation." If
the medium's electricity is excessive, he may repel the spirit messengers in the same way that similarly polarized magnets repel one
another. The "subjugation of our prejudices and anxious feelings"
enables us to "obtain truthful and reliable communications" with
the spirit world, Davis said. Anxiety makes the mediums' electricity too positive, he declared, and then they derange the communication with the spirit world.77 Within a context of this sort,
we may better understand the Whitman persona as he prepares to
enter into his ecstatic state in section 4 of "Song of Myself." The
"complacent, compassionating, idle" persona puts aside doubt and
despair; he dismisses "trippers and askers," "linguists and con-
tenders," and declares that "*Apart* from the pulling and hauling
stands *what I am*" (that is, his quiescent associate spirit or higher
consciousness stands outside his body, prepared to set off on its
dream journey). Similarly, after tallying the miseries of the world
in "I Sit and Look Out," the persona calls attention to his passive
readiness to receive the inspirational afflatus:

All these—all the meanness and agony without end I sitting look
    out upon,
See, hear, and am silent.78

The persona's clairvoyant mediumship is extensively demonstrated in four poems—"Song of the Answerer," "Salut au Monde!" "The Sleepers," and "Song of Myself."

"Song of the Answerer," adapted from two earlier poems, names the "spiritualist" as one of those who "underlie the maker of poems" and endows him with "the pass-key of hearts" to all men and women, whom he "strangely transmutes" by his very presence. In the poem's final version he appears as a Christ-like clairvoyant "who answers for all." Undertaking to translate the "signs" sent by the unseen brother (perhaps no longer alive) of a young man who visits him, the persona holds the visitor's hands in order to equalize the visitor's electricity with his own, in the very manner that Deleuze had prescribed:

> And I stood before the young man face to face, and took his right
> hand in my left hand, and his left hand in my right hand,
> And I answered for his brother, and for men, and I answered for
> THE POET, and sent these signs.

The clairvoyant persona, in whom are fused a mesmeric medium and an omniscient god, interprets these occult "signs," which include an inspiring promise of "the flowing [that is, magnetic] character you could have" by living in harmony with the cosmic laws.[79]

"Salut au Monde!" pictures the persona apparently being put into a clairvoyant trance and launched on a mystic worldwide journey by a voice which may be that of his own associate spirit, a spirit voice from the world of the dead, or, indeed, the voice of a mesmeric operator.[80] "O take my hand Walt Whitman!" commands the inspirational voice by way of setting up the classical mode of occult communication, and then it "widens" the poet-medium's sight, hearing, and sensitivity into a rapport with all persons in all times and climes. In terms of the poem's suggestive imagery, the hand-holding interlocutor seems to impregnate the visionary persona with wisdom (in a manner comparable to the persona's mystic seduction by the spiritual "I am" in "Song of Myself," section 5), and his wisdom seems to "widen" within him like a fetus within a pregnant woman. (Leaving unexplored the persona's depiction of himself as a mother figure, we may once again observe how his prophetic powers have become excited, or activated, by a sexual experience.) After helping the persona to achieve an electrical equilibrium with the divine heart of nature and to become clairvoyant, his associate spirit leads him on a boundless journey and enables him to make contact with kindred souls. At the end of the vision, the poet–medium declares:

> My spirit has pass'd in compassion and determination around the
>   whole earth,
> I have look'd for equals and lovers and found them ready for me in
>   all lands;
> I think some divine rapport has equalized me with them.

After the trance, he reports that he is fully conscious of what he has experienced and that he knows his selfhood is immortal.

"The Sleepers" is a sustained dream vision in which the persona appears as a clairvoyant sleepwaker whose associate spirit, seemingly liberated from his body, communes without limitation with the spirits of men and women, living and dead.[81] A clue to the poem's obsession with death is Townshend's tenet that "the mesmeric state is a far truer image of death than sleep is"; it is the condition in which we suppress our earthly senses and activate those faculties which we shall keep after death—the analogue of immortality that helps us to "bridge our way across the gulf of death" and "connect this world with the future." During "spiritualization," as John B. Newman calls mesmerism, the spirit attains an increasing dominance over the body. The final stages of the process are clairvoyance, during which the spirit controls and almost negates the body, and death, or absolute spiritualization.[82] Hence, the more the persona's supersensory faculties become spiritualized on his cosmic dream journey, the more risky may be his tantalizing gamble with physical self-annihilation.

At the beginning of "The Sleepers," the persona has already entered into the somnambulistic trance:

> I wander all night in my *vision*,
> Stepping with light feet, swiftly and noiselessly stepping and
>   stopping,
> Bending with *open eyes* over the shut eyes of sleepers,
> Wandering and confused, *lost to myself*, ill-assorted, contradictory,
> Pausing, gazing, bending, and stopping.

Walt Whitman and the Body Beautiful

Beholding the maimed, the bored, the imprisoned, and the unrequited, he engages in mesmeric healing:

> I stand in the dark with drooping eyes by the worst-suffering and
>   the most restless,
> I pass my hands soothingly to and fro a few inches from them,
> The restless sink in their beds, they fitfully sleep.

Thereafter, he shares "all the dreams of the other dreamers," entering into their interior worlds by the aid of the "journeymen divine"—the associate spirits or mediumistic faculties. (For, as Andrew Jackson Davis observed, "When spirits speak to us, they address our interior and spiritual sense of hearing.")[83] He "becomes" the sleeping woman, her imaginary lover, and the night that holds them both.

As we have seen, however, the expanded senses—particularly the sense of touch—which can bring such bliss to the sleep-waker can also turn his dream into a nightmare. Thus the persona's clairvoyance now opens up terrifying visions of self-abuse, betrayal, and sorrow. The first section of the poem (in the 1855 edition) ends with an excursion into the sleeper's past—the adolescent's entry into manhood. The thrill of masturbation is succeeded by agonies and intimations of evil. "[M]y sinews are flaccid," moans the sexually exhausted man-child as he descends his "western course" into the midnight realm of death and despair and enters into the innermost consciousness of the aged, the drowning swimmer, the witness to a shipwreck, and the victim of the shipwreck (sections 2–4). He plunges ruefully into the past, beholding a military defeat of the Revolutionary War and scenes of the idyllic ways of life that are forever gone (sections 5–6). In utter despair, he lashes out against Lucifer, a satanic father-figure ("I am his sorrowful terrible heir," he cries). Afraid that he can never prevail against a brutish and meaningless world, the sleeper imagines himself to be the very Melvillean whale, whose "tap is death."[84]

Beginning with section 7 of "the Sleepers," however, the sexually and emotionally spent persona regains his electro-spiritual equilibrium and becomes receptive to a new influx of inspiration. In the timeless moment of his mesmeric sleep, he envisions the unity of the past and the future, the healing of his afflicted fellows, and the resolution of his personal doubts. His soul "comes from its embower'd garden" (a suggestive birth-death image) to behold the perfect bodies and perfect genitalia which will create a flawless human race. The happy prophecy is completed as he sees the naked sleepers "flow hand in hand over the whole earth" in love, friendship, and health, then "pass the invigoration of the night and the chemistry of the night, and awake" (section 8). The persona, too, the poem implies, will awake from his luminous dream with total recall.

"Song of Myself" encompasses the clairvoyant persona's extended sleep-waking experience one summer's day from early morning to "the last scud of day." Although the affinities of this sui generis, many-faceted poem to what James E. Miller calls "the traditional mystical experience" have often been acknowledged, many of its structural and thematic elements relate it to Whitman's other mesmeric dream poems.[85] "Stout as a horse, affectionate, haughty, electrical," the poem's persona becomes passive and possibly cataleptic, attains a balance with the universe, and, in startlingly sexual imagery, seems to become possessed by his "soul" or associate spirit (section 5).[86] Then, having apparently entered into the mystical state, he makes his first halting efforts to interpret nature's "uniform hieroglyphic" or "uttering tongues" ("A child said, *What is the grass?*"; section 6). Thereafter (sections 7–15) he sees more clearly "through the broadcloth and gingham," even though his associate spirit (or inner self) has not yet achieved complete rapport with the associate spirits of those whom he observes. His visionary powers grow increasingly acute as he comes to understand that all creatures are obedient to "the same old law" (section 14)—a law which this experience of spiritual illumination will eventually enable him to decode and explain. The first phase of the vision concludes with the magnificent catalog in section 15 (over sixty lines long)—a kaleidoscopic panorama of sensory experiences that crowd so fast upon him that he can only relate them in a rapid, impressionistic manner:

> And these tend inward to me, and I tend outward to them,
> And such as it is to be of these more or less I am,
> And of these one and all I weave the song of myself.

Having established his centrality in the cosmos by becoming equalized with all its forces and objects, the persona proceeds to a higher spiritual plane, becoming a clairvoyant Daniel who interprets the mystic graffiti on the surfaces of the universe:

To me the converging objects of the universe perpetually flow,
All are written to me, and I must get what the writing means.

He becomes the spokesman for the "many long dumb voices" and translates "the pleasures of heaven" and "the pains of hell * * * into a new tongue"; he acts as the mystic galvanometer of the divine spirit. Speech has become "the twin of my vision" (section 25); his senses of hearing and touch are expanded (sections 26–29) to afford him still keener perception and more inspired utterance (sections 30–32). By section 33, his clairvoyant powers have become fully liberated; the constrictions of "Space and Time" are destroyed:

My ties and ballasts leave me, my elbows rest in sea-gaps,
I skirt sierras, my palms cover continents,
I am afoot with my vision.

Section 33 also contains the poem's second great panoramic catalog of sensory perceptions. But whereas the catalog in section 15 merely dramatizes the persona's newly expanded powers of observation, this later catalog reveals a quantum growth in his perceptual-clairvoyant faculties. Now that his associate spirit has become able to commnicate fully with the associate spirits of other persons, he can identify with all joys and agonies of the past, present, and future, with the prisoner, the "fancy-man," and the Christ.

Having plumbed the depths of misery with his mediumistic senses and being almost overcome by empathic despair (like the persona in "The Sleepers"), he checks himself with the cry:

Enough! enough! enough! * * *
I discover myself on the verge of a usual mistake.

His "mistake" goes beyond philosophical pessimism. By giving way to despair, he has deranged the electrical balance so essential to his mediumistic communication with the spirit world and with the subconscious (the associate spirits) of living men and women. If his dream journey is to continue in a positive direction, he must regain his calm and quiescence. Once he has successfully done so, he is seen as a "flowing savage": "emanations * * * descend in new forms from the tips of his fingers"; they emerge from his body and breath and "the glance of his eyes" (section 39). Now "flowing" (that is, charged) with creative electricity, like the sun itself, he appears to be a clairvoyant healer of bodies, minds, and souls (sections 40–41), a teacher of the highest wisdom, and a spiritual being who can meet the gods on equal terms.

The persona's spiritual progress may be measured by the three occurrences of the bread-of-life imagery in "Song of Myself." In section 3, the yet-unmesmerized persona has a premonitory illumination wherein God, "the hugging and loving bed-fellow," presents him with covered baskets containing the bread of life. In section 19, partway in his clairvoyant journey, the sleep-waking persona partakes freely of this sacred food—"the meal equally set" for liberated spirits. But in section 46 he becomes the *dispenser* of the bread of life: literally, he is the Lord. And here his dream journey reaches its outermost limits. After recapitulating for the reader the truths he has perceived, the persona closes his visionary adventure with a deep sleep, his body "wrench'd and sweaty." Space and time telescope back into their mortal aspects. He departs with the promise that his associate spirit and that of the reader may meet some day.

When Whitman first met Poe in 1845, the latter had just published his "Mesmeric Revelation"—the purported eyewitness account by a mesmerist-physician of the dying moments of his clairvoyant patient. From the edge of eternity, the clairvoyant reiterates the mesmeric tenet that the human spirit is composed of "unparticled matter"—a version of Deleuze's theory that the "magnetic fluid" is a superfine essence of which the soul and the Godhead are made. This infinitely fine matter, says the dying clairvoyant, is the substance through which heavenly bodies roll, and it is likewise "the thoughts of God. . . . The universal mind is God." For the construction of perishable mortal bodies, coarse particulate matter is necessary. But the "ultimate body" (the spirit-body composed of the superfine "unparticled" matter) survives death, and in this "ultimate body" the survivors are angels. "Divested of corporate investiture, [man] were God," says Poe's clairvoyant, who, as he shuffles off his mortal coil of coarse matter, declares himself to be God-like and filled with an awareness that "the divine VOLITION creates all."[87]

In a similar vein, Andrew Jackson Davis alleged that the

spirit, or "interior self," is composed of tangible matter "in a very high state of refinement and attenuation" and that the realm of the dead (which he called the "second sphere") is an electrical ambience. He said that the spirits of the deceased are limited beings, aware of their own distance from perfection, attracted to those who live on after them, and sympathetic to their mortal sufferings.[88] His comments thus provide a crude gloss for "Crossing Brooklyn Ferry," wherein the "impalpable sustenance of me" (the unparticled matter of the dead poet's spirit) tells the spirits of living men and women that the dead wish to be near them and assures them of their own deathlessness:

> I project myself—*also I return*—I am with you, and know how it
>   is * * * *
> These, and all else, were to me the same as they are to you,
> I project myself a moment to tell you—*also I return* * * * *
> Closer yet I approach you * * * *

As the persona's spirit in its electrical ambience, hovering above the East River, empathizes with the joys and sorrows and guilt feelings of those who are still mortal, his extrasensory faculties momentarily fuse with theirs:

> Curious what is more subtle than this which ties me to the woman
>   or man that looks in my face,
> Which fuses me into you now, and pours my meaning into you.

The dead poet-visionary repeatedly instructs the living that a "necessary film" (a body formed of particulate matter) continues to "envelop" their souls:

> Every thing indicates—the smallest does, and the largest does,
> A necessary film envelops all, and envelops the Soul for a proper
>   time.

But he concludes that the "dumb, beautiful ministers" (apparently the intimations of cosmic truths apprehended by the spiritual and extrasensory faculties) "furnish your parts toward eternity." Stage by stage and transformation by transformation, asserts the spirit-persona, the soul grows with, and through, the body.[89]

   The dual and coextensive nature of the body and the soul (a belief which the spiritualists shared with more traditional mystics) is frequently pictured in Whitman's poems. Take, for example, this celebrated passage in "Starting from Paumanok":

Was somebody asking to see the soul?
See, your own shape and countenance, persons, substances, beasts,
   the trees, the running rivers, the rocks and sands.

All hold spiritual joys and afterwards loosen them;
How can the real body ever die and be buried?

Of your real body and any man's or woman's real body,
Item for item it will elude the hands of the corpse-cleaners and
   pass on to fitting spheres,
Carrying what has accrued to it from the moment of birth to the
   moment of death.[90]

In these "fitting spheres" emerges one's "real body," that is, the
spiritual double composed of what Poe's dying clairvoyant had
called "unparticled matter." And like the impalpable spirit of Au-
gustus Bedloe, liberated by the electric shock of death in Poe's "A
Tale of the Ragged Mountains," the "real body" looks uncon-
cernedly at its useless corpse.

The permanence of the immortal "real body" was an article of
spiritualist faith. The Seeress of Prevost said that the spirit body or
"nerve-spirit is the remnant of the body, and after death, sur-
rounds the soul with an aeriel form." Jung-Stilling specified that
"there is in the human frame, a subtle luminous body, an ethereal
covering of the immortal rational spirit, which has undeniably
manifested itself in magnetism . . . with this body the rational
spirit is eternally and inseparably connected." The American ho-
meopath and spiritualist Dr. William Henry Holcombe explained
that the physical body is only a temporary sheath for the spirit
body, which has "an organic form composed of indestructible
spiritual substances in which the soul or vital principle lives and is
finited, differentiated from God and from all other souls." After
death, the immortal body inhabits a spiritual realm, with its own
scientific laws, government, and personal relations, including
"mental" sex and spiritual marriages. But this realm is not one of
pure thought, Holcombe said; it is (as "Crossing Brooklyn Ferry"
implies) a continuation of life as we mortals know it.[91]

The principle of the immortal "real body" may be illustrated
by two stories. Andrew Jackson Davis related that he had once
witnessed the death of an Irish laborer who perished in a caved-in
well, six feet below the ground. Knowing what to expect, the
clairvoyant Davis stood by the site of the accident to watch as bits

of the dead Irishman escaped from under the ground to cohere into an electric likeness (or spirit body) of the laborer's self in the same manner, he said, as the fetus coheres about the electric nucleus in the womb to form a child.[92] And Emanuel Swedenborg, a clairvoyant whose teachings may have been known to Whitman, related that John Calvin arrived in heaven still mistakenly believing that he was alive and that he was clothed in his mortal body. "I have the same body, the same hands, and the like senses," Calvin allegedly told the angels; but the latter "instructed him that he was now in a substantial body," whereas on earth he had been clad not only "in the same but in a material body, which invested the substantial; and that the material body had been cast off and the substantial remained, which is man. . . ."[93] In Whitman's words, Calvin's substantial body could be said to have eluded the "corpse-cleaners" and passed on to "fitting spheres."

The belief in the duality of the body may be called Platonic and Christian. The "Phaedo" declares that when the living soul parts from the body to go into the invisible world, the soulless, voided body becomes useless.[94] And mesmerists approvingly cited St. Paul's declaration that the relatively coarse-grained physical body "connected with the economy of this world" is prior, and anterior, to "the more lasting [spiritual] body which is to connect us with the universe in general."[95] This spiritualist and Platonic principle is clearly articulated in "A Song of Joys":

> For not life's joys alone I sing, repeating—the joy of death!
> The beautiful touch of Death, soothing and benumbing a few
> moments, for reasons,
> Myself discharging my excrementitious body to be burn'd, or
> render'd to powder, or buried,
> My real body doubtless left to me for other spheres,
> My voided body nothing more to me, returning to the purifi-
> cations, further offices, eternal uses of the earth.

The existence of an immortal spiritual body which temporarily co-exists with the mortal body is affirmed in "Eidólons" (1876):

> Thy body permanent,
> The body lurking there within thy body,
> The only purport of the form thou art, the real I myself,
> An image, an eidólon.[96]

Evolution and Hereditary Perfection

"The Stale Cadaver Blocks Up the Passage"

6

BETWEEN 1832, WHEN MRS. FRANCES TROLLOPE'S saucy remarks about the sickly Americans appeared in her *Domestic Manners of the Americans*, and 1866, when her famous son commented on the "hard, dry, and melancholy" appearance of Western women, in his *North America*, a generation of foreign travelers reported that the Americans appeared weak and prematurely aged.[1] They blamed overwork, lack of exercise, wretched diet, poorly ventilated buildings, democratic manners, and all sorts of causes. A certain "Rurio" derided the slope-shouldered American men, sometimes "as narrow as females" under the nape of the neck, and alleged that among American women the "prominent part of female loveliness seemed to be altogether lacking. . . . They are as flat as their own horrid sea-coast." A lady traveler commented that the women of New York City were inferior to those she saw in Europe; rarely did she behold a blooming cheek in Manhattan. After looking down Whitman's beloved Broadway, Fredrika Bremer, one of his favorite authors, reported that the men she saw there reminded her of "over-driven, worn-out horses. . . . The restless, deeply-sunk eyes, the excited, wearied features, to what a life they bore witness," she lamented. "Better lie and sleep on Ocean Hill than live thus on Broadway!"[2]

Many of Whitman's countrymen also believed that Americans—formerly a healthy and heroic people—no longer possessed the characteristic ruggedness of their Revolutionary ancestors. Experts pointed to evidence that the health of the urban masses had worsened. For example, the crude death rate in New York City reportedly rose from 1 in 46.5 persons in 1810 to 1 in 27 in 1859, when half of the city's children were said to be dying before their fifth year. Moreover, the period before the Civil War registered an alarming increase in deaths from consumption—particularly in the cities.[3]

Whitman's attitude toward the apparent deterioration of the American masses was not unlike that of Catharine E. Beecher, the pioneer of physical education in the American public schools. Through neglecting the bodies of their children, Miss Beecher maintained, parents had in effect trained them "to become feeble, sick, and ugly." Her lifelong study of physical fitness convinced her that children in the 1850's were less handsome, less rosy-cheeked, and less cheerful than youngsters had been forty years earlier. Because parents had scorned the laws of health, she claimed, "the great majority of the present generation have grown up with bones and muscles to a greater or lesser extent weaker, smaller, and less healthful than their Creator designed they should be." American women at mid-century were sicklier than their British sisters and weaker than their native-born grandmothers had been. Her explanation of this deplorable situation, like Whitman's, was rooted in the profound faith that the "laws of health," which are as truly the "laws of God as they that were inscribed by his finger on tablets of stone," dictate that the children of two sickly parents will be born sickly and degenerate. The offspring of this second generation, if no physical improvement intervenes, will be born even more enfeebled. And thus (drawing a popular analogy that Whitman himself employed) the nation which once seemed destined to become a second Greece of the Golden Age could miss its chance to achieve greatness.[4]

Horace Greeley voiced similar ideas in a book which Whitman read. Attributing physical retrogression to the division of labor which characterized American capitalism, he complained that the factory system was producing not whole men, but one class of factory "hands" and another of idlers. He believed that a radical overhaul of physical and moral training, which had "decidedly retrograded since the days of Greek freedom and glory," could produce "a *race* of Heroes of Humanity—a People elevated to Love and Universal Blessing." Like Whitman, he asserted that "the loftiest ambition possible finds its essence in perfect, simple Manhood." The nation's best hope, he felt, was the physical regeneration of its masses. Suggesting the profound genetic implications of Whitman's new Adam, and using the very phrase which the poet used to entitle a group of his poems, Greeley declared: "Yes, a brighter day dawns for us, sinning and suffering children of Adam. Wiser in its very follies, less cruel and wanton even in its crimes, our Race visibly progresses toward a nobler and happier realization of its capabilities and powers."[5]

Although the validity of what Dr. Holmes ridiculed as the "universal-degeneration theory applied to American life" was open to challenge,[6] the belief that Americans had become a deteriorating race profoundly affected Whitman and his literary contemporaries. "Guaranty us against physical degeneracy," said Thomas Wentworth Higginson, a physical culture enthusiast, "and we can risk all other perils."[7] Horace Mann warned that an infinite series of physical woes, transmitted from parent to child and "doubled at each remove," had contaminated America's ancestral "fountains" and would continue to injure the physical system of each individual unless the abuses were checked by some ancestor whose "obedient and virtuous life" could prevent the entailing of these defects and maladies.[8] After four or five generations of such deterioration, Dr. Dixon commented, the debilitated stock would lose its reproductive powers and die out.[9] In "Terminus" Emerson attributed his own debility to the waning of the ancestral vigor from its former Germanic ("Baresark") ruggedness and to his "legacy of ebbing veins, / Inconstant heat and nerveless reins." And Hawthorne symbolized the degenerate descendants of the stalwart race that landed on Plymouth Rock in Hepzibah Pyncheon's run-down chickens.

Whitman responded to the theory of physical degeneracy by enunciating an evolutionary gospel of racial betterment and by contrasting a gallery of eugenically superb prototypes to the debilitated urban specimens who surrounded him. Some of his ancestors, as pictured in *Specimen Days*, exemplify the excellent birth stock which formerly characterized the nation, and paragons of manhood and womanhood are paraded throughout *Leaves of Grass*. But he deprecated the "outworn and weary" New York shop girls and the "jaunty crew of the downtown clerks, a slender and round-shouldered generation, of minute leg, chalky face, and hollow chest," whose flashy dress could not conceal their physical weakness:

White, shaved, foreign, soft-fleshed, shrinking,
Scant of muscle, scant of love-power,
Scant of gnarl and knot, modest, sleek in costumes,
Averse from the wet of rain, from fall of snow, from the grit of
     the stones and soil,
A pretty race, each one just like hundreds of the rest,
A Race of scantlings from the strong growth of America.

But with a touch of pity, he reaffirmed his kinship with these unfortunate city types:

They who piddle and patter here in collars and tailed coats I
     am aware who they are . . . . and that they are not worms or
     fleas,
I acknowledge the duplicates of myself under all the scrape-lipped
     and pipe-legged concealments.[10]

The supposed debility of the American masses had strong political implications for Whitman. In 1856 he found the officers at every level of government to be "empty, feeble old men, professional politicians, dandies, dyspeptics, and so forth." Nowhere in public life did he "observe a single, bold, muscular, young, well-informed, resolute American man"; nowhere did he see leaders emerging "from among the ranks of the healthy young men of the common people," whom he implored to raise up a race of rulers to settle the West and revitalize America. Looking about him in 1871, he concluded that American cities had produced few splendid specimens of manhood, womanhood, and old age:

Confess that to severe eyes, using the moral microscope upon humanity, a sort of dry and flat Sahara appears, these cities, crowded with petty grotesques, malformations, phantoms, playing meaningless antics. Confess that everywhere, in shop, street, church, theatre, barroom, official chair, are pervading flippancy and vulgarity, low cunning, infidelity—everywhere the youth puny, impudent, foppish, prematurely ripe—everywhere an abnormal libidinousness, unhealthy forms, male, female, painted, padded, dyed, chignon'd, muddy complexions, bad blood, the capacity for good motherhood decreasing or decreas'd. . . .[11]

His faith in America's future was often stated in eugenic terms. He voiced confidence in the healthy, hard-working family, the fruits of whose labor assured them "individual liberty," a modest income, and the ownership of their own "homestead, fee sim-

Walt Whitman and the Body Beautiful

ple." When Horace Traubel, a reform socialist, tried to persuade him of the need to change the social order, Whitman conceded that political and economic reforms are necessary, but insisted that the "whole business finally comes back to the good body—not back to wealth, to poverty, but to the strong body—the sane, sufficient body." And he added: "I think all the scientists would agree with me, as I agree with the scientists, that a beautiful, competent, sufficing, body is the prime force making towards the virtues in civilization, life, history." [12] Although he viewed the physical decline of his countrymen and countrywomen as a portent of moral decay, he believed that living in harmony with nature's laws and observing a proper regimen of diet, exercise, and fresh air could enable them to become the parents of superior children who, in turn, would raise up a progeny of noble men and women. This rationale was related to the cult of regeneration through physical culture which was so popular in intellectual circles.

At the outset of his poetic career, Whitman singled out a race of splendid parents as the secret of America's impending greatness: "Produce great persons and the producers of great persons . . . . all the rest surely follows. What has been but indicated in other continents, in America must receive its definite and numberless growth. . . . The time is arrived and the land got ready and every present age is to pass the sinewy lesson and add to it." [13] This idea is elaborated in "So Long!":

> When America does what was promised,
> When each part is peopled with free people * * *
> When there are plentiful athletic bards, inland and seaboard,
> When through These States walk a hundred millions of superb persons,
> When the rest part away for superb persons, and contribute to them,
> When fathers, firm, unconstrained, open-eyed—When breeds of the most perfect mothers denote America,
> Then to me ripeness and conclusion.

And "Starting from Paumanok" forecasts a breed of genetically perfect Americans: "A new race, dominating previous ones, and grander far. . . ." [14]

Whitman describes these idealized Americans of the future as "that prolific brood of brown faced fathers and sons who swarm over the free states, and form the bulwark of our republic, mightier than walls or armies. . . ." The "new race dominating previous ones" (and, by implication, less developed ones) exemplifies the stages-of-society dogma that those "races" which have evolved farthest toward civilization are qualified by instinct to rule their racial inferiors. In justifying the American conquest of Mexico—an action which he later deplored—Whitman boasted that native white Americans know instinctively how to exploit the Mexican lands (much as James Fenimore Cooper had maintained that educated whites possess "civilizing gifts") and called this supposedly universal racial concept "a law superior to parchments." Because of its important place in his thought, his attitude toward the race of the future is significant: "We have lofty views on the scope and destiny of our American Republic," he said. "It is for the interest of mankind that its power and territory should be extended—the farther the better." [15] Following the Civil War, he still acclaimed "the [white] American races, north or south," as "the last-needed proof of democracy" and exulted in America's "grand common stock! to me the accomplish'd and convincing growth, prophetic of the future; proof undeniable to sharpest sense, of perfect beauty, tenderness and pluck, that never feudal lord, nor Greek, nor Roman breed, yet rival'd." His final hosanna in "The Mystic Trumpeter" (1872) salutes this idealized, disease-free race, which will emerge when "universal man" becomes "the conqueror at last": "A reborn race appears—a perfect world, all joy!" [16]

Whitman's Polish friend Count Adam de Gurowski defined this new breed of Americans as archetypal Anglo-Saxon supermen: "the Yankee, the man of the Free States, the child of free labor, of the free comprehension of life," who "brings civility, culture, restless but productive nimbleness, shrewdness, clear-sightedness, industry and order, inseparably combined, and above all, so to say, the innate power and faculty of social constructiveness." [17] Gurowski's American democrats resemble the breed of new Western men who appear in this "Calamus" verse:

> Those that go their own gait, erect, stepping with freedom and
>   command—leading, not following,
> Those with never-quell'd audacity—those with sweet and lusty
>   flesh, clear of taint, choice and chary of its love-power,
> Those that look carelessly in the faces of Presidents and
>   Governors, as to say, *Who are you?* [18]

Fathering healthy children is nobler than statesmanship, Whitman maintained, because only pure-bodied men and women can become the parents of the nation's greatest statesmen and poets. The 1855 preface argued that "nothing for instance is greater than to conceive children and to bring them up well. . . ." Like many of his contemporaries, he viewed the production of healthy children as the best measure of American progress.[19] In a manuscript jotting he asserted that "plenty of perfect-bodied, noble-sould [sic] men and women" are more valuable than riches to America.[20] And he further explained that "I bring civilization, politics, the topography of a country, and even the hydrography to one final test,—the capability of producing, favoring, and maintaining a fine crop of children, a magnificent race of men and women . . . a race of really fine perfectionists."[21]

Because Whitman implied that America could achieve her destiny through creating "bully breeds of children," Oscar Cargill has called him the poet of American fecundity—"the natural voice of breeding and prolific America, the Priapus of a new continent."[22] Whitman's emphasis on procreation did indeed express a national ideal. Although Malthus had prescribed population controls to guard against mass starvation in Europe, American expansionists pointed to the large crops of native-born children as proof that this country was exempt from European-style crises. Said Congressman Andrew Kennedy of Indiana: "Go to the West, and see a young man with his mate of eighteen; after a lapse of thirty years, visit him again and instead of two, you will find twenty-two. That is what I call the American multiplication table." Whitman's reasoning was not far different. After viewing the miles of sparsely settled open spaces on his trip to Denver, he asserted that America possessed immense resources for feeding its masses.[23]

Whitman's hoped-for super-race is Nordic; the Americans whom he idealizes are essentially those he calls "ever sturdy, ever instinctively just, by right of Teutonic descent."[24] "I Sing the Body Electric," "Faces," and "Song of the Broad-Axe" depict this superior breed, in the conventional symbolism of the era, at the head of a long evolutionary procession, their inferiors trailing behind them more or less in the order of their eugenic merit. Like his contemporaries, Whitman could not conceive of a society that was at once multiracial and egalitarian; but to judge his racial views solely by today's norms, as some critics have done, is historically dishonest, because his opinions on the subject reflect the thinking of government officials, scientists, and most of the liberal intellectuals of his own day. By mid-century the concept of progress as an evolutionary parade, with the advanced races in the vanguard and their inferiors in the rear, had become a commonplace. "Society," said Henry Adams, "offered the profile of a long, straggling caravan, stretching loosely towards the prairies, its few score of leaders far in advance and its millions of immigrants, negroes, and Indians far in the rear, somewhere in archaic time."[25] Perhaps the best literary adaptation of this social metaphor is Whitman's "Pioneers! O Pioneers!" wherein the "darlings" of the "resistless restless race!" appear "well in order" at the head of an advancing procession moving across the mythic Western lands and bearing "the brunt of danger," even though the "elder races" may be lagging behind or standing still.[26]

In general, Whitman's attitudes toward non-Teutonic peoples were inconsistent or unfavorable. He professed that "Africans" had an instinct for slavery just as the white Americans had an instinct for freedom. "Our Old Feuillage" pictures Southern slaves "in good health," happily at work "in piney woods" or "in the coalings, at the forge, by the furnace-blaze, or at the corn-shucking," and presents that staple of Southern apologist fiction, "the aged mulatto nurse" affectionately greeting "the planter's son." In other poems, the men and women in a slave gang are called "clumsy, hideous, black, pouting, grinning, sly, besotted, sensual, shameless," and an "Ethiopian" former slave woman is said to be "hardly human." On the other hand, Whitman describes black laborers loading barges as "more superb" than Greek statues.[27] Magnificent specimens of black manhood adorn "Song of Myself" and "I Sing the Body Electric," and a noble savage appears in "Salut au Monde!": "You dim-descended, black, divine-souled African, large, fine-headed, nobly-formed, superbly-destined, on equal terms with me." Another passage from "Salut au Monde!" with its conclusion that the dark-skinned peoples "away back there" bring up the rear of the evolutionary procession, illustrates Whitman's version of the racial myth:

> You Hottentot with clicking palate!
> You wooly-haired hordes! you white or black owners of slaves!

Walt Whitman and the Body Beautiful

You owned persons, dropping sweat-drops or blood-drops!
You human forms with fathomless ever-impressive countenances
  of brutes!
You poor kobo whom the meanest of the rest look down upon,
  for all your glimmering language and spirituality!
You low expiring aborigines of the hills of Utah, Oregon,
  California!
You dwarfed Kamtschatkan, Greenlander, Lapp!
You Austral negro, naked, red, sooty, with protrusive lip,
  grovelling, seeking your food! * * *
You peon of Mexico! you Russian serf! you slave of Carolina,
  Texas, Tennessee!
I do not prefer others *so very much* before you either,
I do not say one word against you, *away back there*, where you
  stand,
(You will come forward *in due time* to my side.) [28]

The physical deformities and wretched physiognomies of the grotesque and animalistic hordes "away back there" in the march of human evolution confirm their racial inferiority. The popular sentiment, repeated here, that American Indians (and particularly the Indians of the Pacific Slope) were poor specimens of humanity helped to assuage the national conscience during the systematic uprooting of these peoples by white Americans, whose westward movement Whitman and his contemporaries equated with national progress.

The poet's implication that the colored races must "part away" for superb white persons rather than amalgamate with them reflects the influence upon him of the propaganda, disseminated by scientists and government agencies, proclaiming that when white racial stock is interbred with Negro or Indian stock, its "viability" (or reproductive power) is diminished and that continued hybridization eventually produces racial sterility. The Surgeon-General declared that "a mixture of the white and Indian [or white and black] races, produces offspring of less viability than either of the original races. . . . the offspring of the mixture of these two races is a hybrid, and incapable of propagating itself beyond the third or fourth generation"; and "their union is an insult to nature and a sacrilegious defiance of God." [29] Small wonder that Whitman, who reportedly felt that "there was in the constitution of the negro's mind an irredeemable trifling or volatile element, and that he would never amount to much in the scale of civilization," maintained that "Nature has set an impassable seal" against the amalgamation of the black and Nordic races. He, too, assumed that racial "intermixtures" preclude "fine reproductivities" for "psychological, physiological reasons" and made the avowedly "Darwinian" quip that "the nigger, like the Injun, will be eliminated: it is the law of races, history, what-not: always so far inexorable—always to be. Someone proves that a superior grade of rats comes and then all the minor rats are cleared out."[30]

Basil De Selincourt came close to the truth when he declared that Whitman's vision of human equality represents a belief in "the faculty of endless development" which all men and women share and that Whitman's visionary liberty is essentially a faith in "the last achievement of the human spirit."[31] Inevitably, however, Whitman's benign vision was tempered—and indeed warped—by the quasi-official and quasi-scientific racist propaganda which he accepted in good faith.

Whitman, who felt that the sum total of "all Geologies—Histories—of all Astronomy—of Evolution, Metaphysics all" is the sense of the race "going somewhere," "surely bettering" itself through space and time, declared that *Leaves of Grass* is built on the truth of evolution.[32] Although he respected the teachings of Darwin, he acknowledged Huxley's admonition that evolution is ultimately incapable of explaining beginnings and ends.[33] It is therefore not surprising that, directly or indirectly, he drew his evolutionary ideas largely from the doctrines of Jean-Baptiste Lamarck. His poems and his Adam-hero illustrate Lamarck's concept of a plastic hereditary process whereby all creatures strive instinctively to adapt and improve themselves and to transmit to the next generation what they have struggled for and acquired.[34]

Lamarck's four hereditary "laws" echo throughout *Leaves of Grass*.[35] According to the first, "Life, by its own force, tends continually to increase the volume of every living body and to extend the dimensions of its parts, up to a limit which it imposes." In "Crossing Brooklyn Ferry," Whitman translates this "law" into a poetic injunction: "Expand, being than which none else is perhaps more spiritual * * * *" And in an impromptu jotting, he notes: "Yes, I believe in the Trinity—God Reality—God Beneficence or

Walt Whitman and the Body Beautiful

Love—and God Immortality or Growth."[36] Frequently, his writings assert a mystic link between physiological growth and spiritual dilation.[37]

Lamarck's second "law" declares that "the production of a new organ in an animal body results from a new need (*besoin*) which continues to make itself felt, and from a new movement that this need brings about and maintains."

Lamarck's famous law of exercise maintains that "the development and effectiveness of organs are proportionate to the use of these organs." The failure to exercise any organ weakens and gradually atrophies that organ in a creature and its descendants.

Lamarck's final "law" states that "everything acquired or changed during the individual's lifetime is preserved by heredity and transmitted to that individual's progeny." The protracted conditioning of an organ in a given species will gradually modify that organ over the centuries and millennia.

Two Lamarckian offshoots vitally affected *Leaves of Grass*. Vulgar Lamarckians modified Lamarck's law of exercise in order to prove that *individuals* can *consciously* and *substantially* modify their bodily organs *during* their lifetimes and that a temporarily improved organic condition can promote a corresponding *permanent* improvement in the offspring. This wishful faith is strikingly exemplified in the first three editions of *Leaves of Grass*. Neo-Lamarckians, later deviators from Lamarckian orthodoxy, emphasized an unconscious sexual-evolutionary will (or urge for perfection) which supposedly acts within all species as the agent of progress—a concept incorporated into many of Whitman's later poems.

The vulgar Lamarckian belief that physical characteristics may be upgraded during a parent's lifetime and transmitted in their improved state to his children was an article of perfectionist faith. Dr. Sylvester Graham, the dietary reformer, warned that "as long as hereditary faults are transmitted," the human race could experience no "mental and moral improvement."[38] Whittier linked the advent of God's "benign order" to the compliance with the natural, Biblically enjoined law which makes a sin of "the hereditary transmission of moral and physical disease and debility" and the bequeathing of "loathesomeness, deformity, or animal appetite, incapable of the restraint of the moral faculties!" Dr.

William Wesselhöft, a noted homeopathic physician, counseled, "Through physical education and gymnastics, we must form a soil in the human body on which a dyscrasy cannot continue to flourish; and that which is not allowed to advance will go backwards. . . . Through endeavors prolonged through several generations for the healthy development of the human body, health and beauty would return to the earth."[39] Only "when mankind properly LOVE and MARRY and then rightly GENERATE, NURSE, and EDUCATE their children," said Fowler, "will they be indeed and in truth the holy happy sons and daughters of the 'Lord Almighty'" and realize "the boundless capabilities and perfection of our God-like nature."[40]

Reviewing Jacques's *Hints Toward Physical Perfection*, Whitman wrote that "the form and features of even the fully mature man and woman (and much more those of the child) may be modified at will, and to an almost unlimited extent . . . we have the power to change, gradually but surely, the shape and arrangement of bone, fiber, and fluid, thus growing, day by day, more beautiful or more ugly, according to the direction given to the vital forces. . . ." He said that "laws of health," like those presented in Jacques's "manual of rules," could instruct girls how to enhance their attractiveness, young men how to develop "those high qualities of physical vigor and manliness which will command the admiration of their own sex no less than the love of the other," and both young men and women how to transmit their improved physical and moral qualities to their offspring.[41]

The first three editions of *Leaves of Grass* illuminate this vulgar Lamarckian faith that everyone, from prostitute to poet, may better herself or himself, up to a limit imposed by nature, and that *in time* America will evolve a race of heroes by interbreeding her best specimens and breeding out her unwholesome biological strains. This benign process is the theme of the important 1856 poem, "To You, Whoever You Are," wherein the persona asserts that a latent excellence—an "effulgently flowing" halo—lurks beneath all impotent disguises, meaningless routines, the "shaved face, the unsteady eye, the impure complexion * * * the deform'd attitude, drunkenness, greed, premature death. . . ." The sexually transmitted evolutionary urge is ameliorative, personal, and never-ending: "Amelioration is the blood that runs through the body of the universe," Whitman says.

Walt Whitman and the Body Beautiful

> Through birth, life, death, burial, the means are
> provided, nothing is scanted,
> Through angers, losses, ambition, ignorance, ennui,
> what you are picks its way.[42]

The "Children of Adam" poems, John Burroughs explained (in words that were influenced, if not written, by Whitman), have a political significance because they proclaim the need to father or conceive a race of splendid beings: "the sexual acts" are solemnly celebrated in his poems "mainly with reference to offspring, and the future perfection of the race, through a superior fatherhood and motherhood."[43] Half humorously, editor Whitman admonished his fellow bachelors to get married: "Buy candles and double beds; make yourself a reality in life—and do the state some service."[44] And poet Whitman pictured eugenic matings, such as the "Bridegroom night of love" in "I Sing the Body Electric," occurring between healthy husbands and wives who have carefully hoarded their sexual resources for the strenuous couplings that will be crowned with perfect sons and daughters. The "brawny embraces from the well-muscled woman I love" are matched by Adam's heroic "love-spendings" to produce a heroic progeny; for only parentage "with sweet and lusty flesh, clear of taint, choice and chary of its love-power," can create superb children.[45]

Whitman's Adam-hero personifies the chaste, physically and morally flawless parent, obedient to the genetic laws, who possesses the perfect seed necessary to inaugurate a eugenic paradise. He illustrates the vulgar Lamarckian notion that the Biblical Adam had sown his seed improperly and the principle that American parents must purge themselves of physical taint if they are to create a new Garden of Eden. Resurrected symbolically after five thousand years, "with potent original loins, perfectly sweet," Whitman's evolutionary paragon supplants his Biblical namesake, the symbol of tainted manhood and sower of the faulty seed, who appears briefly in "Passage to India."[46] Whitman's new Adam is reminiscent of George Bernard Shaw's description of "the Noble Savage in the happy hunting ground with all his faculties restored" and of Alcott's prophecy that the "twentieth century should be able to produce an Adam with no Cain in his loins, this time, to curse posterity and blacken its prospects."[47] As Whitman pictures him, the new Adam is "more than a rival of the youthful type heroes of the [conventional] novels and love poems"; he is "a fully complete, well-developed man, eld, bearded, swart, fiery."[48] His genetic garden is phallic and vulval. It resonates, as John Addington Symonds declares, with the universal, sexual "bass-note of the world," the creative-evolutionary drive that governs all existence.[49] In this garden, Adam celebrates the cyclic resurgence of his masculine potency, the electric miracle of fatherhood, and the climax of his mating which will be crowned with untainted offspring:

> To the garden the world anew ascending,
> Potent mates, daughters, sons, preluding,
> The love, the life of their bodies, meaning and being,
> Curious here behold my resurrection after slumber * * *
> My limbs and the quivering fire that ever plays through them, for
>   reasons, most wondrous:
> Existing I peer and penetrate still * * * * [50]

The new Adam is the hero of a trio of "Children of Adam" poems: "Spontaneous Me," "One Hour to Madness and Joy," and "A Woman Waits for Me."[51] Despite an element of autoerotic fantasy, "Spontaneous Me" glorifies the sexual-genetic urge. Inflamed by his paternal passion to transmit his electric procreant seed to its next transmitter, the Adam-hero celebrates

> The great chastity of paternity, to match the great chastity of
>   maternity,
> The oath of procreation I have sworn, my Adamic and fresh
>   daughters,
> The greed that eats me day and night with hungry gnaw, till I
>   saturate what shall produce boys to fill my place when I am
>   through * * * *

In "One Hour to Madness and Joy," Adam rejoices in the electric and "mystic deliria" of the sex drive, declaring that sexual acts are vested in sacredness: "I bequeath them to you my children, I tell them to you, for reasons, O bridegroom and bride."

In "A Woman Waits for Me," Adam personifies the magnificent breeders whose matings will produce a nation of heroes. The poem celebrates the inherited traits of the perfect father and mother and the implantation of these traits in their children during the sexual bout of pleasure-plain so gargantuan that only Adam's proclaimed goal of begetting perfect children tempers the poem's suggestive prurience. It expresses love for no individual woman. Its motivation appears to be Adam's sexual-parental drive, translated into a priapean and polygamous fantasy of fertilizing every perfectly formed woman in America. Eugenically, it is related to Spurzheim's contention that the fortunate few who are farthest advanced along the evolutionary scale ought to become the chosen breeders of nations; to Stephen Pearl Andrews's vision of a future in which a woman will "accept only the noblest and most highly endowed of the opposite sex to be the recipients of her choicest favors, and the sires of her off-spring, rejecting males of a lower degree"; and to Charles Knowlton's ideal marriage in which only "the best of breeders" will have children, and thus "improvement would progress from generation to generation, until there would again be 'giants in the land,' both physical and mental." [52] Whitman-Adam's solemn and awesome procreative exertions help to usher in this hopeful genetic dispensation.

The poem's arrogance and its depiction of sexual intercourse as a somber task for both partners prompted Elizabeth Cady Stanton's barb that Whitman "speaks as if the female must be forced to the creative act, apparently ignorant of the great natural fact that a healthy woman has as much passion as a man, that she needs nothing stronger than the law of attraction to draw her to the male." [53] But although it may be an inadequate depiction of the naturalness and the joys of female sexuality, "A Woman Waits for Me" conveys much of the fervor and the intellectual flavor of Whitman's eugenic programme. The "robust" Adam persona declares unambiguously:

> A woman waits for me, she contains all, nothing is lacking,
> Yet all were lacking if sex were lacking, or if the moisture of the
> right man were lacking.

Proclaiming "the deliciousness of his sex," he demands "warm-blooded," sexually active women for his mates—women who are strong, athletic, compassionate, and self-possessed. This magnetically irresistible embodiment of vulgar Lamarckianism couples with his perfect bedmates solely to engender a race of heroes. Though his tone may be vainglorious, his purposes are humanistic and patriotic:

> I draw you close to me, you women,
> I cannot let you go, I would do you good,

I am for you and you are for me, not only for our own sake, but
    for others' sakes;
Envelop'd in you sleep greater heroes and bards,
They refuse to awaken at the touch of any man but me.

It is I, you women, I make my way,
I am stern, acrid, large, indissuadable, but I love you,
I do not hurt you any more than is necessary for you,
I pour the stuff to start sons and daughters fit for these States, I
    press with slow rude muscle,
I brace myself effectually, I listen to no entreaties,
I dare not withdraw till I deposit what has so long accumulated
    within me.

Through you I drain the pent-up rivers of myself,
In you I wrap a thousand onward years,
On you I graft the grafts of the best-beloved of me and America,
The drops I distil upon you shall grow fierce and athletic girls,
    new artists, musicians, and singers,
The babes I beget upon you are to beget babes in their turn,
I shall demand perfect men and women out of my love-spendings,
I shall expect them to interpenetrate with others, as you and I
    interpenetrate now,
I shall count on the fruits of the gushing showers of them, as I
    count on the fruits of the gushing showers I give now,
I shall look for loving crops from the birth, life, death,
    immortality, I plant so lovingly now.

Whitman's poems, particularly those published after 1865, often stress the neo-Lamarckian urge toward perfection. Relating this principle to Lamarck's second law, Edward Carpenter explained that "there is a force at work throughout creation, ever urging each type [or species] onward into new and newer forms" in a search for physical and moral perfection. This neo-Lamarckian concept, he pointed out, is linked to Whitman's rich poetic imagery of exfoliation or the unfolding of the germ and the seed.[54] In fact, Whitman proclaims that each man is the inheritor of the evolutionary-sexual urge and the reservoir of the birth-stuff from which heroes are created:

(Ever the heroes on water or on land, by ones and twos appearing,
Ever the stock preserv'd and never lost, though rare, enough for
    seed preserv'd.)

This seed may lie "unreck'd for centuries," waiting to sprout into heroes on "God's due occasion." [55]

"Myself and Mine" (1860) relates the persona's vows to perfect himself into an athletic father in order "to beget superb children" and to discharge his genetic duty by transmitting this evolutionary seed, or germ, "the semen of centuries," from which "plenteous supreme gods" will be created. "Song of the Redwood-Tree" glorifies the spermatic treasury of life—the "vital, universal, deathless germs," responsive to the "hidden national will lying in [America's] abysms"—germs which are creating a race of self-reliant Western giants "proportionate to Nature." And "Song of the Universal" credits this evolutionary seed with transmitting the universal life-urge toward perfection, even though its path lies "in spiral routes by long detours":

> In this broad earth of ours,
> Amid the measureless grossness and the slag,
> Enclosed and safe within its central heart,
> Nestles the seed perfection. [56]

The marriage act is the eugenic and spiritual center of *Leaves of Grass*, and the poetic and personal lures that attracted Whitman to write about it are related to the reverence that his era paid to the institution of marriage. Like Victorian writers from Robert Dale Owen to Coventry Patmore, he praised chaste and married love:

> (Bravas to all impulses sending sane children to the next age!
> But damn that which spends itself with no thought of the stain,
>   pains, dismay, feebleness it is bequeathing.) * * * *

> I see the bearer of the great fruit which is immortality . . . . the
>   good thereof is not tasted by roues, and never can be. [57]

Whitman's concern with the "chaste blessings of the well-married couple" may suggest an unwholesome fixation on the marriage bed and on his own begetting (the bed on which he slept in Mickle Street had once belonged to his mother), [58] but the preoccupation with sound begetting was not his alone. A century earlier Tristram Shandy reflected quizzically that his parents, in their heedless coupling, had ignored the fact that they were engaged in "the production of a rational Being" whose physical and mental endowments "might take their turn from the humours and dispositions which were then uppermost. . . . Believe me, good folks, this is not so inconsiderable a thing as many of you may think it." [59] A similar genetic truism is intended in the rhapsodic comment by Henry Ward Beecher, a proud paterfamilias, that "there is nothing more exquisitely refined, and pure, and sacred than the [bed] chamber of the house." To him, "the mother's chamber," containing "the household bed" and the crib and the cradle beside it, was the "heart of the family. . . . It is the Holy of Holies." [60]

In Whitman's poetry, heterosexual couplings occur "purely with reference to offspring" and in conformity with the genetic laws. As the poet indicated in "Song of Myself," pure fathers and mothers are the key to spiritual and racial development:

> All tends to the soul,
> As materials so the soul,
> As procreation, so the soul—if procreation is impure, all is
>   impure * * * *
>
> And a compend of compends is the meat of a man or woman,
> And a summit and flower there is the feeling they have for each
>   other,
> And they are to branch boundlessly out of that lesson until it
>   becomes omnific,
> And until one and all shall delight us, and we them. [61]

The sexual ecstasies and temblor-like orgasms of the "Bride-groom-night of love" are predicated on the sort of couplings which some physicians and genetic reformers deemed necessary to secure the best conceptions; they held that young men could, and should, live without losing a drop of semen until the marital passion has liberated the seminal floods required for the best fatherings, that reserving the semen between the wife's fertile periods is a source of physical and moral strength, and (in a strangely Victorian amalgam) that virtuous marital continence heightens the sexual pleasures of husband and wife and improves the product of their dynamic coupling. [62] *Leaves of Grass* idealizes lusty married lovers whose flesh is "choice and chary of its love-power," the release of "the deposit of what has so long accumulated within me," "the great chastity of paternity," "the great chastity of maternity," and "the chaste blessings of the well-married couple." [63] (Let us observe, in passing, that when the Adam-persona wastes his own precious seed in masturbation or spermatorrhea, he lessens his powers as a begetter.)

Dr. Trall further elucidated the connection (which is apparent in Whitman's poems) between chastity, ideal parentage, and ecstatic sexual couplings. Those parents "who would have beautiful children [ought] to be in their best bodily and mental condition when the fruitful orgasm is experienced," he explained. Otherwise, they will bring children into the world who are inferior to themselves:

> There can be no question that the most perfect organization of the offspring requires the most perfect commingling of elements, or magnetism, or whatever else the parents impart or contribute in the sexual embrace, and that there should be the most perfect harmony and enjoyment with each other. They should be as much of *at-one-ment* as possible, so that, at the moment of conferring life upon a new being, each should almost lose, in the intensity of pleasurable sensation, the consciousness of individual or independent existence. I cannot understand how this condition can be so well acquired, and maintained, as by *temperate* sexual indulgence. . . .

The generative act, explained Dr. Frederick Hollick, is "the most exalted that the animal organization can perform"; its great and convulsive expenditures of energy are essential to proper impregnation. Citing the "latest findings" of French and German physiologists, Hollick claimed "that the vivid and overpowering emotion of sexual excitement should be experienced by both parents in order to give impulse to the new organization which is necessary for the most perfect development." The marital embrace, maintained Dr. Henry C. Wright, should occur only in "the hour of the highest spiritual communion, when heart and soul are merged in the consciousness of but one existence, one life, one eternity. Then, the whole being may and must thrill in unison with such harmony. Passional intercourse is meant to be an ecstatic expression of the soul."[64]

A Wisconsin senator, astutely grasping the eugenic implications of Whitman's amatory verses, informed the poet of a judicial ruling (grounded on these same physiological assumptions) which held that conception follows from "an embrace in which the mental, moral, and physical powers and susceptibilities are wrought to such an intensity of orgasm, mutual and reciprocal, that Nature crowned her beatitude with the production and endowment of a new identity." (Whitman was sufficiently intrigued by the senator's letter to ask the opinion of the celebrated Dr. Samuel D. Gross, who reportedly concurred in this interpretation of the sexual process.) [65]

The Adam-persona's concern with the proper sowing of his seed dramatizes the vulgar Lamarckian thesis that the characteristics of children are determined by the precise condition of each of the parents' bodily functions at the moment of conception as well as by the mother's health and her serenity while carrying the child. The parents of gifted children, and particularly the mothers of great men of letters, were said to bring a spiritual attitude to the engendering and nurturing of their offspring.[66] On the other hand, health reformers warned, promiscuous parents cannot expect to have healthy descendants. As Fowler observed, those parents who "content themselves with that merely animal relief can never enjoy that spiritual intercommunion already shown to be so promotive of parental pleasure, and so indispensable to mental endowment of offspring." He cautioned that "those who incur this liability of becoming parents EXCEPT when this function is wrought up to the highest pitch of intensity, are BAD CITIZENS, and deserve the curse of their progeny." [67]

The Adam-persona is qualified to become an ideal parent precisely because he is rugged and grizzled. The poet's deprecation of marriages between "green" (immature) partners, whose marital exertions cannot endow their offspring with a full complement of physical and moral excellence, is clarified by Dr. Dixon's complaints about the enfeebling sexual practices of immature parents and by Alcott's lament about the current generation of unchaste youth, who, "like old sinners, are eager to pluck forbidden fruits from the stem, the brazen following fast childhood's golden period." ("A chaste generation would restore Paradise," he remarked wistfully.) Drunkenness, gluttony, tobacco, sexual excesses, and what Dixon labeled "the dull, tired, stale bed" were said by physicians to result in the production of sickly and feeble-minded children; those begotten in lust, particularly during the wedding night, were thought to be predisposed to idiocy.[68] As a matter of fact, two of Whitman's early stories illustrate the principle that children born of youthful, oversexed, licentious, or debilitated

Walt Whitman and the Body Beautiful

parents are visited with afflictions. The child born of the illicit passion between Father Luke and the Indian girl in "The Half-Breed" is deformed, a "half-idiot, half-devil," and the child born of "intemperate" parents in "The Old Black Widow" is deaf and mute.[69]

This concern with wholesome breeding characterizes the pageant of progress in "Song of the Broad-Axe." The axe, used by pioneers to trim logs, symbolizes the triumph of the new American personality, free of "delicatesse" and feudal inhibitions. Through life and death, the poem avers, humanity progresses, "and nothing endures but personal qualities." Only selfhood and the coming together of the healthiest fathers and mothers have permanent genetic value in inaugurating the civilization of the future. Denied the hearthside and the fatherhood which he sometimes seemed to crave, the bachelor poet projected himself into a dreamworld of happy domesticity and joyous marriage—a world symbolized by the products of the broad-axe—the cabin, the marriage-bed, and the cradle:

> The shapes arise * * *
> The shape got out in posts, in the bedstead posts, in the posts of
>   the bride's bed,
> The shape of the little trough, the shape of the rockers beneath, of
>   the babe's cradle,
> The shape of the floor-planks, the floor-planks for dancers' feet,
> The shape of the planks of the family home, the home of friendly
>   parents and children,
> The shape of the roof of the home of the happy young man and
>   woman, the roof over the well-married young man and
>   woman,
> The roof over the supper joyously cook'd by the chaste wife, and
>   joyously eaten by the chaste husband, content after his day's
>   work.[70]

To those persons whose progress toward perfection has been thwarted by their physical and moral shortcomings, the poem offers a glowing promise of their own improvability and the prototype images of the Whitman-Adam persona and his perfect Eve peopling a brave new Western world with magnificent human beings.

According to the following visionary lines in "The Sleepers," and the 1847 notebook jotting on which they are apparently based,

the descendants of "decent progenitors," favored by proper physical and moral conditioning, are well launched on the road to perfection, but the offspring of diseased or debased parents are ineligible for spiritual progress unless they improve the faulty organisms
which they have inherited:

> The soul is always beautiful,
> The universe is duly in order, every thing is in its place,
> What has arrived is in its place and what waits shall be in its place,
> The twisted skull waits, the watery or rotten blood waits,
> The child of the glutton or venerealee waits long, and the child of
>   the drunkard waits long, and the drunkard himself waits
>   long,
> The sleepers that lived and died wait, the far advanced are to go on
>   in their turns, and the far behind are to come on in their
>   turns * * * *[71]

"The universe is duly in order" because it is governed by cosmic
laws, including the laws of hereditary perfection and decay. Diseased and debilitated persons and their unredeemed posterity are
ineligible to advance along the evolutionary roadway because their
"vital, universal, deathless germs" cannot transmit the best genetic
codes. The "twisted skull" probably denotes ill-balanced mental
faculties, warped personality, or syphilitic ravages; the "watery"
blood is poorly oxygenated, lacking the electric vitality essential to
dynamism and sex; the "rotten" blood is diseased.

Similarly, "Song of the Open Road" and certain other poems
stipulate that only the best specimens are fit to march alongside the
persona in the evolutionary vanguard:

> The stale cadaver blocks up the passage—the burial waits no
>   longer * * * *
> He traveling with me needs the best blood, thews, endurance,
> None may come to the trial till he or she bring courage and health.
> Come not here if you have already spent the best of yourself,
> Only those may come who come in sweet and determin'd bodies,
> No diseas'd person, no rum-drinker or venereal taint is permitted
>   here.[72]

The blocked-up "passage" is no mere rhetoric. An unhealthy body
(the ineligible "stale cadaver") cannot be the vehicle of spiritual
perfection "till" it becomes physically sound and pure. The man
who has not been "choice and chary of his love-power" and has

"already spent the best" of himself (the seminal treasure of his healthy manhood) or who has been the "slave of laborious routines" is unsuited to achieve heroic fatherhood. Factors that inhibit evolutionary-genetic progress are also specified in "Song of the Broad-Axe":

> The shape of the pill-box, the disgraceful ointment-box, the
>   nauseous application, and him or her applying it * * * *
> The shape of the slats of the bed of a corrupted body, the bed of
>   the corruption of gluttony or alcoholic drinks * * * *

And "A Hand-Mirror" (1860) presents a searing case study of a man whose "fair costume" cannot disguise the fact that he has violated nature's physical laws and cheated his posterity of their birthright. All "ashes and filth" within, deprived of buoyancy, sensitivity, and the "magnetism of sex," he has ruined his body through drink, gluttony, venereal disease, and unwholesome living, and now his blood circulates "dark and poisonous streams."[73]

Whitman tested every aspect of life by its hereditary consequences. Any misconduct which blocks physical or moral development, he believed, must be revenged on one's self and on the children whom one begets or conceives. He applied this hereditary touchstone to the ill effects of tobacco, salacious literature, drunkenness, adultery, prostitution, luxury and idleness, and the lack of personal idealism. Suggesting that softness, boredom, and sensualism undermine health and thus impede evolutionary progress, his 1856 letter to Emerson cautioned that "to be ripe beyond further increase is to prepare to die." And invoking the familiar analogy between America's loss of ruggedness and the corruption which brought about the fall of ancient Greece and Rome, he warned, in "By Blue Ontario's Shore":

> Fear grace, elegance, civilization, delicatesse,
> Fear the mellow sweet, the sucking of honey-juice,
> Beware the advancing mortal ripening of Nature,
> Beware what precedes the decay of ruggedness of states and
>   men.[74]

As a New Orleans journalist, he had speculated that the Victorian practice of swaddling nude statues or disguising the true appearance of the human body "may have aided in the effect of diminishing the average amplitude and majesty of the form, which effect must be confessed to when comparing present times to the age of the old Greeks and Latins." Later, he translated this caveat into a fervid declaration:

> I say the human shape or face is so great, it must never be made
>   ridiculous * * *
> And that exaggerations will be sternly revenged in your own
>   physiology, and in *other persons' physiology* also,
> And I say that clear-shaped children can be jetted and conceived
>   only where natural forms prevail in public, and the human
>   face and form are never caricatured * * * *[75]

Even skepticism toward nature's benevolent purpose can block genetic progress by thwarting the evolutionary urge—the neo-Lamarckian "will" that exists within every living creature:

> Not mere results of sin and law alone,
> Sometimes I see in ye, Disease and Death!
> The fear of evolution, knowledge, growth,
> Reaching beyond the bounds—and so cut short.[76]

These hereditary laws are universal and inexorable. "To Think of Time" testifies that they apply even to the "interminable hordes of the ignorant and wicked." And "Song of Prudence" affirms that they govern all spiritual development:

> The indirect is just as much as the direct,
> The spirit receives from the body just as much as it gives to the
>   body, if not more.
>
> Not one word or deed, not venereal sore, discoloration, privacy of
>   the onanist,
> Putridity of gluttons or rum-drinkers, peculation, cunning,
>   betrayal, murder, seduction, prostitution.
> But has results beyond death as really as before death.

A passage of the 1855 preface, closely paralleling these lines, declares that "not one" such defect "ever is or ever can be stamped on the [eugenic] programme but it is duly realized and returned, and that returned in further performances . . . and they returned again."[77] And Whitman's doctrine of Personalism, in *Democratic Vistas*, also has a distinctly eugenic basis: "Parentage must consider itself in advance. (Will the time hasten when fatherhood and motherhood shall become a science—and the noblest science?) To our model, a clear-blooded, strong-fibred physique is indispensable;

Walt Whitman and the Body Beautiful

the questions of food, drink, air, exercise, assimilation, digestion, can never be intermitted. Out of these we descry a well-begotten selfhood . . . and a general presence that holds its own in the company of the highest." [78] The clear meaning of the statement is that "selfhood," the completed American personality for whose emergence the poet yearned, must be "well-begotten" by the proper mating of prime physical specimens.

Whitman's programme stressed married love as the artery of genetic progress, but it blurred the issues of masturbation and homosexuality as deterrents to physical evolution. In his time, doctors still frightened girls and boys (among whom, Fowler alleged, masturbation was almost universal) [79] with the hoary warning that self-abuse induces insanity and physical decay. Whitman's complaint, in *Democratic Vistas*, that American youngsters are "prematurely ripe" [80] and his adulation of the "chaste married couple" become even more meaningful in the light of Dr. Dixon's contention that masturbation causes premature sexual development, weakens the body's power to resist disease, induces "fatuity and epileptic fits," and is "the actual root of tubercular or scrofulous phthisis, or consumption." Masturbation, Dr. Dixon argued, destroys male virility and renders women "not infrequently sterile, and indifferent to the pleasures of the marriage bed." [81] According to some physiologists, the semen is the finest of the body humors, purportedly of the same essence as the brain fluid and possibly interchangeable with it. (The brain and the sexual organs, Dr. Hollick alleged, are related like the "two poles of a Galvanic Pile.") Hence the derangement of the seminal fluid through masturbation might have dire effects on one's sanity. Sexual frenzy, madness, and inspiration were assumed to be associated in some complex and ambiguous manner. [82] And in Whitman's poems, we may observe, the imagery of sexual release sometimes blurs and overlaps the imagery of artistic–creative ecstasy.

Whitman refers poetically to "the sick-gray faces of onanists"; a notebook fragment, hinting at his aversion to masturbation, echoes the popular notion that its victims are recognizable by their scrofulous and skulking appearance. [83] The man-child in "The Sleepers" who becomes hysterical and disconsolate after his auto-erotic experience illustrates the textbook behavior of the hapless self-abuser: "a strong tendency to gloomy and despondent feelings, with dark forebodings of impending evil, and not infrequently a strong inclination to suicide."[84] Mindful of the hereditary and personal consequences of this supposedly ruinous act, the persona expresses his terrified guilt for having put his hand upon "the headland" ("Song of Myself") and for being "a solitary committer" ("Crossing Brooklyn Ferry").[85] Even the persona's pride in swimming may be viewed in the light of the fact that daily bathing was prescribed as a remedy for masturbation. Yet Whitman's attitude toward autoeroticism was contradictory. *Leaves of Grass* may not clearly glorify this much-deplored practice, but its episodes of self-stimulation are always succeeded by radiant passages in which the persona becomes inspired. For example, "Spontaneous Me" involves, in equal measure, the self-stimulated liberation of the persona's pent-up sexuality and the passionate and frenzied emergence of his creative, artistic spirit.

A similar contradiction characterizes Whitman's bravura lyrics in praise of "manly love." The Adam-hero personifies Adhesiveness, the principle of national comradeship, which one phrenologist defined as the faculty which "makes the nation's heart beat with one pulse."[86] But he also personifies that Adhesiveness which draws man to man, and thus he appears to be a spokesman for homosexuality, the abominated "disordered amativeness" whose very mention was shunned in the medical books. By declaring, in a "Calamus" poem, that homosexual love exists in an "ethereal" sphere, Whitman tried to exempt it from his eugenic programme and place it in its own rarefied realm. But his implication that homosexuality is separable from the other factors governing genetic evolution only intensifies the contradictions between the Adam who depicts a fatherly eugenic hero and the Adam who is a refraction of Whitman's real or fancied relationships with men. The poet had to warn himself to suppress his own excessive Adhesiveness and tried, not always successfully, to dissimulate this tendency. John Addington Symonds, Edward Carpenter, and Havelock Ellis, students of classical antiquity to whom masculine love was attractive, attempted to discover if the poet had been an active homosexual. Burroughs was disturbed by his girlish way of kissing male friends and the soldier boys whom he met on the streets of Washington, but apparently did not fathom his behavior. And if Dr. Bucke, widely recognized for his psychiatric expertise, saw the implications of Whitman's "magnetic love

Walt Whitman and the Body Beautiful

[which] always drew him hungeringly toward manly men," he kept his secret.[87]

Indeed, Whitman-Adam fuses contradictory images of the poet. As a projection of Whitman's conscious and subconscious drives, he is a devotee of pleasures and sensations, a lonely man eager to be pursued by male lovers toward whom he reacts with a rather feminine passivity. As an Epicurus figure, he desires to attract and possibly to dominate a cluster of affectionate young men. As a romantic hero, he displays the opposition between the poet's awareness of his physical and emotional shortcomings and his wish to assert his male potency and his heterosexual allure. As a eugenic hero (the aspect of the persona with which this study is most concerned), Whitman-Adam combines the elements of sexual bravado, perfect health, and a gift for healing the masses and inspiring them with personal and democratic virtues. The many Adams of *Leaves of Grass* seem sometimes to complement one another and sometimes to oppose one another in a dialectic tension that electrifies the whole work. But without its eugenic Adam— and its eugenic Eve—*Leaves of Grass* would lack physiological relevance and philosophical wholeness.

"Hardy and Well-Defined Women"

7

Leaves of Grass PORTRAYS A RACE OF PHYSICALLY and spiritually liberated women, freed from ignorance about their bodies and from distrust of their sexual instincts. Although these rugged figures are sometimes infelicitous from a literary standpoint, they demonstrate Whitman's determination to establish health and sexuality as cultural norms. Whitman's "hardy and well-defined women" contrast sharply with the sexless, sheltered, and wispy females who pervade nineteenth-century literature. The latter are mocked in *The Blithedale Romance* by Zenobia, Hawthorne's round-armed, deep-bosomed specimen of "womanliness incarnated," who taunts Miles Coverdale because he prefers the modishly delicate Priscilla to her voluptuous self: "As she has hardly any physique," Zenobia chides, "a poet, like Mr. Miles Coverdale, may be allowed to think her spiritual." These stylishly enervated "monthly-magazine made" American girls, remarked Henry Adams, "had not a feature that would be recognized by Adam." [1] But in depicting the beauty of fully developed healthy women in his writings, Whitman sought to establish woman's dignity and independence, without which, he felt, a democratic society could not endure. Despite certain limitations in his outlook which now seem obvious, he worked steadily toward a positive feminism in the poems, and, in *Democratic Vistas*, he predicated social evolution and Personalism—the flowering of the individual—on the existence of "perfect Women, indispensable to endow the birth-stock of a new World." [2]

American Victorians did not altogether deny woman's sexual nature, of course. Sometimes, like Hawthorne and Howells, they equated sexual dynamism with a flawed moral character. Sometimes they relegated sexuality to nonwhite girls, as if to say that a proper Caucasian lady simply has no libido. James Fenimore Cooper's Cora, with her trace of Negro blood, is permitted to reveal the passionate element in her nature, but the white damsels in Cooper's society novels are—like the proper maidens celebrated by Gilbert and Sullivan—"demurely coy, divinely cold." Melville's sexually aggressive Annatoo, in *Mardi*, and his sexually playful Fayaway, in *Typee*, are Melanesian girls and are therefore outside the Anglo-Saxon moral code, but his genteel white protagonist in "After the Pleasure Party" is tormented because she must dissimulate her sexual longings.

Like a true son of his age, Whitman sketched a number of dark-skinned passionate women. A prose vignette describes a voluptuous New Orleans octoroon (the "*em bon point* of her form is full of attraction"), and his temperance novel *Franklin Evans* depicts an octoroon who is so attractive to the white hero that he marries her.[3] "Song of Myself" pictures a noble savage heroine, the trapper's bride: "She had long eyelashes, her head was bare, her coarse straight locks descended upon her voluptuous limbs and reach'd to her feet." Another young Indian woman with long, straight hair, "tall-borne face and full and pliant limbs," and "wonderful beauty and purity" appears in "The Sleepers." Perhaps Whitman hoped to compose a full-fledged lyric about this tawny charmer, for he reminded himself, about 1860, to "make a Picture of the Indian girl looking at the turtle by an Aboriginal American Creek."[4]

In making physical fitness, sexual appetite, and a capacity for motherhood the criteria of excellence in all women, Whitman subscribed to a reformist trend which ran counter to the Victorian mainstream but was promoted by a forthright and important group of his contemporaries. Robert Dale Owen, in the first birth-control tract published in America, insisted that the powerful sexual instinct "that entwines itself around the warmest feelings and best affections of the heart" must not be thwarted if mankind is to achieve happiness. Owen's protégé, Dr. Charles Knowlton, termed the sexual drive "as much of heavenly origin as any other part of the human constitution."[5] Richard Hildreth, the philosopher-historian, observed that the sexual urge "probably is more powerful in women than in men" and that the hypocritical denial of woman's sexuality is a device to restrain natural and frank female behavior. He warned against the terrible repressive artifices in the Victorian moral armory, the "cruelties and disgraces intended to operate upon the fear of death and bodily pain, and the still more potent sentiment of self-comparison, by which it is sought to restrain and counterbalance this powerful impulse" in women.[6] And the English sociologist George Drysdale denounced the "rosewater morality" that maligned woman's sexual instincts:

> To have strong sexual passions is held to be rather a disgrace for a woman, and they are looked down upon as animal, sensual, coarse, and deserving of reprobation. The moral emotions of love are indeed thought beautiful in her; but the physical ones are rather held unwomanly and debasing. And this is a great error. In woman, exactly as in man, strong sexual appetites are very great virtues; as they are the signs of a vigorous frame, healthy sexual organs, and a naturally developed sexual disposition. The more intense the venereal appetites and the keener the sense of sexual gratification, provided it does not hold a diseased proportion to the other parts of the constitution, the higher is the sexual virtue of the individual. . . . Instead of a girl being looked down upon for having strong sexual passions, it is one of her highest virtues; while feeble or morbid desires are a sign of a diseased or deteriorated frame. Those who have the most healthy desires are the chosen children of Nature, whom she deems worthiest to continue our race. . . .

Drysdale associated sexual frustrations with female debility, hysteria, and perverted or abnormal development. Like Whitman, he proclaimed the need to speak openly and frankly about these matters.[7]

Whitman's portrayal of female sexuality should be seen as an attack on the restrictive Victorian morality that thwarted self-knowledge. Like Margaret Fuller, he felt that women had the right to develop every facet of their personalities. But whereas Miss Fuller had emphasized the intellectual and emotional faculties, Whitman gave priority to the physical, and particularly the sexual-maternal, qualities. He espoused the "hereditary" argument—by no means original with him—that no woman could rear a normal child unless she brought sexual energy to the marriage bed and carried, nursed, and trained her child in a healthful way. Sexuality, he argued, is the most wonderful fact of life—the sign and proof of wholesome femininity and noble motherhood. Prior to 1855, he said:

> As to the feeling of a man for a woman and a woman for a man, and all the vigor and beauty and muscular yearning—it is well to know that neither the possession of these feelings nor the easy talking and writing about them, and having them powerfully infused in poems is any discredit. . . . No woman can bear clean and vigorous children without them.— Most of what is called delicacy is filthy or sick and unworthy of a woman of live rosy body and a clean affectionate spirit.— At any rate all these things are necessary to the breeding of robust wholesome offspring.

Three decades later, he observed that "the current prurient, conventional treatment of sex is the main formidable obstacle" blocking "the movement for the eligibility and entrance of women amid new spheres of business, politics, and the suffrage."[8]

Like Swedenborg, he insisted that sexual vigor qualifies all human behavior. Thus he reaffirmed his belief that the woman who denies her sexuality is pitiful and incomplete:

> They are not quite full—not quite entire:—the woman who has denied the best of herself—the woman who has discredited the animal want, the eager physical hunger, the wish of that which though we will not allow it to be freely spoken of is still the basis of all that makes life worth while and advances the horizon of discovery. Sex: sex: sex: whether you sing or make a machine, or go to the North Pole, or love your mother, or build a house, or black shoes, or anything—anything at all—it's sex, sex, sex: sex is the root of all: sex—the coming together of men and women: sex: sex.[9]

Whitman's belief in the essential equality of the sexes was announced in the first edition of *Leaves of Grass*, wherein "A Song for Occupations" salutes

> The wife, and she is not one jot less than the husband,
> The daughter, and she is just as good as the son,
> The mother, and she is every bit as much as the father.[10]

And his faith in woman's essential role in shaping America's destiny was emphasized in the evangelical 1856 edition of the poems. Addressing the "just maturing youth" who are inaugurating a new America for "the hundred, or two hundred millions, of equal freemen and freewomen, amicably joined," Whitman says:

Walt Whitman and the Body Beautiful

> Anticipate the best women;
> I say an unnumbered new race of hardy and well-defined women
>   are to spread through all These States,
> I say a girl fit for These States must be free, capable, dauntless, just
>   the same as a boy.

He assures these youngsters that they are indispensable to America's physical-spiritual evolution, for they must produce the great mothers who will conceive "the ever-welcome defiers"—"the sages, poets, saviors, inventors, lawgivers of the earth." To the young men, he counsels manliness, and to the young women:

> Think of womanhood, and you to be a woman;
> The creation is womanhood;
> Have I not said that womanhood involves all?
> Have I not told how the universe has nothing better than the best
>   womanhood? [11]

In a similar vein, the prose preface to the 1872 edition predicts that America will "become the grand Producing Land of nobler Men and Women—of copious races, cheerful, healthy, tolerant, free . . . not the Man's Nation only, but the Woman's Nation—a land of splendid mothers, daughters, sisters, wives," and it declares that *Leaves of Grass* "is, in its intention, the song of a great composite *Democratic Individual*, male or female." [12] Great womanhood, no less than great manhood, announces "Song of the Redwood-Tree," is needed to fulfill America's golden promise:

> You average spiritual manhood, purpose of all, pois'd on yourself,
>   giving not taking law,
> You womanhood divine, mistress and source of all, whence life
>   and love and aught that comes from life and love * * * * [13]

The women who are depicted in the poems exhibit healthy sexuality and the capacity for excellent motherhood, but Whitman elevates these physiological attributes to aesthetic ideals. In *Leaves of Grass* feminine beauty is equated with ideal maternal qualities. By overlooking this truism, readers may misjudge both the poet's intent and his achievement in the portrayal of women.

Whether or not Whitman ever experienced any significant heterosexual love affairs, he had a keen eye for the ladies. Self-revelation and self-mockery combine in the declaration of the twenty-one-year-old journalist that "it behoves a modest personage like myself not to speak upon a class of beings [women] of whose nature, habits, notions, and ways he has not been able to gather any knowledge, either by experience or observation." Posing as a naïf bachelor for his newspaper readers in the 1840's and 1850's, he delighted in making gallant comments about the handsome women—particularly actresses—whom he saw on his editorial rounds. He inscribed a warm journalistic tribute to the "Brooklyn Belles," declaring that they "have those lithe graceful shapes such as the American women only have—the delicately cut features, and the intellectual cast of head. Ah, woman!" he concluded, "the very sight of you is a mute prayer for peace."[14] Later, he reported on the "hundreds and thousands of delicious New York girls, going to their work" on the Bowery; on a popular actress who displayed "a pair of pretty legs"; on the good-looking women who frequented the German beer halls; on a lovely lady descending from her carriage to go to the opera and revealing an opulent figure, splendid hair and eyes, and "sinewy and superb grace." One of his notebooks contains the penciled drawing of a pretty waiter-girl—short-skirted, deep-bosomed, and endowed with shapely arms and legs.[15]

The poet's susceptibility to female beauty may be judged by his comments about some of the women he knew. Recalling the Brooklyn girls of his youth, he mused, "what pretty girls some of them were!"[16] In his old age, he confessed a boyhood crush on the charismatic Frances Wright, "one of the few characters to excite in me a wholesale respect and love: she was beautiful in bodily shape and gifts of soul. . . ." "I never felt so glowingly towards any other woman. . . . she possessed herself of my body and soul." Yet it has been suggested that Whitman was really attracted by a certain masculine quality in her.[17] He relished his first impression of the youthful English actress Fanny Kemble and a later view of her as "just matured, strong, better than merely beautiful" when "she came to give America that young maturity and roseate power in all their noon, or rather forenoon, flush." Yet the actress impressed Melville as "unfemininely masculine."[18] After seeing the corpulent contralto Marietta Alboni in 1852, Whitman called her "a fully developed woman, with perfect-shaped feet, arms, and hands. Some thought her fat—*we* always thought her beautiful.—

Walt Whitman and the Body Beautiful

Her face is regular and pleasant—her forehead low—plentiful black hair, cut short, like a boy's—a slow and graceful style of walk—attitudes of inimitable beauty and large black eyes. . . ." Later he enshrined Alboni in "Proud Music of the Storm" as a "teeming" (that is, fertile) and "blooming mother," a "Venus contralto . . . Sister of loftiest gods." [19]

Some credence should be given to the saucy observation of the actress Adah Isaacs Menken that Whitman was never seen in the company of a young woman. During his Bohemian days, she and the poet attained a degree of intimacy; he attended her stage performances, visited her during her illness, and served as best man when she married Robert H. Newell ("Orpheus C. Kerr"), and she became an ardent admirer of *Leaves of Grass*.[20] Even so, Whitman hinted in his old age at the love affairs he had formerly enjoyed and bragged that girls in Washington and other places were "sweet" on him (he did not assert that he was sweet on *them*). He liked the vivacious Ellen O'Connor "very much," he admitted, but he described her as a dyspeptic ninety-pound slip of a woman who was "rather intellectual than physical." Whether he recognized Mrs. O'Connor's passionate attraction to him or felt any reciprocal passion for any woman who may have been drawn to him is questionable, for she pointedly remarked that he was more capable of meaningful relationships with men than with women.[21] A mature and healthy beauty characterized Mrs. Anne Gilchrist, who began her transatlantic wooing of the poet in 1869 and moved to America in 1876 to be near him, but although he called her "harmonic, orbic . . . more than a woman" and paid poetic tribute to her as "my noblest woman friend," he recorded no tender expressions of affection for her like those that adorn his letters to former soldier boys.[22] Confronted in his last years by the disquieting report that some of his young British fans viewed him as a fellow homosexual, he attempted to bolster the myth of his Adamic *machismo* by inventing the pitiful tale that he had sired six illegitimate children during his lustier days.

Whatever the truth about Whitman's personal relationships, his sympathy with womankind was genuine. He cherished feminine beauty and feminine sexuality and the prospect of a race of happy and liberated women. There are elements of truth in D. H. Lawrence's indictment of Whitman's "athletic mothers of these

States" as so many faceless "muscles and wombs" and in Richard Chase's quip that they differ from his literary "males" only in being procreative machines that exude a divine nimbus.[23] But such mockery misses the point that Whitman defined feminine beauty by idealizing the athletic, passionate woman, fit for childbearing, and by rejecting the traditional svelte, pallid, romantic model of femininity whose life-style, he believed, circumscribed woman's independence.

Equating female beauty with the capacity for motherhood was not unusual in Whitman's day. In a book with which the poet was familiar, Orson S. Fowler defined female beauty in terms of female function—that is, fitness for maternity—and advised prospective bridegrooms who intended to beget healthy offspring to marry women with an ample waist and "a deep broad chest." He cautioned that the fashionable hourglass figure, achieved by wearing tightly laced corsets reaching well above the waist, ruins the "vital" temperament, which is best suited to bearing healthy children; deprives the lungs of air; constricts the nipples, bosom, and stomach; induces curvature of the spine; blocks the circulation of the blood; and muddies the complexion. Likewise, Dr. Dixon blamed tight lacing, together with ornate dress, poor hygiene, and the emotional stimulation of sentimental literature and dancing parties, for creating a generation of prematurely ripened American girls who carried the seeds of tuberculosis and reproductive ailments. The premature ripening of young women, which Whitman deplored, was said by Dixon to induce the early onset of menstruation, with physiologically ruinous results.[24] Whitman issued editorial warnings against tight lacing because he resented the prurient ogling of the tightly laced ladies by the "be-chained, be-ringed, and be-spangled things, called dandies," and because he believed that the practice permanently deforms the female figure, injures the abdominal organs, and induces consumption.[25]

Clues to Whitman's standards of feminine beauty are provided by Hiram Powers's celebrated life-sized statues of female nudes, which the poet admired, and by Jacques's *Hints Toward Physical Perfection*, which he praised. Powers's sensationally popular "Eve Before the Fall," "Greek Slave," and "California" radiate robustness; their arms and legs are sturdy; their necks are strong, as though to show off a prominent cerebellum (the phrenological

Walt Whitman and the Body Beautiful

organ of "Amativeness"); their breasts are round and full; their hips are broad; their pubic zones protrude. They represent serene physical ripeness and a fitness to mate with the flawless Adam-father. In fact, Dr. Trall counseled young men to examine "Powers's Greek Slave, or his statue of Eve, to learn the outline of a good vital organization" and behold "the *normal* female form." [26] Jacques, whose manual was illustrated by line drawings of Powers's statues, said that loveliness and health are inseparable and that both may be acquired through diligent effort. He argued, as Whitman did, that American women are less healthy and attractive than were their granddames because they have traded domestic chores for labor-saving conveniences. Insisting that physical exertion is good for women, he urged them to work hard and to run, walk, skate, swim, row, dance, and engage in gymnastics. Defining female beauty largely in terms of the capacity for motherhood, Jacques attributed the greatest physical attractiveness to the girl with a "vital" temperament who is sturdy, broad-limbed, and large in the bust and pelvis—and preferably flaxen-haired. Obviously, both Powers and Whitman accepted the aesthetic premise that those women are most attractive who possess the greatest "child-bearing capacities." [27]

Not surprisingly, the beauty of the young and old women who appear in Whitman's writings is delineated largely in terms of their health and their sexual and maternal qualities. Whitman's attitude is revealed in his avuncular advice to his brother Jeff to rear his rather spoiled daughter Mannahatta so that "the dear little creature" will become "a splendid specimen of good animal health . . . the foundation of all, (righteousness included)—as to her mental vivacity & growth, they are plenty enough of themselves, and will get along quite fast enough of themselves . . . don't stimulate them at all. . . ." In art, as in upbringing, he championed "good animal health." [28] He jotted a reminder in his notebook: "Intersperse here and there [among the poems] pictures of athletic women—sometimes just a word or two—sometimes elaborate descriptions." He portrayed the heroine of *Franklin Evans* as "about twenty-five, and very handsome; not with unformed and unripened loveliness, but in the rich swell, the very maturity of physical perfection." He personified "Asia, the all-mother," in "A Broadway Pageant" (1860), as a full-blown woman, "florid with blood * * * hot with passion," her matronly physique clad in "ample and flowing garments." And he contemplated a full-dress "poem illustrative of the woman under the 'new dispensation,'" featuring "illuminative characters—from history—Molly Pitcher—the best mothers—the healthiest women—the most lovely women."[29] This objective, hinted at in several poems, was apparently never undertaken; the "new" woman appears only in partial portraits.

"A Woman Waits for Me" celebrates the athletic females, "ultimate in their own right," who are the suitable mates for the rugged Adamic fathers of young America:

> Without shame the man I like knows and avows the deliciousness
>   of his sex,
> Without shame the woman I like knows and avows hers.
>
> O! I will fetch bully breeds of children yet!
> I will dismiss myself from impassive women,
> I will go and stay with her who waits for me, and with those
>   women that are warm-blooded and sufficient for me;
> I see that they understand me, and do not deny me,
> I see that they are worthy of me—I will be the robust husband of
>   these women.
>
> They are not one jot less than I am,
> They are tanned in the face by shining suns and blowing winds,
> Their flesh has the old divine suppleness and strength,
> They know how to swim, row, ride, wrestle, shoot, run, strike,
>   retreat, advance, resist, defend themselves,
> They are ultimate in their own right—they are calm, clear, well-
>   possessed of themselves.[30]

The "impassive women" scorned by the heroic breeder-persona, those who feel no overpowering desire for sexual union, were considered to be unripe for conception; marriage reformers held that motherhood should never be forced upon them. In the folklore of birth control, impassiveness in the female was a reputed means for limiting offspring. (Incidentally, passive women were sometimes said to conceive daughters rather than the splendid sons for whom the persona yearned. Compare the declaration by an electrical biologist that "the sex of the infant is determined by which parent is more firmly charged at the time of conception"

Walt Whitman and the Body Beautiful

with Whitman's idealized mother-figure in "I Sing the Body Electric" who "is both passive and active, / She is to conceive daughters as well as sons, and sons as well as daughters.")[31]

The renunciation, in "A Woman Waits for Me," of "impassive women" affirms Whitman's emphasis on the nobility of the sexual-maternal drive, and the poem's healthy, self-sufficient women illustrate the sort of feminine independence advocated by many reformers. For example, Elizabeth Cady Stanton said in 1851: "The girl must be allowed to romp and play, climb, skate and swim; her clothing must be more like that of a boy . . . that she may be out at all times, and enter freely into all kinds of sport. Teach her to go alone, by night or day, if need be, on the lonely highway, or through the streets of the crowded metropolis. The manner in which all courage and self-reliance is educated out of the girl, her path portrayed with dangers and difficulties that never exist, is melancholy indeed."[32] Reflecting the impact on massed audiences of women activists such as Eliza W. Farnham, Amelia Bloomer, and Lydia Folger Fowler, especially when they were garbed in their "athletic" Bloomer costumes, Whitman included "the athletic American matron speaking in public to crowds of listeners" as part of his poetic panorama of the nation in "Our Old Feuillage" (1860).[33]

"Bridalnight" (incorporated into section 5 of "I Sing the Body Electric") glorifies the female in terms of her maternal powers. Instead of celebrating her fragility and her loving sighs, it presents her as the univeral Eve, "endowed with inexpressible completeness, sanity, beauty," in the consummate moment of her femaleness—the sexual embrace in which she is fulfilled as a woman by conceiving a perfect child. Her sensuous appeal is communicated through the response of the Adam persona, roused to perform the duty of fatherhood which nature has designated for him. Passionately, he declares:

> This is the female form,
> A divine nimbus exhales from it from head to foot,
> It attracts with fierce undeniable attraction * * *
> Mad filaments, ungovernable shoots play out of it, the response
> likewise ungovernable,
> Hair, bosom, hips, bend of legs, negligent falling hands all
> diffused, mine too diffused,

> Ebb stung by the flow and flow stung by the ebb, love-flesh
>   swelling and deliciously aching,
> Limitless limpid jets of love hot and enormous, quivering jelly of
>   love, white-blow and delirious juice,
> Bridegroom night of love working surely and softly into the
>   prostrate dawn,
> Undulating unto the willing and yielding day,
> Lost in the cleave of the clasping and sweet-flesh'd day.[34]

This highly charged woman is the inevitable heroine of "I Sing the Body Electric." The female (that is, negative) magnetism of her dynamic life force is the symbol of her sexual and maternal powers and the proof of her womanly excellence. Similarly, the voluptuous, but rather nebulous, female who is Adam's idealized bedmate in "From Pent-Up Aching Rivers" is electrically charged to attract the hero to "the work of fatherhood" which "the general commanding me" (the God of Genesis, who commands his creatures to be fruitful and multiply?) has ordained to hasten this evolutionary "programme" through the "act divine and you children prepared for."[35]

In "Faces" the image of the passionate "full-grown" lily-woman who invites the "limber-hipp'd" hero-begetter to fill her "with albescent honey" is succeeded, after an internal of years, by the image of a beautiful and serene Quaker grandmother. The lily-woman (personifying the "vital," or maternal, temperament) and the elderly woman are successive stages in the development of the same magnificent person. With a touch of sarcasm, Whitman contrasts this womanly heroine to the undersexed females favored by conventional artists:

> I saw the rich ladies in full dress at the soiree,
> I heard what the singers were singing so long,
> Heard who sprang in crimson youth from the white froth and the
>   water-blue.

These "rich ladies," explained William Sloane Kennedy, are the "Venus women"—listless aristocrats with fickle passions who are "not to be compared to the honored mother of many children," Whitman's truest representation of womanhood.[36] In trial lines of verse, Whitman rejected such privileged ladies in favor of simple proletarian mothers:

not the beautiful girl or the elegant lady with the [?] complexion,
But the mechanic's wife at work or the mother of many children,
    middle-aged or old * * * *37

"Song of Myself" extols the healthy lower-class women rather than these aristocratic ladies and exhibits a small gallery of suitable mates for the stalwart farmers and mechanics of young America: the blushing girl ascending the hill with her lover, "the farmer's girl boiling her iron tea-kettle and baking shortcake," girls and matrons performing domestic tasks, and the popular figure of the "clean-hair'd Yankee girl" working "with her sewing-machine or in the factory or mill." The gallery also displays "the train'd soprano" who "convulses me like the climax of my love-grip" but who, in a trial version of the poem, had been endowed with a "love-grip" of her own.38 These glimpses of elemental womanhood are contrasted with the picture of the lonely and aristocratic twenty-eight-year-old spinster in the poem's eleventh section—the proprietress of "the fine house by the rise of the bank" who "hides handsome and richly drest aft the blinds of the window" to behold the twenty-eight young male swimmers who "float on their backs" like so many Walt Whitmans at Gray's Swimming Bath. In her imagination she is drawn to them, runs down to the beach and joins them in the water, caresses their bodies, "seizes fast to them," and "puffs and declines with pendant and bending arch." This lady sublimating her body hunger for the twenty-eight young male swimmers (one for each day of her menstrual cycle?) is a tragic, self-indulgent figure who toys with her erotic desires but thwarts her natural mating instinct. (In Whitman's eugenic view, a normal girl had best marry a hale farmer or workingman, be his comrade, share his domestic burdens, and provide him with a brood of healthy children.)

Like other depictions of women in Whitman's poetry, however, this one is ambiguous. For if the lady represents an object lesson in misdirected sexuality, she may also be seen as the central figure of an adolescent and voyeuristic fantasy in which a wealthy and mature female aggressor—or possibly the male persona who has identified with her sexual yearnings and predatory gropings—commits a watery rape upon the passive young men as they float supine in the water. Thus a conspicuous oedipal warp seems to run through the eugenic fabric of this episode.39

Despite a steadfast faith in the physiological and spiritual sanctity of motherhood and an insistence on the essential dignity of "every man, every woman, in the inherent nature of things," [40] Whitman's attitudes toward women reveal certain personal and cultural anomalies. The poet was apparently inspired by the belief that America would one day produce a generation of great mothers equal to the rugged women of colonial times and capable of conceiving flawless children. Somehow, thousands of copies of the perfect girl would emerge to mate with Adamic heroes and produce a perfect race for the new Eden. In a "Children of Adam" poem, Whitman-Adam, roaming in his "new garden," announces that "with determined will, I seek—the woman of the future." And in "From Pent-Up Aching Rivers" he expresses the wish

> To talk to the perfect girl who understands me—the girl of The States,
> To waft to her these from my own lips—to effuse them from my own body * * * * [41]

But Whitman sought in vain for the ideal mother type among the masses of American women. As though to mark his disappointment, the poems composed after 1860 rarely celebrate the perfect American girl. In a brief lyric written the year of his physical breakdown, in fact, he despaired of ever finding this archetypal matron (and also, one suspects, of resolving his passionate yearnings in any heterosexual relationship):

> With all thy gifts, America,
> Standing secure, rapidly tending, overlooking the world,
> Power, wealth, extent, vouchsafed to thee—with these and like of these vouchsafed to thee,
> What if one gift thou lackest? (the ultimate human problem never solving,)
> The gift of perfect women fit for thee—what if that gift of gifts thou lackest?
> The towering feminine of thee? the beauty, health, completion, fit for thee?
> The mothers fit for thee?

These misgivings were intensified during his trip to Denver. Expecting to find a new breed of mothers in the West, he discovered instead that the women there were "fashionably dressed and have the look of 'gentility' in face" but were disappointingly "dyspep-

Walt Whitman and the Body Beautiful

tic-looking . . . doll-like" and without "any high native originality of spirit or body." Toward the end of his life, he lamented
the fact that "our [American] women don't seem to be any longer
built for child-bearing. We have gone on for so long hurting the
body that the job of rehabilitating it seems prodigious if not im-
possible. The time will come when the whole affair of sex—copu-
lation, reproduction—will be treated with the respect to which it is
entitled. Instead of meaning shame and being apologized for it will
mean purity and be glorified." [42]

Although Whitman consistently championed the freedom of
women, his feminist views developed slowly. In the years before
the Civil War, as the family-centered rural and small-town life patterns eroded, he expressed a nostalgia for the old-fashioned family
system that had characterized an earlier era. In this period, when
the dwellings of the wealthier classes were being equipped with
hot and cold running water, cookstoves, bathrooms, and air fur-
naces, he praised the "domestic joys" of "womanly housework"
and of "the beautiful maternal cares" and sentimentalized over
the simpler lives of colonial women, "stout, strong, happy, and
hearty," unafraid of animals or Indians—women who "rose early,
worked like beavers, and never spent the hours in dancing." The
granddaughters of these stalwart dames have degenerated, he alleged, because of their "listless idleness, inactivity, thin shoes, late
hours, muslin dresses, horror of fresh morning air," their reading
of "that detestable stuff stitched in pink and yellow covers, which
is flooding the country over," their failure to observe the laws of
health, and their addiction to aristocratic manners. [43] In the depression year of 1857, he deplored the fact that luxury-minded girls
were trained to expect comforts and "fashion," thus thwarting the
marital ambitions of working-class bachelors. Once the girls married, he alleged, their expensive tastes often drove them into the
work force. He rejected the popular argument that women's brains
and physiques were inadequate to permit them to become industrial workers. But he assailed the "miserable system" which slo-
ganeered for the "rights of woman" in order to justify the exploi-
tation of seamstresses at wages so low that many of them were
forced into prostitution. [44]

Although some reformers advocated family planning as a
means to secure personal dignity for women and to relieve the
pressures of poverty, Whitman made no distinction between

"criminal" abortion and birth control, calling the latter a threat to family life and the murder of "inchoate offspring." Birth control was beginning to be favored by middle-class families, among whom information was more freely disseminated, but he condemned it as a vice of the pampered rich that contaminated the lives of the lower classes. He attacked as an incitement to infanticide the advertisement of pills and mechanical devices intended "to regulate or limit the offspring, without injuring the constitution," and he was angered by the manufacturers' boast that "educated and refined ladies" were the chief users of these products. In truth, birth control devices were expensive, but Whitman was chiefly opposed to birth control because he viewed it as a threat to maternal and familial instincts among the American masses.[45]

Whitman's humane regard for prostitutes was also tempered by the conviction that they undermined working-class marriages. Because most workingmen under forty years of age frequented the whores "as an ordinary thing," he warned that prostitution was polluting the stream of inheritance and weakening the physical fibre of the nation: "A generation hence, what a scrofulous growth of children! What dropsies, feebleness, premature deaths, suffering infancy to come!" Voicing an opinion like that expressed in Dr. W. W. Sanger's *The History of Prostitution* (1850), he declared that the adoption of the European system of licensing prostitutes would further threaten the health and the morals of American men, and he decried "the hundreds of quacks" who were "dosing thousands of the best bodies of the land" with drugs and administering medical treatments that inflicted more harm than did the venereal diseases.[46]

He blamed prudery and a false sense of respectability for robbing young women of the physiological knowledge they needed to safeguard their morals and for frustrating their wish to have "a powerful, agreeable, clear-fleshed, sweet-blooded body." He condemned the ladies of the "gay upper circle" who were charitable toward South Seas Missions and "superannuated lap dogs" but ignored the denizens of the city's "stews and purlieus" and "the poor seamstresses" who were "toiling out life and blood and brain for the miserable pittance which the cupidity of men" granted them and could barely manage to evade "the pest houses and brothels." Like Dr. Sanger, he deplored the periodic police roundups of prosti-

Walt Whitman and the Body Beautiful

tutes to the Tombs or Welfare Island prisons and their subsequent release without any intervening efforts at rehabilitation. Just as Dr. Sanger acknowledged that inclination drew many girls into prostitution, so Whitman (whose brother Andrew's wife Nancy walked the streets) avoided the Victorian clichés that prostitutes are invariably the victims of seduction and that they are unreformable. Although he included them in his compassionate sweep when he celebrated himself poetically as the "espouser of unhelped women," his newspaper sketches reveal how shrewdly he observed their ways and understood their victimization; his description of the harlots and establishments in Manhattan, along lower Broadway, resembles one of Dr. Sanger's objective reports.[47] A "New York Dissected" article characterizes a specimen of these "hideous women of the night"—one of the "tawdry, hateful, foul-tongued, and harsh-voiced harlots"—in these terms: "Dirty finery, excessively plentiful; paint, both red and white; draggle-tailed dress, ill-fitting; coarse features, unintelligent; bold glance, questioning, shameless, perceptibly anxious; hideous croak or dry, brazen ring in voice; affected, but awkward, mincing, waggling gait. Harlot."[48]

Whitman wrote three poems about prostitutes. "The New York Beggar" (1854) is a mawkish ballad which laments the girls, some of them mere children, who are driven into a life of vice. "To a Common Prostitute" (1860) is an imagined address to a passing streetwalker by the "liberal and lusty" persona who affects a flippant or ostensibly bawdy manner but is recognizably the Whitman-Christ of the "Messenger Leaves" poems, whose lyrical "leaves" and "words" "glisten and rustle" for all mankind as a gospel of hope. "The City Dead-House" (1867) is a reflection by the quasi-medical persona of "The Wound-Dresser," who stoically witnesses a scene of human misery. Observing the corpse of "a poor dead prostitute" which "lies on the damp brick pavement" beside a running faucet and amidst the "odors morbific" of a Washington city morgue, he laments—in a brilliantly elaborated house-of-life metaphor—the spiritual demise which had long ago preceded the harlot's physical death and the wreck of "that wondrous house—that delicate fair house"—that "poor, desperate house" of her life.[49]

Whitman elevated women to the most exalted levels of human dignity, but prior to his affirmation of woman's rights in *Democratic Vistas*, he rarely admitted them into the highest reaches of the affections except in terms of their motherhood or their eligibility for motherhood. His poems celebrate heterosexual union as the divine avenue of racial amelioration. But outside the bounds of marriage and motherhood, the poet reacts tepidly to feminine attraction. Observe, for instance, the difference in intensity between the persona's affectional responses to the men and women he observes, in these lines from "A Song of Joys":

> O male and female!
> O the presence of women! (I swear, nothing is more exquisite to
>   me than the presence of women;)
> O for the girl, my mate! O for happiness with my mate!
> O the young man as I pass! O I am sick after the friendship of him
>   who, I fear, is indifferent to me.
>
> O the streets of cities!
> The flitting faces—the expressions, eyes, feet, costumes! O I
>   cannot tell how welcome they are to me;
> O of men—of women toward me as I pass—The memory of only
>   one look—the boy lingering and waiting.[50]

Whitman called for a breed of splendid women, but for his own companions he preferred men. *Leaves of Grass* contains no expression of heterosexual elation to rival "We Two Boys Together Clinging" and no love lyric as delightful as "When I Heard at the Close of Day," with its address to the absent male lover. A fragmentary prose sketch condemns the "modesties and prohibitions" that inhibit women in a man's world, but warns the women that "under present arrangements, the love and comradeship of a woman, of his wife, however welcome, however complete, does not and cannot satisfy the high . . . requirements of a manly soul for love and comradeship," because a man is drawn to his male lover "with more passionate attachment than he can bestow on any woman, even his wife. . . ." Whitman rephrases this thesis in "Calamus 38":

> Primeval my love for the woman I love,
> O bride! O wife! more resistless, more enduring than I can tell, the
>   thought of you!
> Then separate, as disembodied, the purest born,
> The ethereal, the last athletic reality, my consolation,

Walt Whitman and the Body Beautiful

I ascend—I float in the regions of your love, O man,
O sharer of my roving life.[51]

Despite the anomalies and the limitations that are evident in Whitman's statements about women, he evolved an advocacy of every woman's right to achieve unqualified opportunities and development in all areas of human endeavor. Throughout his career, he viewed femininity, motherhood, and the family as the foundations of racial advancement. In *Leaves of Grass*, where the terms *mother* and *mothers* together occur more than one hundred times, women attain completion through the physical and moral force of motherhood. The mother—in youth, in childbirth, in old age—is exalted in "Song of Myself," whose twenty-first section asserts that "there is nothing greater than the mother of men"—a sentiment which rejects heterosexual romanticism without doing violence to Whitman's affectional propensities. Whitman undertakes to portray "The Mothers of These States" as the proper emblem for the new America, declaring that "none of the emblems of the classic goddess—nor any feudal emblems—are fit symbols for the republic." Typically, the poet pictures Mother America surrounded by her progeny of sons and daughters:

A grand, sane, towering, seated Mother,
Chair'd in the adamant of Time * * * *[52]

The freest and most self-possessed woman in *Leaves of Grass*, in the prophetic eleventh section of "Song of the Broad-Axe," moves fearlessly through the city streets, uncorrupted by the license and abuse of the loafers:

She is less guarded than ever, yet more guarded than ever,
The gross and soil'd she moves among do not make her gross and
    soil'd,
She knows the thoughts as she passes, nothing is conceal'd from
    her,
She is none the less considerate or friendly therefor,
She is the best belov'd, it is without exception, she has no reason
    to fear and she does not fear,
Oaths, quarrels, hiccup'd songs, smutty expressions, are idle to
    her as she passes,
She is silent, she is possess'd of herself, they do not offend her,

> She receives them as the laws of Nature receive them, she is
> strong,
> She too is a law of Nature—*there is no law stronger than she is*.

What law this admirable woman personifies is specified in a fragmentary draft version of the poem: "She too was a law of nature. . . . [She] was *maternity*."[53]

Like his contemporaries, Whitman extolled family life. The Beecher sisters, for example, described the home as "the incarnation and seedbed of Christian virtue," alleging that Christ's purpose on earth had been to secure the existence of "the family state," which was designed "to provide for the training of our race to the highest possible, intelligence, virtue and happiness. . . ."[54] Whitman was only twenty-one when he composed a tale about two elderly brothers who meet after a long separation. One, though humble, has enjoyed a marriage and children and has found happiness through fathering "brown boys and fair girls." "Oh, Mark," he exclaims to his rich but miserable bachelor brother, "that, *that* is a pleasure—that swelling of tenderness for our offspring—which the rigorous doctrines of your course of life have withheld from you!"[55] Whitman's editorials and reviews in the *Brooklyn Daily Eagle* praised the serene married state and lauded the novels of Fredrika Bremer for showing "how charity and forebearance and love are potent in the domestic circle" and for revealing "how indulgence in stormy passion leads invariably to sorrow—and depicting in especial the character of a *good, gentle mother*." The twenty-eight-year-old bachelor declared: "If we ever have children, they will read, first, the New Testament, and second, Miss Bremer." (He obviously appreciated her description of the "simplicity and gentleness" of the American male's conduct toward women and her sentiment that "in every woman he respects his own mother.")[56] Charles W. Eldridge remarked that Whitman remained "passionately attached to the old fashioned family relations" and that he was particularly attracted to children.[57]

Whitman observed that married love alone reveals "the true nature of sex" and that casual intercourse tends to debase and "imbrute" the soul. Echoing the slogans of feminist reformers, he said that women must always decide the terms on which they will accept sexual love, for "the mothers *are* the foundations of society: mothers need no law."[58] He rejected the romanticizing of hetero-

Walt Whitman and the Body Beautiful

sexual love because romance withdraws attention from the sexual-parental meaning of marriage and focuses on partial and perverse passions. His poetry, explained John Addington Symonds, depicts the "intercourse established in matrimony . . . not so much as an intellectual and moral union, but as an association for the mutual assistance in the labours of life, and for the production of noble human specimens"; its "Adamic hygienic view of marriage, satisfying the instincts of the primeval man," rejects "those dregs of mediaeval sentimentalism and platonism" which set women upon a false pedestal.[59] In fact, Whitman had accused Tennyson, Balzac, George Sand, and Bulwer-Lytton of undermining marriage by glorifying infidelity and idealizing the sort of "love" that pays tribute to "the same unnatural and shocking passion for some girl or woman, that wrenches it from its manhood, emasculated and impotent, without strength to hold the rest of the objects and goods of life in their proper positions." Romantic love "seeks nature for sickly uses," he said. "It goes screaming and weeping after the facts of the universe in their calm beauty and equanimity, to note the occurrence of itself, and to sound the news, in connection with the charms of the neck, hair, or complexion of a particular female."[60]

Whitman's mature expression of feminist ideas, in *Democratic Vistas*, bears comparison with the advanced feminist writings of the 1860's as a noble declaration of the freedom which women may, and must, struggle to achieve. This work shows the impact upon him of contemporary campaigns for women's rights. It is illuminating, for instance, to compare his attitudes toward women in this noble essay to the ideas formulated at great length in Eliza Farnham's *Woman and Her Era*, a pioneering social-historical study which had hailed Whitman as a true feminist and as the only male writer whose works clearly envisioned the advent of a physical-spiritual democracy in which women will exercise and enjoy complete human selfhood. She deplored the personal and social restrictions which blind custom had imposed on woman's progress. Like Whitman, she perceived female sexuality, and particularly the power of motherhood, which she deemed the highest function in all of nature, as positive proof that woman constitutes the most advanced organic form and the greatest virtue that nature has evolved. Like Whitman, she assumed that woman's evolutionary primacy, transcending that of men, signifies that she can become intellectually and spiritually superior to man, once she is divested of false attitudes toward herself and of the prohibitions placed upon her by a male-oriented society. And like the poet, Mrs. Farnham declared that the greatest barrier to woman's self-realization is her addiction to the prevailing romantic myths and fallacies about her capabilities and functions.[61]

The theoretical premise of *Democratic Vistas* is not unlike Mrs. Farnham's argument that woman's potential for personal excellence derives from her capacity for motherhood and that her physical excellence is analogous to, and symbolic of, the personal-spiritual eminence toward which she, and the entire human race, should aspire and struggle. Deploring the postwar American society in which "the men believe not in the women, nor the women in the men," Whitman insists that the attainment of democracy requires "perfect women, to match the general luxuriance" of America's material progress. Fundamental social advance in America is predicated upon the evolution of a new womanhood: "I have sometimes thought, indeed, that the sole avenue and means of a reconstructed sociology depended, primarily, on a new birth, elevation, expansion, invigoration of woman, affording, for races to come, (as the conditions that antedate birth are indispensable,) a perfect motherhood. Great, great, indeed, far greater than they know, is the sphere of women. But doubtless the question of such new sociology all goes together, includes many varied and complex influences and premises, and the man as well as the woman, and the woman as well as the man."[62]

Basic to this "reconstructed sociology," *Democratic Vistas* asserts, is "achieving the entire redemption of woman out of these incredible holds and webs of silliness, millinery, and every kind of dyspeptic depletion—and thus insuring to the States a strong and sweet Female Race, a race of perfect Mothers. . . ." Here, too, Whitman joined hands with the feminist reformers who argued that fashionable dress, stylish conduct, and husband hunting rendered women frivolous, robbed them of self-respect, made them view their situation through the conventional lenses of a male-dominated society, and hindered their progress toward independence. To gain the social equality to which they are entitled by nature, Whitman said, women must attain personal health and reject the romantic-feudal allurements which block their way:

The idea of the women of America, (extricated from this daze, this fossil and unhealthy air which hangs about the word *lady*,) develop'd, raised to become the robust equals, workers, and, it may be, even practical and political deciders with the men—greater than man, we may admit, through their divine maternity, always their towering, emblematic attribute—but great, at any rate, as man, in all departments; or, rather, capable of being so, soon as they realize it, and can bring themselves to give up toys and fictions and launch forth, as men do, amid real, independent, stormy life.[63]

Unambiguously, Whitman demands "the perfect equality of women, and . . . a grand and powerful motherhood." Like Mrs. Farnham, he deplores the fact that traditional literature has never adequately pictured a real woman: "woman portray'd or outlin'd at her best, or as perfect human mother. . . ." To indicate the sort of individual to whom artists should direct their attention, *Democratic Vistas* presents four thumbnail portraits, which Whitman admits "are frightfully out of line from these imported models of womanly personality—the stock feminine characters of the current novelists, or of the foreign court poems . . . which fill the envying dreams of so many poor girls, and are accepted by our men, too, as supreme ideals of feminine excellence to be sought after." His sketches, he asserts, are not merely aesthetic; they are also a response to the revolutionary "mutterings" which he hears in the air: "The day is coming when the deep question of woman's entrance amid the arenas of practical life, politics, the suffrage, etc., will not only be argued all around us, but may be put to decision, and real experiment."[64]

The first of these brief portraits describes a healthy farm girl who works in the city as a domestic and supports her parents, but preserves her self-respect and steadily improves her mind. The second depicts a woman who "carries on a mechanical business" without surrendering "the charm of the womanly nature." The third exhibits a workingman's wife endowed with "such a noble female personality" that in tending her children and keeping house, "she beams sunshine out of all these duties, and makes them illustrious. Physiologically sweet and sound, loving work, practical. . . . Whatever she does, and wherever she is, that charm, that indescribable perfume of genuine womanhood attends her, goes with her, exhales from her, which belongs of right to all the sex, and is, or ought to be, the invariable atmosphere and common aureola of old as well as young." The fourth portrait features an octogenarian "Peacemaker," with "her profuse snow-white hair (uncoif'd by any headdress or cap), dark eyes, clear complexion, sweet breath, and peculiar personal magnetism," who is recognizably a version of the matriarchal heroines depicted in *Leaves of Grass*.[65] Like Egyptian deities, these elderly matrons are characterized by beauty, bodily perfumes, and silvery haloes.

"I know of nothing more beautiful, inspiring, significant," said the poet, than "a hale old woman, full of cheer as of years, who has raised a brood of hearty children, arriving at last at a period of rest, content, contemplation—the thought of things done."[66] "Outlines for a Tomb" (1870) includes two glimpses of matronly fulfillment in its kaleidoscope of a happy future:

> In one, the sacred parturition scene,
> A happy painless mother birth'd a perfect child * * * *
> In one a trio beautiful,
> Grandmother, loving daughter, loving daughter's daughter, sat,
> Chatting and sewing.

The idealized mother in "There Was a Child Went Forth" is seen performing her household duties (those tasks, Catharine Beecher observed, which are designed to perfect a woman physically and spiritually). A matron to whom motherhood has brought the full comprehension and pleasure of life appears in "A Song of Joys":

> O ripen'd joy of womanhood! O happiness at last!
> I am more than eighty years of age, I am the most venerable
> mother,
> How clear is my mind—how all people draw nigh to me!
> What attractions are these beyond any before? what bloom more
> than the bloom of youth?
> What beauty is this that descends upon me and rises out of me?

The venerable Quaker matron, in the concluding section of "Faces," sits on the front porch of her farmhouse; in the glint of the sunshine "her old white head" looks like the aureola of an angel:

> The finish beyond which philosophy cannot go and does not wish
> to go,
> The justified mother of men.

These lovely lines are no mere sentiment; they embody a faith in woman's purpose in the evolutionary scheme of things, well expressed by the Scottish altruist Henry Drummond: "Mothers are the chief end of creation. In plants the mother species heads the list. Beyond the mother with her milky breast the Creator does not go; that is His goal. In as real a sense as a factory is meant to turn out locomotives or locks, the machinery of nature in its last resort is meant to turn out mothers." [67]

The appealing motherly figures, with their clean garments and sacred perfume, who move through the pages of *Leaves of Grass* tempt one to conclude that Whitman had heeded the advice of the elderly Quakeress in *Uncle Tom's Cabin* who exclaimed: "So much has been said and sung of beautiful young girls, why don't somebody wake up to the beauty of old women?" [68] In fact, both Whitman and Mrs. Stowe were responsive to the reformist view that healthy postmenopausal women are serene and delightful persons. To the poet, fascinated by longevity, old folks were objects of veneration and joy. And he could have felt none of the qualms in idealizing elderly women that might accompany his romanticizing of handsome young women and girls.

Of course Whitman's reverence for motherhood represented a profound emotion as well as a cultural ideal. From Frederik Schyberg to Edwin Havilland Miller, critics have viewed his dependency on his mother's love as a vital factor in the development of his psyche. His mother, Whitman hinted, was the incarnation of perfect womanhood: "*Leaves of Grass* is the flower of her temperament active in me," he asserted. Following her death, the preface to the 1876 edition of the poems declared that she was "the most perfect and magnetic character, the rarest combination of practical, moral and spiritual, and the least selfish, of all and any I have ever known—and by me O so much the most deeply loved. . . ." His poetic tribute, "As at Thy Portals Also Death," enshrines her as a beautiful matron whose "divine blending, maternity," qualifies her to be "the ideal woman, practical, spiritual, of all of earth, life, love, to me the best * * * *" [69]

To Whitman, motherhood was a cardinal virtue and woman's sexuality a spiritual force. Motherhood—the female principle—denoted love, stability, and prophetic spirituality, in contrast to the male principle of restless dynamism and self-reliance. Woman's sexuality symbolized the evolutionary yearning to complete the human race and to supply it with physically sound and spiritually sensitive children. Motherhood was an analogue to the poet's own creativity, for the ideal mother gives birth to the great poet, Whitman's archetypal symbol of human supremacy.

Complete Selfhood

"Thy Ensemble Including Body and Soul"

8

"THE POET WRITES THE HISTORY OF HIS OWN BODY," Thoreau observed, and Whitman's physical self *is* the authentic vital center of *Leaves of Grass*. By idealizing his body, Whitman created a model that his fellow Americans could emulate. By hallowing his bodily drives and processes, he sanctified the animal element in everyone's life. By exalting his physique, he demonstrated his fitness to create what he called "the most religious book among books: crammed full of faith." [1] By dramatizing his enthusiasm for health and physical culture, he fashioned the Whitman persona—his poetic alter ego—into a Christ-like healer and prophet of physical and spiritual perfectibility. And by studying physiological facts and phenomena, he found "the stimulus of new perceptions and the material of new analogies and correspondences" that is so vital "in the poet's advance on the frontiers of the mind." [2] His fascination with the healthy human body sometimes became translated into a metre-making argument, the polarized themes of bodily soundness and spiritual infinitude charging *Leaves of Grass* with supernal beauty.

Although many of Whitman's contemporaries could accept his attitudes toward man's physical nature, others were troubled by his frank and vociferous affirmation of the body. What were they to make of a poet who took for his emblem the calamus root, known in folk medicine as a specific to be chewed for sweetening the stomach and for achieving sexual virility? [3] Or who bragged about his "amativeness," commonly understood to mean sexual virility? Or who rhapsodized about his own "mettle," or sperm? In the high noon of American Victorianism, genteel men of letters were irked by what they imagined to be his unseemly delight in chanting about the body and its functions. An anonymous critic alleged that the first edition of *Leaves of Grass* was so "beastly" that its author deserved "no better than the lash." [4] The young Harvard art historian Charles Eliot Norton, who reviewed the first edition, observed that the work was not without merit but that it contained "passages of intolerable coarseness—not gross and licentious, but disgustingly coarse"; Norton feared some moral damage if the book should fall into feminine hands. [5] In 1889, during Victorianism's Indian summer, William Dean Howells confessed an editorial itch to delete from Whitman's poems certain lines that could offend the ladies and innocent young girls who were Howells's arbiters of clean-mindedness. Howells declared that "the five senses do not need any celebration," because "the beast half" of our nature is sufficiently self-assertive. Likewise, the poet Swinburne scathingly denounced the "unhealthy demonstrative and obtrusive animalism of the Whitmaniad" because he found Whitman's attitudes "unnatural and incompatible with the wholesome instincts of human passion." [6] With prurient malice, a Southern reviewer attacked the poet's alleged cult of the body as a rape of the Victorian muse and assailed Whitman as a "rhapsodist . . . sewer-rat astray in the secret parts of Parnassus . . . a monstrosity that can be classed in no geological age, nor Pliocene, nor Miocene; but in one only, of which he is the sole relic, and which by analogy to these we might term conveniently the *Obscene*." [7] Even Edmund C. Stedman's tolerant critique of Whitman's physical and sexual gospel deplored the poet's failure to "do it in a clean way" rather than lugging his preachments onto the "highway" and among the masses where, the banker-critic declared, they do not belong. [8]

Many persons, of course, sympathized with Whitman's intent. William Michael Rossetti demonstrated an understanding of the poet's creed of complete selfhood when he explained Whitman's poems to the British public, in 1866, as "the paean of the natural man—not of the merely physical, still less of the disjunctively intellectual or spiritual man, but of him, who being a man first and foremost, is therein also a spirit and an intellect." [9] The Irish critic Thomas Rolleston described Whitman's poems as exerting a "*physiological* influence" and declared that Whitman demands that great American poetry "make its existence perceived in the bodily as well as in the spiritual life of its readers." (Whitman was "tickled" by Rolleston's remarks, declaring that "I have al-

ways made much of the physiological: I never want it to be ne-
glected, flouted, made light of: I remain in touch with the earth no
matter how high I soar.") [10] Colonel Robert Ingersoll, the famed
orator, championed the liberating power of Whitman's physiological teachings, especially the doctrine that bodily well-being
is consistent with moral virtue. Whitman, said Ingersoll, "announced the gospel of the body. He confronted the people. He denied the depravity of man. He insisted that love is not a crime; that
men and women should be proudly natural; that they need not
grovel on the earth and cover their faces for shame. He taught the
dignity and glory of the father and the mother; the sacredness of
maternity." [11]

Likewise, the Cuban poet and revolutionary José Martí, un-
tinged by the Calvinistic tradition, accused Americans of failing to
recognize Whitman as the advocate of a full and balanced human
development and proclaimed him to be a specimen of noble manhood who ought to be emulated by "their faded, domesticated and
dwarfed species." Extolling Whitman above the "rachitic poets
. . . the literary and philosophical mannequins" of the day, Martí
asserted that Whitman "sees the world as a gigantic bed and for
him the bed is an altar. . . . One of the sources of his originality is
the herculean strength with which he wrestles with ideas as though
to violate them, when he actually desires to give them a kiss with
saintly passion. Another source is the earthy, brutal and corporeal
form in which he expresses his most delicate ideals." [12] In depicting
Whitman as a muscular and sensuous faun capable of uttering solemn truths, Martí laid bare the paradox that tantalized the poet's
hostile critics. A merely bumptious or coarse Whitman they could
have ignored or ridiculed, but confronted by his moving revelations of the sensual elements that are intertwined in everyone's
spiritual promptings, they branded him a threat to their moral
code.

Indeed, the very themes which Whitman transmuted into
poetry—the interdependence of body and soul, the linking of
physical health and artistic greatness, the excitement inherent in
physiological phenomena—were also articulated by some of his
contemporaries. Thus, the English spiritualist George Moore, in a
work the poet had read, cautioned that "if we would avoid injuring the soul, we must treat the body with tenderness and wisdom"
and postulated (like Whitman) that each person receives identity

through his body and is endowed with a benevolent soul that is entrusted with the well-being of the body just as the body is entrusted with the well-being of the soul. In the harmony of body and soul, Moore (like Whitman) found the secret of human fulfillment.[13]

Similarly, Bronson Alcott believed that man finds his place in the divine scheme in the context of his body, through which "the infinitude [doth] shadow forth itself, God in all and all in God." Alcott declared: "The study of the [body's] organs and functions is none other than the study of the Spirit incarnate." And in 1848, when Whitman was already dreaming of becoming a poet, Alcott remarked that American poetry must learn to revere the human organism. "The human body is itself the richest and raciest phrasebook," he said, "and it is at once a proof of the shallowness and indelicacy of our American authors that our rhetoric is so seldom drawn from this armory, and our speech partakes so little of the blood-warmth and flesh-colors of nature."[14] This comment resembles Whitman's contention that great literature "returns to the human body, male or female—[and] that that is the most perfect composition, and shall be best-belovd [sic] by men and women and shall last the longest, which slights no part of the body, and rejects no part of the body." The poet proclaimed: "If perfect health appear in a poem, or any book, it propagates itself a great while. Show health and native qualities and you are welcome to all the rest."[15]

Also paralleling Whitman's physiological views, Henry Ward Beecher—whose words Whitman was fond of quoting—instructed his congregation that the animal passions are not to be "maimed" but to be "trained, guided, restrained . . . for they are the soil in which we were planted." He compared the human being to an oak, whose "earth-buried root" is not scorned by the highest leaf on the tree, for "the top will famish if the root is hungry." To the young men, Beecher asserted that the "foundation of all earthly happiness is physical health. . . . There are many troubles which you cannot cure by the Bible and Hymn Book, but which you can cure by a good perspiration and a breath of fresh air." In a Whitmanesque vein, he said: "Whatever tends to give you a robust and developed physical system is in favor of virtue and against vice, other things being equal." But, like Whitman, he warned that the healthy body is merely one element in man's total development, because "the end of our existence here is that we may be more God-like; and we know we shall become so by being more manly in the world, and that we are placed here to grow strong and noble, not merely to enjoy."[16]

Even the concept that poets should be prime physical specimens was familiar to Whitman's generation. Thus, one year before *Leaves of Grass* first appeared, the English social scientist George R. Drysdale attacked the abstemious and sickly creators of Victorian literature, arguing that health, serenity, vigor, and the "natural tastes and enjoyment of life, which are the characteristics of a healthy and equally balanced mind," are prerequisites for the "healthy writer or thinker. If the body is feeble, puny, and prone to disordered sensations, and if there be not a keen relish for the pleasures of the senses, such as proceeds from healthy and well-exercised organs, his mind will, to a certainty, be wanting in some of the elements which aid in forming true literary excellence." Like Whitman, Drysdale sounded the call for an author-hero who could mediate between the flesh and the intellect and bring "to bear on the problems of life a brain equally trained in spiritual and bodily experience; educated equally in the phenomena of the mental and material universe; unstirred by unhappy party distinctions between spiritualism and materialism, seeking instruction on all parts and sides of nature; omitting equal reverence to none. . . ."[17]

In the light of these popular ideas, Whitman's proclamation in the 1855 preface to *Leaves of Grass* that such a poet-hero had finally arrived on the literary scene seems wholly appropriate.

Whitman consistently related the physical side of human nature to the total creative personality. His 1855 preface presented him as the "equable man" who "supplies what wants supplying and checks what wants checking" and who brings the people health, courage, faith, and a respect for natural forms and models. Arguing the vital interaction between art and genetics, he declared that "exaggerations [perpetrated by artists] will be revenged in human physiology. Clean and vigorous children are jetted and conceived only those communities where the models of natural form are public every day." He refused to divorce spiritual principles from physical or behavioral laws; for all actions, he felt, affect every aspect of one's life. "The indirect is just as great and real as the direct," he said. "The spirit receives from the body just as much as it gives to the body." He defined the "prudent" person (who acts in harmony with nature's cosmic and compensatory laws) as one "who has learnt to prefer real longlifed things, and favors body and soul the same. . . ." He demanded that poetry become a force that serves to create great new individuals and provides positive guidelines to self-knowledge, universal love, liberty, and physical naturalness. In judging the value of a poem, he asked: "Will it help breed one goodshaped and wellhung man, and a woman to be his perfect and independent mate? Does it improve manners? Is it for the nursing of the young of the republic? Does it solve reality with the sweet milk of the nipples of the breasts of the mother of many children?" [18]

His 1856 letter to Emerson (in effect the preface to the second edition of *Leaves of Grass*) reasserted that poetry must inspire the creation of great individuals. The letter, whose barbs seem to be aimed at the genteel New England poets, asserted that literature is ineffectual unless it promotes the life-giving powers of health and sexuality. Attacking the laws and customs that rendered the power of sex unmentionable in polite literature, Whitman insisted that "the unabashed development of sex" must be favored in literature as in life. He forecast equality for women only when honesty and frankness in literature are substituted for gallantry and for "this tepid wash, the diluted deferential love, as in songs, fictions, and so forth." Deploring the fact "that the body of a man or woman, the main matter, is so far quite unexpressed in poems," and maintaining that "the body is to be expressed, and sex is," he said that the main challenge to American poets is

> whether they shall celebrate in poems the eternal decency of the amativeness of Nature, the motherhood of all, or whether they shall be the bards of the fashionable delusion of the inherent nastiness of sex, and of the feeble and querulous modesty of deprivation. This is important in poems, because the whole of the other expressions of a nation are but flanges out of its great poems. To me, henceforth, that theory of any thing, no matter what, stagnates in its vitals, cowardly and rotten, while it cannot publicly accept, and publicly name, with specific words, the thing on which all existence, all souls, all realization, all decency, all health, all that is worth being

Walt Whitman and the Body Beautiful

here for, all of woman and of man, all beauty, all purity, all sweetness, all friendship, all strength, all life, all immortality depend.[19]

Interpreting *Leaves of Grass* to post–Civil War readers in 1867,
John Burroughs described Whitman (in concepts, if not words,
that are the poet's own) as one whose writings create "a modern,
democratic, archetypal" American hero who filters the cosmic
laws through his body and his senses. And acknowledging that the
apparant savagism and "the hirsute, sun-tanned, and aboriginal in
humanity" which the poet glorifies may mislead his readers into
believing that Whitman is essentially crude or narrow-minded,
Burroughs cautioned that "the poet uses these elements only for
checks and balances, and to keep our attention, in the midst of a
highly refined and civilized age, fixed upon the fact that here are
the final sources of our health, our power, our longevity. The need
of the pre-scientific age was knowledge and refinement; the need
of our age is health and sanity, cool heads and good digestion." He
interpreted the poet's declaration that he "will not make a poem,
nor the least part of a poem but has reference to the soul," as the
key to what he called "the curious physiological strain which runs
through the poems," and he declared that Whitman "exalts the
body because in doing so he exalts the soul."[20] The ideal man
whom Whitman celebrates in *Leaves of Grass* is a complete human
being whose "barbaric yawp" signifies the rude animal health
without which humanity is incapable of spiritual self-discovery.
Consistently, the poet equates health with the well-balanced personality. "Perfect health," he says, "is simply the right relation of
man himself, & all his body, by which I mean all that he is, & all its
laws & the play of them, to Nature & its laws & the play of them."
For "perfect health . . . is the last flower and fruitage of civilization & art, & of the best education." Health, he avers, is "the inlet
& outlet of every good."[21] It is this consummating physical quality that he projects in his own poetic self-image and that he demands for his countrymen and countrywomen. His moving conclusion to *Specimen Days* declares that sound health and the natural
modes of life are essential to achieve creative selfhood and to promote "the whole politics, sanity, religion, and art of the New
World." Admitting that other poets may excel him in many ways,
he asserts proudly that he has introduced into literature "the brawn

and blood of the people, the basic animal element, virility, the pure sexuality, which is as indispensable to literature as its finer elements.[22] Hitherto," he snaps, "the blackguards have had the field to themselves."[23]

His insistence on "the plain and easy voicing" of humanity's animal drives and on the full development of the bodily powers must be seen against the backdrop of what he mockingly called the "delicatesse" of his era. Like some of his contemporaries, he believed that physical improvement was the immediate need of the masses of American men and women, who seemed to be in danger of forsaking their ruggedness while they pursued comforts, gentility, and prosperity. He complained that although manual labor and physical exertion are good for them, Americans go in for upholstered furniture and fancy dress as soon as they make a little money; that American boys and girls try to appear erudite and show a tendency "to dyspepsia, to wear glasses, and look interesting"; and that the nation seems to "breed specially *smart men*" whose cunning is inimical to the "splendid & healthy" American qualities. Nevertheless, he did not advocate physical health as a final and sufficient goal, but as a necessary precondition of the complete selfhood that he called "character."[24] The aim of *Leaves of Grass*, he told a British visitor, "is Character: what I sometimes call Heroism—Heroicism. Some of my friends say it is a sane strong physiology; I hope it is. But physiology is a secondary matter. Not, as in Homer's 'Iliad,' to depict great personalities, or as in Shakespeare's plays, to describe events and passions, but to arouse that something in the reader which we call Character."[25]

Whitman's watchword to those engaged in arguing the relative importance of body and soul seems to have been "hold your horses, hold your horses—don't be too confident that you know the whole story—the kernel, the beginning, the end." His seeming overemphasis on physiology was intended to counterbalance the entrenched power of prudery. Hence, he declared unambiguously: "After the long period in which the other view was upheld—the contempt of the body, the horrible, narrow, filthy, degenerate, poisonous distaste expressed in ascetic religions for the physical man—I confess that even materialism is a relief, like a new day, like sunlight, like beauty—yes, like truth itself." He affirmed the need of "a powerful loyalty to the body—to the body's desires, passions, appetites, all of them, well in rein, but alive, serving the soul, like a faithful steed." But he concluded that there is ultimately much more to the great scheme "than the most superb bodies." [26] Reacting to a Unitarian minister who had exalted the soul above the body, he said: "I do not believe in the body as the end, of course, but as the beginning, or rather, as a necessary item in the combinations of material that go to making a man. The body is the other side of the soul." [27]

Whitman steadfastly maintained a belief in humanity's "ensemble including body and soul." [28] Predicting that the nation is destined "to become a grand Producing Land of nobler Men and Women—of copious races, cheerful, healthy, tolerant, free," his 1872 preface to *Leaves of Grass* insisted that the highest development to which Americans are eligible can only be defined in spiritual terms. A letter to the Danish critic Rudolf Schmidt explained that "sometimes by directions, but oftener by indirections," his poetry seeks to portray "a sound, large, complete physiological, emotional, moral, intellectual & spiritual *Man* . . . & *Woman* also . . . to arouse, brace, dilate, excite to the love & realization of health, friendship, perfection, freedom, amplitude." In the same vein, he told the Irish author Edward Dowden that the poems "seek to typify a living Human Personality, immensely animal, with immense passions, immense amativeness, immense adhesiveness—in the woman immense maternity—& then, in both, immenser far, a *moral conscience*, & in always realizing the direct & indirect control of the divine laws through all and over all forever." [29]

His prose preface to the 1876 *Leaves of Grass* explained that the "brawn" which suffuses the poems is "thoroughly spiritualized everywhere" and "that LEAVES OF GRASS entire is not to be construed as an intellectual or scholastic effort or Poem mainly, but more as a radical utterance out of the abysms of the Soul, the Emotions and the Physique—an utterance adjusted to, perhaps born of, Democracy and Modern Science, and in its very nature regardless of the old conventions, and, under the great Laws, following its own impulses." The purpose of the poems is to drive home the truth that these "great Laws" govern the development of personalities and that the triumph of any man is that he fills his proper sphere, "preserves his physique, ascends, developing, radiating himself in other regions," and succeeds in elevating his self-consciousness and spirituality to the divine "Yourself." Whitman recapitulated: "To sing the Song of that divine law of Identity, and of Yourself, consistently, with the Divine Law of the Universal, is the main intention of those LEAVES." [30]

His last preface, "A Backward Glance O'er Travel'd Roads" (1888), repeated the claim that his masterpiece "is avowedly the song of Sex and Amativeness, and even Animality," but he cautioned once again that these themes have been "lifted into a different light and atmosphere." The depiction of man's physical nature in the poems, Whitman said, gives the "breath of life to my whole scheme"; without it the total meaning could not converge. "The vitality of it is altogether in its relations, bearings, significance—like a clef in a symphony. At last analogy the lines I allude to, and the spirit in which they are spoken, permeate all 'Leaves of Grass,' and the work must stand or fall with them, as the human body and soul must remain an entirety." [31]

From the start of his poetic career to his last backward glance, Whitman rejected the dualism of body and soul that had been ingrained in American religious and secular thought. For him the body cannot be vile, for it is the sensuous link to the world of experience; it *is* the world of experience. It is the only context in which we may understand the world, apprehend the truth, or achieve a state of higher consciousness. This attitude toward the body permitted Whitman to identify with all that is earthy and to translate all promptings and spiritual correspondences into a sensuous, emotion-charged poetic language. The exploration of *Leaves of Grass* as a work of art and as a spring-source of modern poetry must begin with Whitman's treatment of the human body.

Notes

ABBREVIATIONS

Am Ph J	*American Phrenological Journal* (title varies).
Barrus	Clara Barrus, *Whitman and Burroughs: Comrades* (Boston and New York, 1931).
B D Eagle	*Brooklyn Daily Eagle*.
B D Times	*Brooklyn Daily Times*.
"Book-Reviews"	Thomas Brasher, "Whitman's Book-Reviews in *The Brooklyn Eagle*, 1846–48" (M.A. thesis, Hardin-Simmons University, 1951).
Bucke	Richard M. Bucke, *Walt Whitman* (1883; reprint New York and London, 1970).
Corr.	*The Correspondence of Walt Whitman*, ed. Edwin H. Miller (New York, 1961–64, 1977), 6 vols.*
CW	*The Complete Writings of Walt Whitman*, ed. Richard M. Bucke, Thomas B. Harned, and Horace L. Traubel (New York and London, 1902), 10 vols.
DV	*Prose Works 1892*, vol. 2, *Democratic Vistas*, ed. Floyd Stovall (New York, 1964).*
EPF	*The Early Poems and the Fiction*, ed. Thomas L. Brasher (New York, 1963).*
In Re W W	*In Re Walt Whitman*, ed. Richard M. Bucke, Thomas B. Harned, and Horace L. Traubel (Philadelphia, 1893).
ISL	*I Sit and Look Out: Editorials from the Brooklyn Daily Times*, ed. Emory Holloway and Vernolian Schwarz (New York, 1932).

*Part of the New York University edition, *The Collected Writings of Walt Whitman*, ed. Gay Wilson Allen and Sculley Bradley (New York, 1961–).

LC	*Walt Whitman: A Catalog Based upon the Collection of the Library of Congress* (Washington, 1955). Bibliographical references identify elements of the collection.
LG	*Leaves of Grass: Comprehensive Reader's Edition*, ed. Harold W. Blodgett and Sculley Bradley (New York, 1965).*
LG1855	*Leaves of Grass* (Brooklyn, 1855; facsimile eds., New York: The Eakins Press, 1966, and San Francisco: Chandler Publishing Co., 1968).
LG1856	*Leaves of Grass* (Brooklyn, 1856).
LG1860	*Leaves of Grass* (Boston, 1860; facsimile ed., Ithaca, N.Y.: Cornell University Press, 1961).
LG Inc	*Leaves of Grass (Inclusive Edition)*, ed. Emory Holloway (New York, 1925).
Lowenfels	*Walt Whitman's Civil War*, ed. Walter Lowenfels (New York, 1960).
Memoranda	*Walt Whitman's Memoranda During the War [&] Death of Abraham Lincoln*, ed. Roy P. Basler (Bloomington, Ind., 1962).
N&F	*Notes and Fragments, Left by Walt Whitman*, ed. Richard M. Bucke (London, Ont., 1899).
NYD	*New York Dissected*, ed. Emory Holloway and Ralph Adimari (New York, 1936).
PW1892	*Prose Works, 1892*, ed. Floyd Stovall (New York, 1964), 2 vols.*
Rubin	Joseph Jay Rubin, *The Historic Whitman* (University Park, Pa., and London, 1973).
SD	*Prose Works, 1892*, vol. 1: *Specimen Days*, ed. Floyd Stovall (New York, 1964).*
SS	Gay Wilson Allen, *The Solitary Singer: A Critical Biography of Walt Whitman* (New York, 1955).
Trent	*A Bibliography of Walt Whitman: Being the Catalog of the Trent Collection of the Duke University*, ed. Ellen Frances Frey (1945; reprint Port Washington, N.Y., 1965). Bibliographical references generally identify items in the collection.
UPP	*The Uncollected Poetry and Prose of Walt Whitman*, ed. Emory Holloway (Garden City, N.Y., 1921), 2 vols.
W-Eagle	Thomas L. Brasher, *Whitman as Editor of the Brooklyn Daily Eagle* (Detroit, 1970).
W W Civ War	*Walt Whitman and the Civil War*, ed. Charles I. Glicksberg (1933; reprint New York, 1963).
WWWC	Horace L. Traubel, *With Walt Whitman in Camden*, 5 vols.: I (Boston, 1906); II (New York, 1908); III (New York, 1914;

I-III reprinted New York, 1961); IV, ed. Sculley Bradley (Philadelphia, 1953); V, ed. Gertrude Traubel (Carbondale, Ill., 1964).
WWR   *Walt Whitman Review*

Chapter 1. "A Perfect and Enamour'd Body"

1. The quoted phrase occurs in Ramon Guthrie, "Coda," *The Asbestos Phoenix* (New York, 1968), p. 57.
2. *WWWC*, II:234.
3. *W, Poems by Walt Whitman*, ed. William Michael Rossetti (London, 1868), pp. 6, 8.
4. Compare *LG1860*, 5, and *LG*, 15; *LG1860*, 364, and *LG*, 126; *LG*, 525, and *LG*, 1.
5. *B D Times*, September 29, 1855, in Bucke, 195–96 (bracketed date in Bucke's text).
6. *LG*, 26.
7. W underlined this definition in a magazine clipping on the subject of massage (*LC*, Item no. 81). W reviewed Erasmus Wilson, *A Treatise on Healthy Skin*, 1847 ("Book-Reviews," 156n.). On the pseudophysiology of redness, see Orson S. Fowler, *Self-Instructor in Phrenology and Physiology* (New York, 1859), p. 62.
8. *LG*, 495; see also *LG*, 466.
9. "Walt Whitman and His Poems," *United States Review*, reprinted in *In Re W W*, 15–21; review of *Maud and Other Poems* and *LG* in *Am Ph J*, October, 1855, reprinted in *LG1856*, 369–73; and Milton Hindus, ed., *Walt Whitman: The Critical Heritage* (New York, 1971), pp. 41–45.
10. Frances Wright D'Arusmont, *A Few Days in Athens* (1822; reprint Boston, 1869), p. 22 and *passim*. On W's Epicurus, see *LG*, 649.
11. *W, Manuscripts, Autograph Letters, First Editions and Portraits of Walt Whitman* . . . (New York: American Art Association / Anderson Galleries, Inc., 1936), p. 26.
12. *NYD*, 130.
13. Rubin, 259–67; Charles E. Feinberg, "A Whitman Collector Destroys a Whitman Myth," *Papers of the Bibliographical Society of America* 52 (1958):73–92; Charles E. Feinberg, *An Exhibition of the Works of Walt Whitman* (Detroit, 1955), pp. 3–4. See also Bucke, 24; Odell Shepard, ed., *The Journals of Bronson Alcott* (Boston, 1938), p. 290; Bliss Perry, *Walt Whitman: His Life and Work* (New York, 1906), pp. 55–56; Isaac Hull Platt, *Walt Whitman* (Boston, 1907), p. 36.
14. Barrus, 339; Thomas Donaldson, *Walt Whitman, the Man* (New York, 1896), p. 201.
15. John Burroughs, *Notes on Walt Whitman as Poet and Person* (1867; reprint New York, 1971). Gay Wilson Allen terms the book "a collaboration, for parts of it were actually written by Whitman himself, and he freely edited the whole manuscript" (*The New Walt Whitman Handbook* [New York, 1975], p. 5).
16. John Burroughs, *Walt Whitman: A Study* (Boston, 1896), pp. 40–41. Compare similar passages in "My Preparation for Visits," in *SD*, 51–52; Bucke, 39.
17. Burroughs, *Notes on Walt Whitman*, pp. 13–14.
18. Bucke, 55–56, 127.

19. William O'Connor, *Three Tales* (Boston and New York, 1891), pp. 257, 301, 304. See also *SS*, 364; Bucke, 99, 103.
20. *LG*, 748.
21. John Burroughs, "Walt Whitman and His 'Drum-Taps,'" *The Galaxy* 2 (1866):608–609; Burroughs, *Notes on Walt Whitman*, p. 31.
22. Douglas Grant, *Whitman and His English Admirers* (Leeds, 1962), p. 10. For typical exaggerations of W's cleanliness, see Platt, *Walt Whitman*, p. 76; Alma Calder Johnston, "Personal Memories of Walt Whitman," *The Bookman* 46 (1917):409; Barbara Marinacci, *O Wondrous Singer! An Introduction to Walt Whitman* (New York, 1970), p. 326.
23. W reviewed Irving's biography: *W-Eagle*, 131n. See *Walden*, ch. 18 ("Conclusion"). For Alcott's remarks, see *WWWC*, III:243–44. See also Martin K. Doudna, "The Atlantic Cable in Whitman's 'Passage to India,'" *WWR* 23 (1977):50–52.
24. *LG*, 414–18. On "Ulysses," see *N&F*, 115; Herbert H. Gilchrist, *Anne Gilchrist: Her Work and Writings* (London, 1887), p. 232.
25. *LG*, 421–23; *SS*, 452, 458–59.
26. John Johnston and J. W. Wallace, *Visits to Walt Whitman in 1890–1891 by Two Lancashire Friends* (New York, 1918), p. 127.
27. Quentin Anderson, introduction to *Walt Whitman's Autograph Revision of the Analysis of Leaves of Grass* (New York, 1974), p. 29.
28. *WWWC*, III:582.
29. Florence B. Freedman, "New Light on an Old Quarrel: Walt Whitman and William Douglas O'Connor—1872," *WWR* 11 (1965):49.
30. Clara Barrus, ed., *The Heart of Burroughs's Journals* (Boston and New York, 1928), p. 69; see also John Burroughs, "The Flight of the Eagle," in *The Complete Writings* (New York, 1924), VI:188–90; John Burroughs, "A Poet of Great Physique," *The Critic* 22 (June 3, 1893):372.
31. William Sloane Kennedy, *Reminiscences of Walt Whitman* (London, 1896), pp. 1, 3, 109; Sadakichi Hartmann, *Conversations with Walt Whitman* (New York, 1895), p. 9.
32. Harold Jaffe, "Bucke's *Walt Whitman*: A Collaboration," *WWR* 15 (1969): 190–94.
33. *LG*, 549, 580–81, 508–509, 513.
34. Bucke, 47–49; Richard M. Bucke, *Cosmic Consciousness: A Study of the Human Mind* (1901; reprint New York, 1940), pp. 61, 216–18, 225. See also Frederick W. Conner, *Cosmic Optimism: A Study of the Interpretation of Evolution by American Poets* (Gainesville, Fla., 1949), pp. 65–66.
35. *SD*, 9–10; *WWWC*, IV:501; Bucke, 18.
36. John Bovee Dods, *The Philosophy of Electrical Psychology* (1850; reprint New York, 1885), p. 246; *LG1860*, 233. According to Charles Knowlton, *Fruits of Philosophy* (1831; reprint Mt. Vernon, N.Y., 1937), p. 18, "boys commonly resemble their mother, and girls their father, and . . . men of great talents generally descend from mothers of superior organization."
37. *SD*, 3–4; Burroughs, *Notes on Walt Whitman*, p. 79; Bucke, 15; Johnston and Wallace, *Visits to Walt Whitman*, p. 135. On W's ancestry, see also *SS*, 15, 595.
38. Orson S. Fowler, *Hereditary Descent* (New York, 1843), pp. 168–69. W gutted his copy of the book to cover a scrapbook on manly training (*LC*, Item no. 81). See also "Notes . . . on Elias Hicks," in *PW1892*, 626–53.
39. Louis J. Bragman, "Walt Whitman, Hospital Attendant and Medical Critic,"

Medical Life 39 (1932):611; Anderson, *Walt Whitman's Autograph Revision*, p. 30; Josiah C. Trent, "Walt Whitman—A Case History," *Surgery, Gynecology, Obstetrics* 87 (July, 1948):114; Philip Marshall Dale, *Medical Biographies* (Norman, Okla., 1952), p. 205.

40. Dale, *Medical Biographies*, p. 199. For a photograph of Jeff, see *WWR* 13 (1967):36.

41. Bucke, 15; *SS*, 145; Ellen M. Calder, "Personal Recollections of Walt Whitman," *Atlantic Monthly* 99 (1907):828.

42. *EPF*, 86; *LG*, 365, 444–45; *LG1855*, 74.

43. Trent, "Walt Whitman—A Case History," pp. 113–21; Katherine Molinoff, *Some Notes on Whitman's Family* (New York, 1941 [monograph]); Harold D. Barnshaw, "Walt Whitman's Physicians in Camden," *Transactions and Studies of the College of Physicians of Philadelphia* 31 (January, 1964):229–30; Dale, *Medical Biographies*, p. 203; *WWWC* IV:473–74; V:450. See also *SS*, 8; *Corr.*, IV:293; Barrus, 82–83.

44. Dale, *Medical Biographies*, p. 203.

45. Rubin, 256; Perry, *Walt Whitman*, pp. 19–20; *In Re W W*, 34–36.

46. Clarence Gohdes and Rollo G. Silver, eds., *Faint Clews & Indirections: Manuscripts of Walt Whitman and His Family* (Durham, N.C., 1949), pp. 222–23, 227. On W's explosive temper, see also William Sloane Kennedy, *The Fight of a Book for the World* (West Yarmouth, Mass., 1926), pp. 111–12; Johnston and Wallace, *Visits to Walt Whitman*, p. 129; *SS*, 480.

47. *WWWC*, I:55; IV:93, 378–79; Burroughs, *Notes on Walt Whitman*, p. 81. W was apparently recalling the opening sentence of Carlyle's essay "Characteristics."

48. *LG1855*, 92.

49. Platt, *Walt Whitman*, pp. 8–10; Bertha H. Funnell, *Walt Whitman on Long Island* (New York and London, 1971), p. 58; *In Re W W*, 34–36; *CW*, IX:200.

50. Roger Asselineau, *The Evolution of Walt Whitman: The Creation of a Personality* (Cambridge, Mass., 1960), p. 26; Joseph Jay Rubin and Charles H. Brown, eds., *Walt Whitman of the New York Aurora* (State College, Pa., 1950).

51. *Leaves of Grass: Selected and with an Introduction by Christopher Morley* (New York, 1940), p. *v*. Morley gives the amount of the policy as $2,500; Rubin, 154, gives it as $500. Walt's photograph is reproduced in *Specimen Days*, ed. Lance Hidy (Boston: David Godine, 1971), p. 130; the volume provides a fine photographic record of W.

52. Rubin, 154, 223–24; *ISL*, 5; "Book-Reviews," 7–9.

53. *WWWC*, II:559.

54. L. N. Fowler, "Phrenological Description of W. [. . .] Whitman"; see *Trent*, 66–67; Gohdes and Silver, eds., *Faint Clews & Indirections*, pp. 233–36.

55. *In Re W W*, 39; *WWWC*, IV:223–24; *ISL*, 106–108.

56. *WWWC*, IV:223–24; V:467; Burroughs, "Walt Whitman and His 'Drum-Taps,'" p. 606; *PW1892*, 612; *Corr.*, V:215.

57. *NYD*, 125; *LG*, 178.

58. *UPP*, I:248–49; *B D Eagle*, June 10, 1846; Rubin, 111, 228; Feinberg, "A Whitman Collector," p. 84.

59. *WWWC*, II:21.

60. Grace Gilchrist, "Chats With Walt Whitman," *Temple Bar Magazine* 103 (February, 1898):207–208; *LG*, 478.

61. *NYD*, 147.

62. Walter Harding and Carl Bode, eds., *The Correspondence of Henry David*

Thoreau (New York, 1958), pp. 441–45; Shepard, *Journals of Bronson Alcott*, pp. 286–87; Richard Herrnstadt, ed., *The Letters of A. Bronson Alcott* (Ames, Iowa, 1969), p. 229.

63. Moncure Daniel Conway, *Autobiography: Memoirs and Experiences* (Boston and New York, 1904), I:215–19; Kennedy, *Reminiscences of Walt Whitman*, pp. 71–72; Bucke, 49. W. warns that Conway "romances" about him (*WWWC*, III:16).

64. *LG*, 733; *LG1860*, 224 (italics mine).

65. Bucke, 28; Kennedy, *Fight of a Book for the World*, p. 15; Howells, *Literary Friends and Acquaintance* (New York and London, 1902), p. 74; Winter, *Old Friends: Some Literary Recollections of Other Days* (New York, 1909), pp. 50, 84–91, 114; Higginson, *Cheerful Yesterdays* (Boston and New York, 1898), pp. 230–31.

66. Dale, *Medical Biographies*, pp. 201–202.

67. Perry, *Walt Whitman*, p. 133n.; *WWWC*, III:204.

68. Barrus, 4, 15, 17.

69. Burroughs, *Walt Whitman: A Study*, p. 58. W's military pass describes him as six feet tall, ruddy, and stout (Lowenfels, 307–308).

70. Donaldson, *Walt Whitman, the Man*, pp. 20–21; Bucke, 28. W was fascinated by the character as revealed in the walk (*LC*, Item no. 81; *N&F*, 206; *Trent*, 67).

71. Calder, "Personal Recollections of Walt Whitman," pp. 827, 831–32.

72. *WWWC*, IV:260–61.

73. Dale, *Medical Biographies*, p. 202.

74. *Corr.*, I:254; Dale, *Medical Biographies*, p. 202.

75. *SS*, 449.

76. Burroughs, "Flight of the Eagle," p. 189. The passage is in W's handwriting (Barrus, 161).

77. Charles E. Feinberg, "Walt Whitman and His Doctors," *Archives of Internal Medicine* 114 (1964):835, 840.

78. *Corr.*, II:192–224; *WWWC*, IV:332; III:208; Feinberg, "Walt Whitman and His Doctors," pp. 836–37; Trent, "Walt Whitman—A Case History," pp. 115–16; *SS*, 447–48. On Dr. Drinkard, see C. H. A. Kleinschmidt, "Death of Dr. Wm B. Drinkard," *Medical Society of the District of Columbia Transactions* 4 (1877):64–75; Samuel C. Busey, *Personal Reminiscences and Recollections* (Washington, D.C., 1895), pp. 183–86.

   On W and massage, see "Notes on Manly Training" (manuscript, Feinberg Collection); *WWWC*, III:52–53, 348; IV:387; *Corr.*, V:52; *SD*, 151, 168; Bert A. Thompson, "Edward Wilkins: Male Nurse to Walt Whitman," *WWR* 15 (1969):194–96. Emil Kleen, *Handbook of Massage* (Philadelphia, 1892), pp. 57, 277–78, and *passim*, describes Dr. S. Weir Mitchell's massage therapy and prescribes massage treatment for neurasthenia, constipation, melancholia, and as a substitute for daily exercise.

79. Feinberg, "Walt Whitman and His Doctors," pp. 836–37.

80. *SD*, 119.

81. *Corr.*, II:240, 389; III:312; Trent, "Walt Whitman—A Case History," p. 116; Feinberg, "Walt Whitman and His Doctors," p. 837.

   W implied that more than one Philadelphia doctor used the battery on him. See *Corr.*, II:211, 215; *WWWC*, V:53. Harold D. Barnshaw, "Walt Whitman's Medical Problems While in Camden," *Academy of Medicine in New Jersey Bulletin* 16 (December, 1970):35.

82. Barnshaw, "Walt Whitman's Physicians in Camden," p. 227.

83. *SD*, 118–20, 143, 150.
84. *LG*, 744.
85. Edward Carpenter, *Days with Walt Whitman* (London, 1906), pp. 4–9; Gilchrist, "Chats With Walt Whitman," p. 201.
86. Barrus, 146.
87. *Memoranda*, 30, 34 (introduction); Donaldson, *Walt Whitman, the Man*, pp. 36–42.
88. *SD*, 291.
89. *Corr.*, III:288–89, 311n.; Trent, "Walt Whitman—A Case History," p. 116. On Dr. Benjamin, see George R. Prowell, *The History of Camden County* (Philadelphia, 1886), p. 292. L. B. Godfrey, *History of the Medical Profession of Camden County, N.J.* (Philadelphia, 1896), logs the public activities of all Camden doctors known to have attended W.
90. Henry Cushing, *The Life of Sir William Osler* (New York, 1940), p. 265; *Corr.*, III:406n.
91. *WWWC*, II:415–16; William White, "Walt Whitman and Sir William Osler," *American Literature* 11 (1939):73–77; William White, "Walt Whitman on Osler: 'He Is a Great Man,'" *Bulletin of the History of Medicine* 15 (January, 1944):79–90; Feinberg, "Walt Whitman and His Doctors," pp. 838–40.
92. *Corr.*, IV:80.
93. *Corr.*, IV:225, 243, 269, 276; *WWWC*, I:446; III:240; Barrus, 277–78. On Dr. Wharton, see also J. H. H., "Henry R. Wharton . . .," *Transactions of the American Surgical Association* 44 (1926):590–93.
94. C. Carroll Hollis, "The Correspondence, Vols. IV and V," *WWR* 26 (1970):93.
95. *WWWC*, II:398; Horace L. Traubel, "Walt Whitman at Date," in *In Re W W*, 129.
96. *WWWC*, III:194.
97. *PW1892*, 684–85.
98. *LG*, 510, 534, 546, 556; Kennedy, *Reminiscences of Walt Whitman*, p. 4.
99. *Corr.*, V:259 (italics in original).
100. Trent, "Walt Whitman—A Case History," pp. 119–20. Dr. Trent conjectured that W's pink body and presumably homosexual temperament indicated possible eunuchoidism, the syndrome produced by an androgen deficiency.

Chapter 2. "I Am He Bringing Help for the Sick"

1. Grace Gilchrist, "Chats With Walt Whitman," *Temple Bar Magazine* 103 (February, 1898):210.
2. Charles E. Feinberg, "Walt Whitman and His Doctors," *Archives of Internal Medicine* 114 (1964):834; Daniel Longaker, "Last Sickness and Death of Walt Whitman," in *In Re W W*, 397.
3. Richard Maurice Bucke, "Leaves of Grass and Medical Science," in *In Re W W*, 250.
4. Samuel C. Busey, *Personal Reminiscences and Recollections* (Washington, D.C., 1895), p. 334. For a similar opinion, see Edward H. Dixon, *Back-Bone, Photographed from the "Scalpel"* (New York, 1866), p. 116.
5. Russell Thacher Trall, *The Hydropathic Encyclopedia: A System of Hydropathy and Hygiene* (New York, 1853), I:35; II:174. The "cold effusion practice" refers to the induced seepage of serous or purulent fluids.
6. Dixon, *Back-Bone*, pp. 94–95, 116. Bleeding was supposed to deny oxygen

to diseased matter in the blood, thus aiding the victim's recovery from disease (Justus Liebig, *Animal Chemistry, Or Organic Chemistry in Its Application to Physiology and Pathology* [1842; reprint New York, 1964], p. 247).

7. John M. Galt, *The Treatment of Insanity* (New York, 1846), pp. 120, 325, and *passim*; *UPP*, I: 128n.; *W-Eagle*, 74. W believed that insanity can be alleviated through a healthful regimen; see "An Asylum for Idiots," *B D Eagle*, May 12, 1846; *W-Eagle*, 170; Rubin, 289–91; "Causes of Insanity," *B D Times*, May 16, 1859.

8. Richard H. Shryock, *Medicine in America: Historical Essays* (Baltimore, 1966), pp. 16, 21, 90–110.

9. Oliver Wendell Holmes, *Medical Essays, 1842–1882* (Boston, 1889), pp. 203, 231–38.

10. James J. Walsh, *History of Medicine in New York* (New York, 1919), V: 331. On medical practice at mid-century, see also Stephen Smith, "The Comparative Results of Operations in Bellevue Hospital," in *Medical America in the Nineteenth Century: Readings from the Literature*, ed. Gert H. Brieger (Baltimore and London, 1972), pp. 201–209.

11. "The Art of Health," in *The Gathering of the Forces*, ed. Cleveland Rodgers and John Black (New York and London, 1920), II: 199–200; *W-Eagle*, 248–49, 182–86.

12. "Which 'Pathy Will You Have?" *B D Times*, June 19, 1858. See also *B D Eagle*, April 10, 1846. Francois Magendie, a famed surgeon, opposed needless surgical operations.

13. *W-Eagle*, 184.

14. On deviant movements in medicine, see esp. Joseph F. Kett, *The Formation of the American Medical Profession: The Role of Institutions* (New Haven, 1968), pp. 100–64; Martin Kaufman, *Homeopathy in America: The Rise and Fall of a Medical Heresy* (Baltimore, 1971), pp. 19–26; Richard H. Shryock, *Medicine and Society in America, 1660–1860* (New York, 1960), 120–24.

15. Kaufman, *Homeopathy in America*, pp. 25, 45; Dixon, *Back-Bone*, p. 85; Holmes, "Homeopathy and Its Kindred Delusions," *Medical Essays*, p. 53; Kett, *Formation of the American Medical Profession*, pp. 125, 133–39.

16. Dixon, *Back-Bone*, pp. 291–92; *W-Eagle*, 183–84; Kaufman, *Homeopathy in America*, pp. 25–26.

17. *WWWC*, II: 533; *CW*, VII: 55; Parke Godwin, *A Biography of William Cullen Bryant* (New York, 1883), I: 343. See also Charles H. Brown, *William Cullen Bryant* (New York, 1971), pp. 49, 275–76, 388; Walsh, *History of Medicine in New York*, II: 528–38.

18. *WWWC*, III: 384.

19. Kett, *Formation of the American Medical Profession*, pp. 105–107, 122, 125–72; Kaufman, *Homeopathy in America*, pp. 19, 25–26.

20. William Horsell and R. T. Trall, *Hydropathy for the People* (New York, 1851), pp. 230–31; Thomas Low Nichols, *Forty Years of American Life* (London, 1864), II: 21; Harry B. Weiss and Howard R. Kemble, *The Great Water-Cure Craze* (Trenton, N.J., 1967), pp. 25, 61; Shryock, *Medicine in America*, 113–15, 120–23.

21. Catharine E. Beecher, *Physiology and Calisthenics for Schools and Families* (New York, 1856), p. 106; Odell Shepard, ed., *The Journals of Bronson Alcott* (Boston, 1938), pp. 69–71; Fredrika Bremer, *Homes of the New World* (New York, 1853), I: 146–47 [on Alcott]; Edward Bulwer-Lytton, *Confessions of a Water-Cure Patient* (London, 1845), pp. 74, 97–98.

22. *B D Times*, April 23, 1858; *Corr.*, I: 88–89. On Sammis, see also *Corr.*, I: 371; II: 23; Weiss and Kemble, *Great Water-Cure Craze*, p. 145; *Brooklyn*

City Directory and Annual Advertiser for the Year 1848–49 (Brooklyn, 1848), I:198.

23. Madeleine B. Stern, *Heads & Headlines: The Phrenological Fowlers* (Norman, Okla., 1971), pp. 156–63 and *passim*; Frederick Waite, "Dr. Lydia Folger Fowler, the Second Woman to Receive the Degree of Doctor of Medicine in the United States," *Annals of Medicine*, n.s. 4 (1932):290–97; Weiss and Kemble, *Great Water-Cure Craze*, pp. 36–46, 83; Horsell and Trall, *Hydropathy for the People*, pp. 230–31.

24. Trall's obituary, *New York Times*, September 26, 1877; William L. Finkel, "Sources of Walt Whitman's Manuscript Notes on Physique," *American Literature* 22 (1950):326–27; *B D Times*, August 25, 1857.

25. Richard Herrnstadt, ed., *The Letters of A. Bronson Alcott* (Ames, Iowa, 1969), pp. 200–209.

26. *W-Eagle*, 180–81, 248; Rubin, 270–71; "A Plea for Bathing," *B D Eagle*, March 23, 1846, cited in "Book-Reviews," 149. W reviewed the anonymous *Water Cure in America* (*W-Eagle*, 248).

27. "Ablutions," *B D Eagle*, March 24, 1846, cited in "Book-Reviews," 150. Cold-water baths were prescribed to combat mental depression and spermatorrhea (involuntary seminal discharge)—ailments which may have afflicted the author of the classic "wet-dream" poem, "Spontaneous Me"; see Galt, *Treatment of Insanity*, p. 325; Trall, *Hydropathic Encyclopedia*, II:291; Orson S. Fowler, *Amativeness* (New York, 1844), pp. 54–60.

28. *ISL*, 15, 100–104. Clean water and sewage disposal were important reform issues in the 1850's; see Shryock, *Medicine in America*, p. 24; Holmes, *Medical Essays*, p. 259. For some of W's comments on these issues, see *W-Eagle*, 180–81; William Sloane Kennedy, ed., *Walt Whitman's Diary in Canada* (Boston, 1904), pp. 64–65; *UPP*, I:254–55; Rodgers and Black, eds., *Gathering of the Forces*, pp. 201–207.

29. Herman Melville, *Pierre: or, The Ambiguities* (New York, 1957), p. 419.

30. "Hydropathy," *B D Times*, May 21, 1859; *LG*, 157; *LG1855*, 28; *N&F*, 16.

31. Trall, *Hydropathic Encyclopedia*, I:310–11; Edward H. Dixon, *A Treatise on Diseases of the Sexual System* (ca. 1845; reprint New York, 1867), pp. 237–45.

32. *LG*, 130, 95, 480, 15. For more bathing imagery, see *LG*, 122, 181, 419, 422, 496.

33. *UPP*, II:293–94.

34. *SS*, 17; Steven M. Ostrander, *A History of Brooklyn and Kings County* (Brooklyn, 1894), II:32; Ralph Foster Weld, *Brooklyn Village, 1816–1834* (New York, 1938), p. 33.

35. Bucke, 136, 19–20. On W's viewing of medical exhibits, see also *UPP*, II:84.

36. *EPF*, 68–79, 316–17n.

37. *EPF*, 316n.

38. *EPF*, 319–26. On W's interest in handicapped children and his visits to asylums for deaf, dumb, and blind children, see *W-Eagle*, 170–71; Florence B. Freedman, ed., *Walt Whitman Looks at the Schools* (New York, 1950), pp. 112–14, 119–23.

39. Shryock, *Medicine in America*, p. 172. Books that W read by such authors as Frances Wright, Abdiel Abbott Livermore, Henry Ward Beecher, and Horace Greeley were addressed to young men. See *UPP*, I:127–28n.; "Book-Reviews," 141; Freedman, *Walt Whitman Looks at the Schools*, p. 183.

40. *LC*, Item no. 81, consists mainly of notes and clippings from various sources on health and physique.

41. Charles E. Feinberg, "A Whitman Collector Destroys a Whitman Myth,"

Papers of the Bibliographical Society of America 52 (1958):79. See also Rubin, 243.

42. Charles E. Feinberg, *An Exhibition of the Works of Walt Whitman* (Detroit, 1955), p. 7; *N&F*, 176. On W's possible lecture plans in the 1850's and 1860's, see Finkel, "Sources of Walt Whitman's Manuscript Notes on Physique," p. 330; W, *Leaves of Grass Imprints: American and European Criticisms on "Leaves of Grass"* (Boston, 1860), p. 64; Henry Binns, *A Life of Walt Whitman* (1905; reprint New York, 1971), pp. 90–91.

43. W, "1840's? / MANLY TRAINING: notes for a prose series"; "MODEL AMERICAN: ideas for a poem or essay," manuscript fragments in the Feinberg Collection, courtesy of Mr. Charles E. Feinberg. W canceled the bracketed words.

44. New York [State] Division of Archives and History, *Proceedings at the Unveiling of a Memorial to Horace Greeley* (Albany, 1915), p. 203.

45. *W-Eagle*, 180–85.

46. *W-Eagle*, 157–61, 179–87; "Book-Reviews," 146–55; Freedman, *Walt Whitman Looks at the Schools*, pp. 126–27, 245; *B D Eagle*, April 16 and June 4, 1846. The rude diet is prescribed in "A Simpler System of the Table," in *LC*, Item no. 46.

47. *ISL*, 55, 105–106, 193–96, and *passim*; *B D Times*, July 11, 1857, Oct. 18, 1858; Rodgers and Black, *Gathering of the Forces*, II:207–209.

48. *UPP*, II:64.

49. *CW*, VIII:274; the version differs somewhat from *LC*, Item no. 81.

50. Ludovico Cornaro, *The Art of Living Long* (Milwaukee, 1917), pp. 58–59. *LC*, Item no. 81, contains a clipping of a book review of Cornaro's book.

51. *N&F*, 82; for related clippings on old age and longevity, see *Trent*, 67.

52. *PW1892*, 639.

53. Thomas B. Harned, "Walt Whitman and Physique," in *CW*, VIII:261–72; *LC*, Item no. 81. On Whitman's use of manuscript and printed materials, esp. on medical subjects, see Floyd Stovall, *The Foreground of Leaves of Grass* (Charlottesville, Va., 1974), pp. 152–60; Floyd Stovall, "Notes on Whitman's Reading," *American Literature* 26 (1954):337–62; Finkel, "Walt Whitman's Manuscript Notes on Physique," pp. 308–38; "Book-Reviews," 145–63; *UPP*, I:127–30n.

54. *B D Times*, May 7, 1857; September 6, 1858.

55. Horace Traubel, ed., *An American Primer* (Boston, 1904), pp. 4–5, 9, 27–28.

56. *N&F*, 55 (italics in original).

57. *LG1860*, 53; John Burroughs, "The Flight of the Eagle," in *The Complete Writings* (New York, 1924), VI:215–17. On the role of science in *LG*, see Joseph Beaver, *Walt Whitman, Poet of Science* (New York, 1951), pp. 93–99, 131–44.

58. *CW*, X:28; *N&F*, 175; *LG*, 275, 678. W may have considered writing a group of "Health Chants"; see *The Wound-Dresser*, ed. R. M. Bucke (1898; reprint New York, 1949), p. ix.

59. *N&F*, 49.

60. *W-Eagle*, 74.

61. *WWWC*, II:57.

62. *LG1855*, 62.

63. Bucke, 27; James Thomson, *Walt Whitman, the Man and the Poet* (London, 1910), p. 9; *SS*, 201; William Sloane Kennedy, *Reminiscences of Walt Whitman* (London, 1896), pp. 73–74.

64. *LG1860*, 446. In a six-week period, eight hundred cholera victims, mostly

poor immigrants, were admitted to the hospital (Walsh, *History of Medicine in New York*, I:106–10, 173–74; III:826). W was haunted by the memory of this epidemic, pledging to include a description of it in *SD* if he ever revised the volume (*Walt Whitman's Diary in Canada*, p. 64; W, *Daybooks and Notebooks*, ed. William White [New York, 1978], p. 348). W reported the cholera epidemic of 1849 in the *Brooklyn Freeman* (Rubin, 291).

65. Rubin, 231, 342–44.
66. W reported the activities of the institution (*W-Eagle*, 147–48, 169–70). A poorhouse opened there in 1832, a hospital and lunatic asylum in 1839, and a hospital facility at the prison in 1849 (Walsh, *History of Medicine in New York*, III:737). Blackwell's Island, in New York City, where many syphilitics were treated, also combined asylum, prison, and hospital.
67. Dr. Edward H. Dixon alleged that liquor may cause a syphilitic "virus" (*The Scalpel* 12 [1860]:263), a possible reference to chancre of the mouth.
68. *W-Eagle*, 249.
69. *LG1860*, 53.
70. A likely possibility is Dr. John William Draper, physician, scientist, and rationalist historian. W wrote a notice of Draper's *Text-Book on Chemistry* ("Book-Reviews," 136) and apparently read parts of his *Human Physiology*, 1856 (W, *Daybooks and Notebooks*, p. 779). W's reference to a Dr. Draper (*W W Civ War*, 87) could allude to him or to his sons, both prominent physicians.
71. *NYD*, 130, 227; Edward Preble, "John Wakefield Francis," *Dictionary of American Biography*, VI:581; John Wakefield Francis, *Old New York; or, Reminiscences of the Past Sixty Years* (New York, 1865), pp. 300–301, 306–11. See also Dixon, *Back-Bone*, p. 179. The fact that Dr. Dixon was Dr. Francis's son-in-law strengthens the likelihood that Whitman knew him personally.
72. *NYD*, 27–40, 204–207; *CW*, VII:54; *N&F*, 15. On W's interest in Egyptology, see also Rubin, 194–95, 298.
73. Rodgers and Black, eds., *Gathering of the Forces*, II:305–306; *UPP*, I:131. Testimonials in Dixon's volume expressed sentiments like those voiced in W's review; see *Woman and Her Diseases; From the Cradle to the Grave* (1847; reprint New York, 1867), pp. v–viii. On Dixon's career, see *The Scalpel* 2 (1850):211, 337–38; 3 (1851):23–24; 4 (1853):194–97; Edward H. Dixon, *Organic Law of the Sexes: Positive and Negative Electricity* (New York, 1861); Dixon, *Back-Bone*, pp. 48, 179; Martin Kaufman, "Edward H. Dixon and Medical Education in New York," *New York History* 51 (1970):394–409.
74. W, *An 1855–56 Notebook Toward the Second Edition of Leaves of Grass*, ed. Harold W. Blodgett (Carbondale, Ill., 1959), p. 51.
75. *B D Times*, July 11, 1857; February 3, 1858; April 23, 1858.
76. *B D Times*, July 11, 1857; December 12, 1857; February 3, 1858; April 23, 1858.
77. W quotes Dixon's epigraph *B D Times*, July 11, 1857, and April 23, 1858; his reservations are stated in the latter item. On W's praise of Dr. Dixon's forthrightness, see Rubin, 291.
78. *LG*, 342–43, 349, 590, 480; *LG1860*, 141.
79. *LG1860*, 220, 111. Compare the "corpse" imagery in *LG*, 343, 709 [1855 preface].
80. *LG1860*, 129–31, 135, 264, 260.
81. *W-Eagle*, 154–56.
82. *SD*, 156–57; Harold Jaffe, "Bucke's *Walt Whitman*: A Collaboration," *WWR* 15 (1969):192.

83. *B D Times*, July 11, 1857. W wrote skeptically of miasma in *B D Times*, February 3, 1858. See also *W W Civ War*, 38; *N&F*, 28; Kennedy, *Reminiscences of Walt Whitman*, p. 6.

84. Liebig, *Animal Chemistry*, pp. 104, 115; Rubin, 94.

85. "Book-Reviews," 158–59. William Wesselhöft, a noted homeopathic physician, explained that noxious matter, properly diluted, can be used to effect cures; see Elizabeth P. Peabody, *Memorial to Dr. William Wesselhöft* (Boston, 1859), p. 48.

86. *Trent*, opp. p. 6.

87. "On Imagination," in *Selected Writings of Edgar Allan Poe*, ed. David Galloway (Baltimore, 1967), p. 497.

88. Binns, *Life of Walt Whitman*, p. 86; 1 Corinthians 15 (italics mine).

89. *LG*, 368–70 (italics mine). On the same theme, see "Light and Air," *LG*, 652–53.

90. *LG*, 149–59.

91. *LG*, 29–30, 89, 430, 403, 410.

92. Samuel Sheldon Fitch, *Six Lectures on the Uses of the Lungs* (New York, 1847), pp. 37–38. W reviewed this book and Jacob Servoss Ross, *Consumption, a Curable Disease* (New York, 1847), in *B D Eagle*, June 17 and 18, 1847.

93. Russell T. Trall, *Sexual Physiology* (New York, 1871), p. 252.

94. Samuel Tissot, *Remarks on the Disorders of Literary Men* (Boston, 1825), pp. 29–39; Trall, *Hydropathic Encyclopedia*, II:49–50, 75–76; Dixon, *Back-Bone*, pp. 365–69.

95. J. Henry Clark, *Sight and Hearing: How Preserved and How Lost* (New York, 1856); W, *1855–56 Notebook*, pp. 19, 41.

96. *EPF*, 275; *W-Eagle*, 113; *B D Times*, July 28, 1857; *SD*, 150–53.

97. F. O. Matthiessen, *American Renaissance*, (1941; reprint London and New York, 1968), p. 98.

98. *Moby-Dick*, ch. 80.

99. Oliver Wendell Holmes, *The Autocrat of the Breakfast-Table* (Boston and New York, 1891), pp. 174–76.

100. *LG1855*, 77–82; *LG*, 93–101.

101. *Trent*, opp. p. 12; *LG*, 98. On anatomical and art exhibits and the physiques of working men, see also *CW*, X:10, 15; *W-Eagle*, 213; W, *1855–56 Notebook*, p. 13.

102. *LG1860*, 7, 398–99, 403.

103. *LG1860*, 362, 354–55, 349; Richard G. Lillard, *The Great Forest* (New York, 1948), p. 29.

104. *UPP*, II:288–92; *B D Times*, July 11, 1857; *W W Civ War*, 159–60, 169. W's impressions are confirmed in Walsh, *History of Medicine in New York*, III:740–41. See also *SD*, 30; Lowenfels, 105–106; *CW*, VII:122.

105. *B D Times*, April 10, 1858. On these institutions, see Ostrander, *A History of Brooklyn and Kings County*, II:115.

106. The "City Photographs" essays are reprinted in *W W Civ War*, 24–47; the quotations in the text are from this source. The name "Van Velsor Brush" combines the maiden surnames of W's mother and his paternal grandmother.

107. D. B. St. John Roosa, *The Old Hospital and Other Papers* (New York, 1899), pp. 3, 7–8, 12, 259; anonymous, *Society of the New York Hospital* (New York, ca. 1921), pp. 28–30.

108. On the celebrated Dr. Post, see Walsh, *History of Medicine in New York*, IV:11.

109. Roosa, *Old Hospital*, p. 19.

Notes: "I Am He Bringing Help for the Sick"

110. On Dr. Watson, who opened the nation's first skin and venereal disease dispensary, see Walsh, *History of Medicine in New York*, I:214; *The Scalpel* 3 (1851):250.
111. Anonymous, *Society of the New York Hospital*, p. 95; *National Cyclopaedia of American Biography*, VI:390–91.
112. *B D Times*, September 5, 1857; December 11, 1858.
113. *SD*, 18–19; Charles I. Glicksberg, "Walt Whitman in 1862," *American Literature* 6 (1934):273.
114. *SS*, 267–79; Roosa, *Old Hospital*, p. 13; Bliss Perry, *Walt Whitman: His Life and Work* (New York, 1906), pp. 131–32.
115. John Burroughs, *Walt Whitman: A Study* (Boston, 1896), pp. 24–25.
116. Thomas Donaldson, *Walt Whitman, the Man* (New York, 1896), pp. 205–206; the remarks are poorly recalled or poorly transcribed. The eminent Dr. Roosa lived to 1908. A Dr. James Macdonald is mentioned in *W W Civ War*, 37. Dr. Flint may be the younger Austin Flint, later a distinguished doctor.
117. Walsh, *History of Medicine in New York*, I:192, IV:29; *National Cyclopaedia of American Biography*, X:349; *New York Times*, March 9, 1908, p. 7.
118. *W W Civ War*, 20, 44. The procedure was named for the Scottish surgeon James Syme.
119. *W W Civ War*, 30–31; Walsh, *History of Medicine in New York*, V:458–60; *National Cyclopaedia of American Biography*, XI:259; anonymous, *Society of the New York Hospital*, p. 95.
120. *W W Civ War*, 42–43 (italics mine).

Chapter 3. "I Pacify with Soothing Hand"

1. *LG*, 281.
2. Louis J. Bragman, "Walt Whitman, Hospital Attendant and Medical Critic," *Medical Life* 39 (1932):607.
3. *Corr.*, I:69. On this period, see, esp., *SS*, 280–321; *W W Civ War*; *Memoranda*.
4. *CW*, VII:92, 81, cited in *W W Civ War*, 3–4. The "missionary" was named a "Delegate" of the Christian Commission on January 20, 1863; his authorization is reproduced in *Specimen Days*, ed. Lance Hidy (Boston: David Godine, 1971), p. 15. He apparently resigned from the group a few weeks later. W's name does not appear on the roster of the five-thousand-member pietistic organization whose official duties included "Preaching, Business, and Working." See Lemuel Moss, *Annals of the Christian Commission* (Philadelphia, 1869), pp. 142–44, 563, 602–58.
5. *New York Times*, February 26, 1863, cited in Lowenfels, 91.
6. *B D Eagle*, March 19, 1863, cited in Lowenfels, 94.
7. *Corr.*, I:125, 118, 109, 81–82; *WWWC*, I:233.
8. F. De Wolfe Miller, ed., *Walt Whitman's Drum Taps (1865) and Sequel to Drum Taps (1865–66)* (Gainesville, Fla., 1959), p. xxiv; *Memoranda*, 32–33, 36; *Corr.*, I:153; Barrus, 21.
9. Thomas Donaldson, *Walt Whitman, the Man* (New York, 1896), p. 167.
10. *W W Civ War*, 145–48; Lowenfels, 145–47.
11. Charles E. Feinberg, "Walt Whitman and His Doctors," *Archives of Internal Medicine* 114 (1964):834.
12. Donaldson, *Walt Whitman, the Man*, p. 168.
13. *LG*, 352.
14. *Memoranda*, 26–27; *SD*, 65–67.

15. *Memoranda*, 55–56.
16. Lowenfels, 91–92; *Memoranda*, 25–26.
17. *Memoranda*, 37–38.
18. John Johnston and J. W. Wallace, *Visits to Walt Whitman in 1890–1891 by Two Lancashire Friends* (New York, 1918), p. 45.
19. *SD*, 42–43, 155–56; *WWWC*, I:116; Lowenfels, 96–97. W had kind words for some of the young women who enlisted as nurses, but he preferred healthy, unsqueamish matrons for the task; see *SD*, 58, 88; *Memoranda*, 17, 40; Lowenfels, 106.
20. Louisa May Alcott, *Hospital Sketches*, ed. Basil Z. Jones (Cambridge, Mass., 1960), pp. xxv, 63.
21. *Corr.*, I:112, 122, 153, 157, 231, 261; *Memoranda*, 8–9, 38–39; Lowenfels, 111–27.
22. *Memoranda*, 9–10.
23. *W W Civ War*, 92–98; *Corr.*, I:106, 194–95, 207.
24. Ellen M. Calder, "Personal Recollections of Walt Whitman," *Atlantic Monthly* 99 (1907):826; *Memoranda*, 50–51; *Corr.*, I:132. On W and Dr. Bliss, see also *Corr.*, I:94, 106, 154, 259; *SD*, 103; *WWWC*, II:109; *SS*, 290, 312.
25. Donaldson, *Walt Whitman, the Man*, pp. 168–69.
26. On Dr. Bliss, see C. B. Burr, ed., *Medical History of Michigan* (Minneapolis and St. Paul, 1930), I:689, II:492; Samuel C. Busey, *Personal Reminiscences and Recollections* (Washington, D.C., 1895), pp. 270–91; Martin Kaufman, *Homeopathy in America: The Rise and Fall of a Medical Heresy* (Baltimore, 1971), pp. 73, 88–91; *Corr.*, I:91n.
27. Richard H. Shryock, *Medicine in America: Historical Essays* (Baltimore, 1966), p. 107.
28. *Memoranda*, 3, 5; Henry Cushing, *The Life of Sir William Osler* (New York, 1940), p. 1317.
29. Alcott, *Hospital Sketches*, pp. xix, xlv, *passim*; Caroline Ticknor, *Louisa May Alcott: A Memoir* (Boston, 1928), p. 55; Taylor Stoehr, *Hawthorne's Mad Scientists* (Hamden, Conn., 1978), pp. 46–47, 279. In 1863, W tried unsuccessfully to persuade James Redpath, who had published Louisa's book, to bring out his *Memoranda of a Year* (*SS*, 308).
30. *Corr.*, I:68–69.
31. *LG*, 324.
32. Lowenfels, 312.
33. *LG*, 319.
34. *WWWC*, II:66; "Death of Abraham Lincoln," in *Memoranda*, part 3, pp. 12–13.
35. *LG*, 302–303, 306–307, 300–301. *W W Civ War*, 79, has a prose draft of "A Sight in Camp."
36. *LG*, 303–305; *W W Civ War*, 142.
37. *LG*, 317–18; *W W Civ War*, 121–23.
38. *LG*, 305–306; *W W Civ War*, 123–25. The Battle of White Oak (W calls it White Oaks) Church was probably an element of the Battle of Glendale; see Newton A. Strait, comp., *Alphabetical List of Battles, 1754–1900* (1905; reprint Detroit, 1968), p. 138.
39. *Memoranda*, 13–15; a similar statement appears in *SD*, 46–47.
40. *W W Civ War*, 82n.; but he had also read the work in 1859 (*Trent*, 24).
41. *LG*, 308–12.
42. *SD*, 73; Lowenfels, 123.

43. O'Connor, "The Carpenter," in *Three Tales* (Boston and New York, 1892), p. 247. "TO WALK THE HOSPITALS—to attend the medical and surgical practice of hospitals as a student under one of the qualified staff" (John S. Farmer and W. E. Henley, *Slang and Its Analogues* [New York, 1965], p. 287).
44. *Memoranda*, 46; Bragman, "Walt Whitman, Hospital Attendant and Medical Critic," pp. 608–609.
45. Shryock, *Medicine in America*, p. 92.
46. Gangrenous wounds and their treatment were described by Dr. S. Weir Mitchell; see Ernest Earnest, *S. Weir Mitchell, Novelist and Physician* (Philadelphia, 1950), pp. 53–54.
47. *Corr.*, I:157.
48. *LG*, 484; *Memoranda*, 44.
49. *DV*, 369, 382, 385. Earlier versions of the theme appear in "Ashes of Soldiers," *LG*, 490–92; *Memoranda*, 57.
50. *LG*, 202.
51. *LG*, 460, 411–21.
52. *LG*, 149–59, 182, 451.
53. Bucke, 136.
54. *WWWC*, IV:198, 492.
55. *Corr.*, III:88, 105; *SS*, 472, 482. Frank Baker (M.D., 1880), an anthropologist affiliated with the Smithsonian Institution who was called "probably the most erudite physician in Washington," had been a friend of W since 1864. The Bakers named their second child, born in 1875, Mabel Whitman Baker. See Fielding H. Garrison, "In Memoriam Dr. Frank Baker," *New York Medical Journal* 108 (November 16, 1918):855–60; *Dictionary of American Biography*, I:519.
56. *WWWC*, IV:332; III:208. See also chapter 1, note 78.
57. *Corr.*, II:240, 289, 315–16; *SS*, 454; Feinberg, "Walt Whitman and His Doctors," p. 827; Josiah C. Trent, "Walt Whitman—A Case History," *Surgery, Gynecology, Obstetrics* 87 (July, 1948):116. W was interested in the Philadelphia medical scene in the 1870's. He visited the University of Pennsylvania Hospital and made the acquaintance of distinguished physicians including Samuel D. Gross and William S. W. Ruschenberger, a former naval surgeon (W, *Daybooks and Notebooks*, ed. William White [New York, 1978], pp. 23, 31–32, 49–50.)
58. *SS*, 505; L. B. Godfrey, *History of the Medical Profession of Camden County, N.J.* (Philadelphia, 1896), pp. 131–284, *passim*. W presented Dr. Ridge with a complimentary book in 1876; Ridge bought a set of books in 1878 (*Corr.*, VI:xxv; W, *Daybooks and Notebooks*, pp. 31, 81). Dr. George Hendry Shivers, closely associated with this group in the Camden District Medical Society, arranged for W to deliver his Lincoln lecture at Haddonfield, N.J., in 1886.
59. *Corr.*, III:311–12; *WWWC*, III:270; George R. Prowell, *The History of Camden County* (Philadelphia, 1886), p. 292; letters to author from Harold D. Barnshaw, M.D.
60. *WWWC*, III:242, 262, 268–69; IV:373; *Corr.*, IV:245–58; William White, "Walt Whitman on Osler: 'He Is a Great Man,'" *Bulletin of the History of Medicine* 15 (January, 1944):86. Dr. Walsh, president of the Camden City Medical Society in 1885, won a Boylston Prize in 1897 for an essay on the anatomy of the hand.
61. *Corr.*, IV:187–89, 192; V:121–22; Bragman, "Walt Whitman, Hospital Attendant and Medical Critic," p. 614; *Who's Who in America, 1914–15*, p. 121.

62. George M. Stevenson, "The Life and Work of Richard Maurice Bucke," *American Journal of Psychiatry* 93 (March, 1937):1132–50; George Moreby Acklom, introduction to R. M. Bucke, *Cosmic Consciousness* (New York, 1940); Harold Jaffe, "Bucke's *Walt Whitman*: A Collaboration," *WWR* 15 (1969):190–94.

63. *SS*, 481–82; Stevenson, "Life and Work," pp. 1145–46; Artem Lozynsky, *Richard Maurice Bucke, Medical Mystic* (Detroit, 1977), pp. 34–41.

64. *SD*, 237–39; *Corr.*, III:187–89, 389; *WWWC*, I:431.

65. *Corr.*, V:219; *WWWC*, I:174, 277, 414, 448, 397; William White, "Inscribed to Dr. Bucke," *WWR* 15 (1969):127–28.

66. Beverley Tucker, "Speaking of Weir Mitchell," *American Journal of Psychiatry* 93 (September, 1936):341–46; Anna Robeson Burr, *Weir Mitchell: His Life and Letters* (New York, 1930).

67. Fred B. Rogers, "Osler and Philadelphia," *Transactions and Studies of the College of Physicians of Philadelphia*, 4th ser. 28 (October, 1970):119.

68. Earnest, *S. Weir Mitchell*, pp. 108, 115–17; Elinor M. Tilton, *Amiable Autocrat: A Biography of Oliver Wendell Holmes* (New York, 1947), p. 435; *SS*, 524; S. Weir Mitchell, *Doctor and Patient* (1887; reprint New York, 1972), p. 162.

69. Artem Lozynsky, "S. Weir Mitchell on Whitman: An Unpublished Letter," *American Notes and Queries* 13 (April, 1975):120–21; Earnest, *S. Weir Mitchell*, p. 258.

70. Earnest, *S. Weir Mitchell*, p. 233; *WWWC*, II:271–72; I:454–55; IV:338–39.

71. Max Neuberger, "Vis Medicatrix Naturae," *Medical Life* 39 (1932):657.

72. *Corr.*, IV:227; *WWWC*, I:415; II:383; III:391.

73. William White, "Walt Whitman and Sir William Osler," *American Literature* 11 (1939):74. Dr. Osler declared that virtue begins with "a sweet fresh body" (William Osler, "A Way of Life," in *Selected Writings 12 July 1849 to 29 Dec. 1919*, ed. Alfred W. Franklin *et al.* [New York, 1951], pp. 234–49).

74. Neuberger, "Vis Medicatrix Naturae," p. 657.

75. *WWWC*, III:384; V:81; Shryock, *Medicine in America*, pp. 98–99; William Osler, "The Resources of Life," in *The Continuing Education*, ed. John P. McGovern and Charles G. Roland (Springfield, Ill., 1969), p. 199. See also Cushing, *Life of Sir William Osler*, p. 267.

76. *WWWC*, III:294.

77. *SD*, 304; *WWWC*, III:251, 534; V:373.

78. Austin Flint, "Conservative Medicine," in *Medical America in the Nineteenth Century*, ed. Gert H. Brieger (Baltimore and London, 1972), p. 139.

79. *WWWC*, II:364; III:435; *SD*, 249. Compare *B D Times*, July 11, 1857; February 12, October 18, 1858.

80. *WWWC*, III:251; IV:56; Herman Melville, *Pierre: or, The Ambiguities* (New York, 1957), p. 21.

81. *WWWC*, I:430; *SD*, 249.

Chapter 4. *"The Ultimate Brain"*

1. Important discussions of phrenological theory include Orson S. Fowler, *Self-Instructor in Phrenology and Physiology* (New York, 1859; hereafter cited as *Self-Instructor*. Titles and contents of the many editions vary). Edward Hungerford, "Walt Whitman and His Chart of Bumps," *American Literature* 2 (1931):350–85; John D. Davies, *Phrenology, Fad and Science: A 19th-Century Crusade* (New Haven, 1955), pp. 177–82; Madeleine B. Stern, *Heads & Headlines: The Phrenological Fowlers* (Norman, Okla., 1971), ix–xv; Arthur

Wrobel, "Whitman and the Phrenologists: The Divine Body and the Sensuous Soul," *PMLA* 89 (1974):17–23; David De Giustino, *Conquest of Mind: Phrenology and Victorian Social Thought* (London, 1975):12–31.

2. Hungerford, "Walt Whitman and His Chart of Bumps," p. 370.

3. Edwin H. Ackerknecht, "Contributions of Gall and the Phrenologists to Knowledge of Brain Function," in *The History and Philosophy of the Brain and Its Functions: An Anglo-American Symposium* (Oxford, 1958), pp. 149–53. See also Joseph F. Kett, *The Formation of the American Medical Profession: The Role of Institutions* (New Haven, 1968), p. 146.

4. *Self-Instructor* (ca. 1890), p. 68.

5. D. H. Jacques, *Hints Toward Physical Perfection* (New York, 1859), p. 127n.; *The Illustrated Annual of Phrenology and Physiognomy for 1872*, ed. S. R. Wells (New York, ca. 1871), p. 41.

6. *Am Ph J* 7 (1845):369–73; see also J. G. Spurzheim, *Education: Its Elementary Principles* (New York, 1847), pp. 5, 15, 26–27.

7. "Summary; or, Concluding Influences and Remarks," *Am Ph J* 6 (1844):38–39; Lorenzo N. Fowler, *Marriage: Its History and Ceremonies* (New York, 1847), p. 120.

8. "Experience," in *Selections from Ralph Waldo Emerson*, ed. Stephen E. Whicher (Boston, 1957), pp. 258–59.

9. O. W. Holmes, "Border Lines in Medical Science," in *Medical Essays, 1842–1882* (Boston, 1889), pp. 245–46; O. W. Holmes, *The Professor at the Breakfast-Table* (Boston and New York, 1901), pp. 197–98; Joseph Ernest, Jr., "Holmes to Whittier re Whitman," *Walt Whitman Newsletter* 4 (March, 1958):77.

10. Harriet Martineau, quoted in *The Illustrated Annual of Phrenology and Physiognomy for 1870*, ed. S. R. Wells (New York, ca. 1869), pp. 52–53.

11. *The Illustrated Annual of Phrenology and Physiognomy for 1868*, ed. S. R. Wells (New York, ca. 1867), pp. 65–66; *Am Ph J* 13 (1851):31; Louise Hall Tharp, *Until Victory: Horace Mann and Mary Peabody* (Boston, 1953), pp. 170–71 and passim.

12. "Phrenology Inculcated from the Pulpit by the Rev. Henry Ward Beecher," *The Zoist* 13 (October, 1855):281–83. See also Nelson Sizer, *Forty Years in Phrenology* (New York, 1884), p. 14; *Self-Instructor* (1859), p. 48. Many literary figures who were enthusiastic about phrenology are named in Stern, *Heads & Headlines*, and in John B. Wilson, "Phrenology and Transcendentalism," *American Literature* 28 (1936):225.

13. Orson S. Fowler, *Hereditary Descent* (New York, 1847), pp. 280–81.

14. *WWWC*, II:256–57.

15. William Godwin, *Lives of the Necromancers* (1834; reprint London, 1876), p. 8; Johann Caspar Lavater, *Essays on Physiognomy for the Promotion of Knowledge and the Love of Mankind* (1804; reprint London, 1878), p. 113. Lavater had identified the man as a physiognomist.

16. For example: *WWWC*, I:36; II:100; V:17; "Preface 1876," in *LG*, 751; *UPP*, II:96; Edward Carpenter, *Days with Walt Whitman* (London, 1906), p. 38.

17. *W-Eagle*, 77, 237–38; "Book-Reviews," 161–63; Thomas L. Brasher, "Whitman's Conversion to Phrenology," *Walt Whitman Newsletter* 4 (June, 1958):95–97.

18. For W's exposure to phrenological literature in the 1840's and 1850's, see "Book-Reviews," 152–64; Hungerford, "Walt Whitman and His Chart of Bumps"; Stern, *Heads & Headlines*, pp. 99–123; W, *The Gathering of the Forces*, ed. Cleveland Rodgers and John Black (New York and London,

1920), II:203, 304; *Trent*, 113; *N&F*, 192ff.; William White, *Walt Whitman's Journalism: A Bibliography* (Detroit, 1969), pp. 7–30, 32–61. Additional information on W's reading and book sales courtesy Charles E. Feinberg and Madeleine B. Stern.

19. Rubin, 382.

20. Emory Holloway, "Portrait of a Poet" (typescript, Berg Collection, New York Public Library), p. 155.

21. *Am Ph J*, February, 1844, p. 33.

22. Fowler, *Hereditary Descent*, pp. 168–69. Charles E. Feinberg, *An Exhibition of the Works of Walt Whitman* (Detroit, 1955), p. 18, lists "A Memoir of John Whitman and His Descendants," by Ezekiel Whitman (Portland, Me., 1832). On W's genealogy, see *SS*, 595; *SD*, 4–5.

23. Bookseller W sold phrenological charts and guides and such books as John Bovee Dods's *Six Lectures on the Philosophy of Mesmerism* (New York, 1851), O.S. Fowler's *A Home for All*, and Henry Newcombe's *How To Be a Lady*, which, with other "*How To*" books, W reviewed in the *B D Eagle*. See "Book-Reviews," 140; Stern, *Heads & Headlines*, pp. 105–106. Additional information courtesy Madeleine B. Stern and Charles E. Feinberg.

24. *B D Times*, August 5, 1857; May 24, 1859; December 12, 1857.

25. *ISL*, 45; *B D Times*, February 12 and September 7, 1858.

26. John Bovee Dods, *The Philosophy of Electrical Psychology* (1850; reprint New York, 1885), pp. 44–45.

27. *UPP*, I:132; Stern, *Heads & Headlines*, p. 168; Rubin, 291.

28. *NYD*, 11–12, 162–79; James K. Wallace, "Whitman and *Life Illustrated*: A Forgotten 1855 Review of *Leaves of Grass*," *WWR* 17 (1971):135–39; Stern, *Heads & Headlines*, pp. 115–23. On references to W in *Am Ph J*, see Rubin, 382–83.

29. *LG1856*, 190.

30. Dods, *Philosophy of Electrical Psychology*, p. 44.

31. John Burroughs, *Notes on Walt Whitman as Poet and Person* (1867; reprint New York, 1971), p. 19; *LG1856*, 384; *Corr.*, I:44.

32. G. S. Weaver, *Lectures on Mental Science* (New York, 1854), 52.

33. *American Whig Review* 3 (January, 1846): 33, 44. Another article that W preserved, "Physiognomy," *Quarterly Review* (American ed.) 40 (January, 1852):39, declared that the ability to read phrenological and physiognomic signs depends on intuition: "it is the spirit within witnessing, by some wonderful adaptation, with the spirit of the gazer." (See *Trent*, 66–67, 75.)

34. "Mr. George Combe on the Size of Sir Walter Scott's Brain," *Am Ph J* I (1838–39):129–34.

35. James Parton, *The Life of Horace Greeley* (New York, 1854), pp. 431–44.

36. Orson S. Fowler on the humorist-phrenologist Joseph C. Neal, *Am Ph J* 8 (1846):19–23.

37. W, *Leaves of Grass Imprints: American and European Criticisms on "Leaves of Grass"* (Boston, 1860), p. 52; *LG*, 55.

38. Nelson Sizer, "Poets, Poetry, and Phrenology," *Am Ph J* 11 (1849):337–40.

39. "William Cullen Bryant," *The Illustrated Phrenological Almanac for 1850*, ed. L. N. Fowler (New York, ca. 1849), pp. 24–25.

40. Warren U. Ober, et al., eds., *The Enigma of Poe* (Boston, 1966), pp. 83–87. See also Edward Hungerford, "Poe and Phrenology," *American Literature* 2 (1930):209–31; Stern, *Heads & Headlines*, pp. 70–85.

41. *LG*, 169, 723.
42. Fowler, *Hereditary Descent*, pp. 203–204.
43. Spurzheim, *Education*, pp. 15, 185.
44. David George Goyder, ed., *The Battle for Life: The Autobiography of a Phrenologist* (London, 1857), p. 554; Weaver, *Lectures on Mental Science*, pp. 172, 175.
45. J. G. Spurzheim, *Phrenology; or, The Doctrine of Mental Phenomena* (New York, 1855), pp. 238–39.
46. "The Drake-Halleck Review," *Selected Writings of Edgar Allan Poe*, ed. David Galloway (Baltimore, 1967), p. 396.
47. R. L., M.D., "Phrenology Exemplified in Literature," *Am Ph J* 20 (January, 1854): 1–3; Orson S. Fowler, *Creative and Sexual Science* (Philadelphia, 1870), pp. 220–21.
48. *CW*, IX: 62; *Trent*, 66–67; Wrobel, "Whitman and the Phrenologists," p. 22.
49. W's anonymous review of *LG* and *Maud and Other Poems*, reprinted in *Walt Whitman: The Critical Heritage*, ed. Milton Hindus (New York, 1971), pp. 41–45; *CW*, IX: 40; *LG1856*, 181.
50. *PW1892*, 482.
51. Wrobel, "Whitman and the Phrenologists," p. 19.
52. *CW*, IX: 120.
53. *Trent*, 66–67; reproduced in *Faint Clews & Indirections: Manuscripts of Walt Whitman and His Family*, ed. Clarence Gohdes and Rollo G. Silver (Durham, N.C., 1949), pp. 223–36. Incidentally, W was thirty years old, not twenty-nine.
54. Three of W's contemporaries wrote satirical reports of *their* examinations by the Fowlers: Sarah Payson Parton ("Fanny Fern"), *Ruth Hall: A Domestic Tale of the Present Time* (New York, 1855), pp. 318–29; Holmes, *Professor at the Breakfast-Table*, pp. 195–97; Mark Twain, *The Autobiography of Mark Twain*, ed. Charles Neider (New York, 1961), pp. 69–73. See also Stern, *Heads & Headlines*, pp. 183–86, 299.
55. *WWWC*, I: 385.
56. W said his "chart of bumps" was read by "Nelson Fowler (or was it Sizer?)" at the Fowler and Wells cabinet ("Good-Bye My Fancy," *PW1892*, 697; *CW*, VII: 54). Sizer (there was no "Nelson Fowler" with the firm) lectured at Clinton Hall, where the cabinet was located, between 1850 and 1855 (Sizer, *Forty Years in Phrenology*, p. 237), and was long associated with the firm. In 1887 he purchased a copy of *LG* from W (*Corr.*, VI: xxxii; W, *Daybooks and Notebooks*, ed. William White [New York, 1978], p. 427).
57. Arthur Wrobel speculates ("A Poet's Self-Esteem: Whitman Alters His 'Bumps,'" *WWR* 17 [1971]: 129–35) that the capsule analyses W used in his self-reviews may derive from an examination that occurred between 1841 and 1848. But if W had more than one analysis, internal evidence seems to me to point to the post-1849 period.
58. Hindus, *Walt Whitman: The Critical Heritage*, p. 47; *In Re W W*, 25.
59. *LG*, 709–29.
60. Definitions of the various phrenological faculties are taken from the *Self-Instructor*.
61. The quoted phrases are, of course, W's.
62. George Combe, *Phrenological Development of Robert Burns from A Cast of His Skull* (Edinburgh, 1834), p. 7.
63. *LG1860*, 141–42.

64. *LG1860*, 120–21, 113–14, 117, 412–14; George Combe, *Notes on the United States of North America during a Phrenological Visit in 1838–39–40*, cited in *Am Ph J* 3 (April, 1841):379.

65. *LG*, 480–81, 649, 687.

66. *LG1860*, 265; *Self-Instructor* (ca. 1890), p. 166.

67. *LG1860*, 268; *Self-Instructor* (ca. 1890), p. 124.

68. *LG*, 364–66; Spurzheim, *Education*, pp. 56–57; Fowler, *Hereditary Descent*, pp. 130–31, 210, 279. See also Harold Aspiz, "Educating the Kosmos: 'There Was a Child Went Forth,'" *American Quarterly* 18 (1966):655–66.

69. Orson S. Fowler, *Education and Self-Improvement* (New York, 1844), II:17–23, 36, 44–45, 14–15. This is the volume on "Memory" that W read.

70. *The Works of Thomas Carlyle* (London, 1897), XI:13. W was familiar with Carlyle's biography (*WWWC*, III:118–19). Lorenzo N. Fowler's *Marriage*, which W had read, listed the faculties which should be cultivated by mothers and fathers (pp. 202–203); they add up to the same sort of shrewd go-getting father and child-rearing mother depicted by W.

71. W, "Manuscript Notes" (Feinberg Collection); Gall, cited in William Mattieu Williams, *A Vindication of Phrenology* (London, 1894), p. 178.

72. Buchanan, *Outlines of Lectures in the Neurological System of Anthropology* (New York, 1854), relates "gestures and spontaneous movements" to phrenological organs and paths of energy. See also Emmet Field Horine, *Biographical Sketch . . . of Charles Caldwell, M.D.* (Brooks, Ky., 1960), pp. 104–105; *The Scalpel* VII (1855):57.

73. Alexander Lowen, *The Language of the Body* (New York, 1971).

74. *LG1855*, 77–78 (italics mine).

75. *Walt Whitman's Diary in Canada*, ed. William Sloane Kennedy (Boston, 1904), p. 68; *LG*, 382.

76. *Memoranda*, 39. W's "Notes . . . on Elias Hicks," *PW1892*, 626–53, contains bits of physiognomic lore; W used at least one *Am Ph J* article in its preparation; see Feinberg, *Exhibition*, p. 33; Bliss Perry, *Walt Whitman: His Life and Work* (New York, 1906), p. 257.

77. Lavater, *Essays on Physiognomy*, p. 135 and *passim*. *Self-Instructor* (ca. 1890), pp. 45–50.

78. F. Baldensperger, *Études d'Histoire Littéraires* (Paris, 1910), pp. 60–91; Elizabeth Ruth Hosmer, "Science and Pseudo-Science in the Writings of Nathaniel Hawthorne," (Ph.D. diss., University of Illinois, 1948), pp. 245–46.

79. *LG*, 463–67; Lavater, *Essays on Physiognomy*, p. 23.

80. *LG*, 86–87; Bronson Alcott, *Table-Talk* (Boston, 1877), p. 144. Analyses of facial reading in the text are derived chiefly from Lavater, from *Self-Instructor*, and from Nelson Sizer, *Heads and Faces, and How to Study Them* (New York, 1891). See also Harold Aspiz, "A Reading of Whitman's 'Faces,'" *WWR* 19 (1973):37–48.

81. Joan's eyes appear "very wide apart and bulging, as they often do in very imaginative people" (*Saint Joan: A Chronicle Play in Six Scenes and an Epilogue* [New York, 1941], p. 6).

82. *Moby-Dick*, ch. 10.

83. Lavater, *Essays on Physiognomy*, pp. 100, 115; *Corr.*, I:82.

84. *Self-Instructor* (ca. 1890), p. 53; Lavater, *Essays on Physiognomy*, p. 474.

85. Lavater, *Essays on Physiognomy*, pp. 110–11; *N&F*, 82; W, "Is Not Medicine a Frequent Cause of Sickness?" *B D Eagle*, April 16, 1846.

86. *LG1855*, 83.

87. Lavater, *Essays on Physiognomy*, p. 394.
88. *Ibid.*, pp. 243, 282; Sizer, *Heads and Faces*, pp. 92–93. A phrenological analysis of the skull of Black Hawk supposedly revealed the characteristics of the typical stage Indian: piety, eloquence, cunning, unscrupulousness, and stupidity (*Am Ph J* 1 [1838–39]: 51–59).
89. "The Standard Civilized Head," *Life Illustrated*, n.s. 2 (July 5, 1856); see *Trent*, 75.
90. *LG1855*, 68.
91. "A Brooklynite Criticized," *Brooklyn City News*, October 10, 1860, cited in Bucke, 199.
92. Sizer, *Heads and Faces*, p. 174. For a similar description, see D. H. Jacques, *Hints Toward Physical Perfection* (New York, 1859), pp. 41–42.

Chapter 5. *"The Body Electric"*

1. Orson S. Fowler, *Love and Parentage* (New York, 1844), p. 26.
2. D. H. Jacques, *Hints Toward Physical Perfection* (New York, 1859), pp. 56–57, 180; *LG*, 136, 17, 154.
3. Andrew Jackson Davis, *The Philosophy of Spiritual Intercourse* (New York, 1851), p. 20; *LG*, 80–81; *N&F*, 35. For similar ladder imagery in an article that W preserved, see J. D. Whelpley, "Phrenology: A Socratic Dialogue," *American Whig Review* 3 (January, 1846): 40–41; see *Trent*, 75.
4. "Circles," in *Selections from Ralph Waldo Emerson*, ed. Stephen E. Whicher (Boston, 1957), pp. 170, 176.
5. *LG*, 744. W's telegraphic "thread-voice" resembles spiritualist imagery: see Emma Hardinge Britten, *Modern American Spiritualism* (New York, 1870), p. 36; R. Laurence Moore, "Spiritualism and Science: Reflections on the First Decade of Spirit Rapping," *American Quarterly* 24 (1972): 486.
6. *Frankenstein; or, The Modern Prometheus* (London, 1969), pp. 40–41, 57.
7. Chauncey Hare Townshend, *Facts in Mesmerism* (London, 1840), p. 492. W reviewed this book in "Is Mesmerism True?" *New York Sunday Times*, August 14, 1842.
8. Moore, *The Use of the Body in Relation to the Soul*, (New York, 1847), pp. 7–9, 80, 142–43, 152, 301.
9. Channing, *Notes on the Medical Application of Electricity*, (Boston, 1849), pp. 46–48. W's copy is in the Feinberg Collection.
10. *LG*, 93.
11. Fowler, *Love and Parentage*, p. 26 (italics mine).
12. *LG*, 391. On W's evolution–unfolding imagery, see Harold Aspiz, "Unfolding the Folds," *WWR* 12 (1966): 81–87; Gay Wilson Allen, *The New Walt Whitman Handbook* (New York, 1975), pp. 173–81.
13. Edward H. Dixon, *The Organic Law of the Sexes: Positive and Negative Electricity* (New York, 1861), pp. 2–4; *The Scalpel* 4 (1853): 49; I (1849): 105.
14. *LG*, 483.
15. Lorenz Oken, *Elements of Physiophilosophy* (London, 1847), pp. 396–97; Russell Thacher Trall, *The Hydropathic Encyclopedia: A System of Hydropathy and Hygiene* (New York, 1853), II: 444. Jacques, *Hints Toward Physical Perfection*, p. 67, speaks of the "vitalizing fluid" that impregnates the mother.
16. *LG1860*, 268; *LG1856*, 241. (Italics mine.)
17. Samuel Warren, "Electricity the Great Acting Part of Nature," *Am Ph J* 11 (1849): 151.

18. Alfred Still, *Soul of Lodestone* (New York, 1946), p. 128; Frank Podmore, *Mediums of the 19th Century* (1902; reprint New York, 1963), I:45.
19. Orson S. Fowler, *Creative and Sexual Science*, (Philadelphia, 1870), pp. 741–42, 85–86. John Bovee Dods, *Six Lectures on the Philosophy of Mesmerism* (New York, 1851), pp. 44–45, observes that the hand of God constantly shapes new creations out of electrical matter.
20. *LC*, Item no. 63. Another version of W's note characterizes the persona as the "genital master" (Clifton J. Furness, ed., *Walt Whitman's Workshop: A Collection of Unpublished Manuscripts* [New York, 1961], p. 49).
21. *LG1855*, 27. Joseph Beaver, *Walt Whitman, Poet of Science* (New York, 1951), pp. 41–45, has explicated this interplanetary intercourse in astronomical terms.
22. *LG*, 52 (italics mine), 54; *N&F*, 34.
23. *LG1860*, 262, 389; *LG*, 294. Compare *The Journals of Bronson Alcott*, ed. Odell Shepard (Boston, 1938), p. 121: "Mettle is the Godhead proceeding into the matrix of Nature to organize Man. Behold the creative jet! And hear the morning stars sing for joy at the sacred generation of the Gods!"
24. *Trent*, 66–67. For examples of W's praise of magnetic persons, see *SD*, 141, 231, 281; *Corr.*, II:182–83; *PW1892*, 643; W's preface to William Douglas O'Connor's *Three Tales* (Boston and New York, 1892), pp. iii–iv.
25. Park Benjamin, *The Intellectual Uses of Electricity: A Symposium* (London, 1895), pp. 219–23; Mary A. B. Brazier, "The Evolution of Concepts Relating to the Electricity of the Nervous System," and Aubrey Lewis, "J. C. Reil's Concept of Brain Function," in *The History and Philosophy of Knowledge of the Brain: An Anglo-American Symposium* (London, 1958), pp. 154–57, 221–22.
26. *LG*, 183, 177, 390 (italics mine), 238, 120; *LG1860*, 308; *LG*, 90.
27. Dods, *Six Lectures on the Philosophy of Mesmerism*, pp. 62–63; A. E. Newton, ed., *The Modern Bethesda; or, The Gift of Healing, Being Some Account of the Life and Labors of Dr. J. R. Newton, Healer* (New York, 1879), pp. 40, 112.
28. Furness, *Walt Whitman's Workshop*, p. 38; F. O. Matthiessen, *American Renaissance* (1941; reprint London and New York, 1968), p. 553. Oratory is celebrated in "Vocalism," *LG*, 383–84.
29. *LG*, 496, 253; "In Memoriam," section 125; *LG*, 406.
30. *LG*, 501, 458, 293, 117, 17, 24, 25, 501.
31. *LG*, 280, 325, 227, 344, 196–97, 205.
32. *Mesmerism*, ed. Gilbert Frankau (London, 1948), pp. 21, 54–57. See also Still, *Soul of Lodestone*, pp. 185–87.
33. *The Zoist* 1 (1843):134–35; 3 (1845):338, 536; Fred Kaplan, *Dickens and Mesmerism: The Hidden Springs of Fiction* (Princeton, 1975); Margaret Goldsmith, *Franz Anton Mesmer: A Study* (Garden City, N.Y., 1936), p. 243; J. West Nevins, "Phreno-Mesmerism," *Am Ph J* 30 (1870):246–47; Nelson Sizer, *Forty Years in Phrenology* (New York, 1884), pp. 110–35.
34. Joseph F. Kett, *The Formation of the American Medical Profession: The Role of Institutions* (New Haven, 1968), pp. 142–45; "Récamier, Joseph-Claude Anthèlme," *Biographie Universelle (Michaud) Ancienne et Moderne*, XXXV:292–96; Goldsmith, *Franz Anton Mesmer*, p. 223; James Esdaile, *Mesmerism in India, and Its Practical Application in Surgery and Medicine* (1846; reprint Chicago, 1902).
35. T. S. Arthur, *Agnes; or, The Possessed: A Revelation of Mesmerism* (Philadelphia, 1848).

36. "Is Mesmerism True?" *New York Sunday Times*, August 14, 1842.

37. Dods, *Six Lectures on the Philosophy of Mesmerism*, pp. 77–78, 72.

38. John Townsend Trowbridge, *My Own Story: With Recollections of Noted Persons* (Boston and New York, 1903), pp. 361–62.

39. *SD*, 51–52, 308–309; Lowenfels, 104; John Burroughs, *Walt Whitman: A Study* (Boston, 1896), pp. 40–41; Bucke, 103.

40. Harold Aspiz, "Mark Twain and 'Dr.' Newton," *American Literature* 44 (1972):130–36; S. Weir Mitchell, *Doctor and Patient* (1888; reprint New York, 1972), p. 135.

41. Dods, *Six Lectures on the Philosophy of Mesmerism*, pp. 16, 66, 69.

42. W, *The Eighteenth Presidency!*, ed. Edward F. Grier (Lawrence, Kans., 1956); "Definitions," in *UPP*, II:84. See also *LG*, 388.

43. *UPP*, II:71–72 (text emended by Emory Holloway: italics mine).

44. *LG*, 650.

45. *LG1855*, 44–45 (italics mine). This version more clearly displays the persona's mesmeric powers than does the final revision (*LG*, 73–74). W's imagery may reflect the theory of the Od, or Odie, a dynamic force allegedly distinct from electricity, which "sensitives" were said to perceive as color or light emanating from the body or any substance. See Karl Ludwig Reichenbach, *Odie-Magnetic Letters* (New York, 1860), Moore, "Spiritualism and Science," pp. 492–93; Still, *Soul of Lodestone*, pp. 200–22.

46. John R. Newman, *Fascination; or, The Philosophy of Charming* (New York, 1878), pp. 171–72. Newman cites "fascination" and "charming" as synonyms for mesmerizing (*ibid.*, p. 13).

47. Newton, *Modern Bethesda*, pp. 96–97; Herbert W. Schneider and George Lawton, *A Pilgrim and a Prophet, Being the Incredible History of Thomas Lake Harris and Laurence Oliphant* (New York, 1942), pp. 168–76. In Dr. James Esdaile's celebrated surgical operations, performed while the patient was mesmerized, an assistant first breathed on the afflicted part of the body to desensitize it (Esdaile, *Mesmerism in India*, p. 30).

48. *National Cyclopaedia of American Biography*, XI:539–40. On Quimby, see Frank Podmore, *From Mesmer to Christian Science* (1909; reprint New Hyde Park, N.Y., 1963), pp. 250–56.

49. *LG1860*, 391–400.

50. Newton, *Modern Bethesda*, p. 288; Herman Melville, *Pierre: or, The Ambiguities* (New York, 1957), pp. 89–91.

51. *LG*, 628; *LG1860*, 349; *LG*, 615.

52. *LG*, 149–59 (italics mine).

53. *Journals of Bronson Alcott*, pp. 171–72; George Moore, *The Use of the Body in Relation to the Mind* (New York, 1847), p. 13; Dods, *Six Lectures on the Philosophy of Mesmerism*, pp. 27, 39–40.

54. *LG1860*, 318. W altered the phrase to "draughts of space," thus blurring its physiological relevance.

55. John Humphrey Noyes, *History of American Socialisms* (1870; reprint New York, 1961), p. 151; Newton, *Modern Bethesda*, p. 113. See also Joseph Haddock, *Psychology; or, The Science of the Soul* (New York, 1850), pp. 71–73.

56. Karl Marx and Frederich Engels, *The German Ideology*, cited in *Problems of Modern Esthetics*, ed. S. Mozhnyagun (Moscow, 1969), p. 237.

57. Podmore, *Mediums of the 19th Century*, I:154–76.

58. *N&F*, 76–77; *LG*, 705.

59. Allen, *New Walt Whitman Handbook*, pp. 192–201, 260–65; Frederik Schy-

berg, *Walt Whitman* (New York, 1951), pp. 248–327; V. K. Chari, *Whitman in the Light of Vedantic Mysticism* (Lincoln, Neb., 1964); T. R. Rajasekharaiah, *The Roots of Whitman's Grass* (Rutherford, N.J., 1970).

60. Britten, *Modern American Spiritualism*, pp. 101, 149.

61. J. B. Rhine, "Spiritualism," *Encyclopedia Americana* (1951), XXV:421–23.

62. Howard Kerr, *Mediums, Spirit-Rappers, and Roaring Radicals* (Urbana, Ill., 1972), pp. 199, 20–21.

63. Schneider and Lawton, *A Pilgrim and a Prophet*, pp. 14–19; Britten, *Modern American Spiritualism*, p. 213; Arthur A. Cuthbert, *The World-Work of Thomas Lake Harris* (Glasgow, 1908); Gilbert Seldes, *The Stammering Century* (1928; reprint New York and Evanston, 1965), pp. 232–36.

64. "The Christian Spiritualist," in Milton Hindus, ed., *Walt Whitman: The Critical Heritage* (New York, 1971), pp. 80–84; W. H. [William Howitt?], "The Poems of Walt Whitman," *The Spiritual Magazine* (London), n.s. 5 (January, 1870):34–40. Dr. Bucke plainly attributed "clairvoyant powers" to W; see Artem Lozynsky, *Richard Maurice Bucke, Medical Mystic* (Detroit, 1977), p. 173. On American spiritualist publications, see Elizabeth Ruth Hosmer, "Science and Pseudo-Science in the Writings of Nathaniel Hawthorne" (Ph.D. diss., University of Illinois, 1948), p. 62.

65. "Walt Whitman and His Poems," in *In Re W W*, 19.

66. *LG1860*, 189–90 (italics mine), 216; *LG*, 602 (italics mine), 502, 487, 610–11.

67. *B D Times*, August 15, 1857; *LG*, 241.

68. Matthiessen, *American Renaissance*, pp. 539–40. On the mystic state, see also A. P. Sinnett, *The Rationale of Mesmerism* (Boston and New York, 1899), p. 199.

69. Justinus Kerner, *The Seeress of Prevost: Being Revelations Concerning the Inner Life of Man* (London, 1844), pp. 84, 89, 107–109, 217.

70. Haddock, *Psychology*, pp. 73–74.

71. Johann Heinrich Jung-Stilling, *Theory of Pneumatology*, ed. George Bush (New York, 1851), pp. 227–28, 46–47; Kaplan, *Dickens and Mesmerism*, pp. 118–19, 16–17. Jung-Stilling and Kerner were disciples of Mesmer.

72. Haddock, cited in Arthur, *Agnes; or, The Possessed*, p. 114 (documentary supplement).

73. *LG*, 580 (italics mine); *N&F*, 34. On mesmerized prodigies of strength, see Townshend, *Facts in Mesmerism*, pp. 155, 493.

74. Sinnett, *Rationale of Mesmerism*, pp. 49–50; Andrew Jackson Davis, *Philosophy of Spiritual Intercourse*, pp. 107–108. See also Haddock, *Psychology*, p. 102; Podmore, *From Mesmer to Christian Science*, pp. 222–23.

75. Davis, *Philosophy of Spiritual Intercourse*, p. 41; Dods, *Six Lectures on the Philosophy of Mesmerism*, pp. 51–52.

76. *LG*, 347–48, 392.

77. Davis, *Philosophy of Spiritual Intercourse*, pp. 50, 68, 92. On attaining an "exact equilibrium with external electricity," see also Dods, *Six Lectures on the Philosophy of Mesmerism*, pp. 12–14, 28–29.

78. *LG*, 32 (italics mine), 272–73.

79. *LG1860*, 216, 204–208.

80. *LG*, 137–48. In this poem, "we have him clearly in a trance, and the impressing spirit speaking through him:—'Take my hand, Walt Whitman! . . .'" (W. H., "The Poems of Walt Whitman," p. 35). W's clairvoyant voyage theme is also developed in "Pictures" and "Unnamed Lands," *LG*, 642–49, 372–73.

81. *LG*, 424–33 (italics mine).

82. Townshend, *Facts in Mesmerism*, pp. 126, 201; Newman, *Fascination*, pp. 74–77.

83. Davis, *Philosophy of Spiritual Intercourse*, p. 41; Haddock, *Psychology*, p. 18.

84. *LG1855*, 72, 74.

85. *LG*, 28–89; W, *Complete Poetry and Selected Prose*, ed. James E. Miller, Jr. (Boston, 1959), p. xviii.

86. An English medium reportedly went into a "spontaneous" trance, becoming "for part of it quite insensible to all outward things, and perfectly cataleptic from head to foot . . . her body as stiff and inflexible as a log of wood" (Haddock, *Psychology*, pp. 101–2).

87. *The Complete Tales and Poems of Edgar Allan Poe* (New York, 1938), pp. 88–95.

88. Davis, *Philosophy of Spiritual Intercourse*, p. 49. See also Townshend, *Facts in Mesmerism*, p. 168; Kerner, *Seeress of Prevost*, p. 119.

89. *LG1860*, 379–88 (italics mine).

90. *LG*, 23.

91. Kerner, *Seeress of Prevost*, pp. 151–53; Jung-Stilling, *Theory of Pneumatology*, p. 48; William Henry Holcombe, *The Other Life* (1869), cited in Kett, *Formation of the American Medical Profession*, pp. 151–52.

92. Davis, *Philosophy of Spiritual Intercourse*, pp. 129–30.

93. Newman, *Fascination*, p. 94. On W and Swedenborg, see *SS*, 199; *UPP*, II:16–17. W found Swedenborg "confirmed in all my experience" that "a very close connection" exists "between the state we call religious ecstasy and the desire to copulate" (*WWWC*, V:376).

94. *The Dialogues of Plato*, tr. B. Jowett (New York, 1920), I:499.

95. Townshend, *Facts in Mesmerism*, p. 530; Haddock, *Psychology*, 65.

96. *LG*, 182–83, 8. On the same theme, see "Continuities," *LG*, 523–24; "Poem of the Road," *LG1860*, 326.

Chapter 6. "The Stale Cadaver Blocks Up the Passage"

1. Frances Trollope, *Domestic Manners of the Americans* (1832; reprint New York, 1927), pp. 97–99; Anthony Trollope, *North America* (London, 1866), II:304.

2. Thomas Horton Jones ("Rurio"), *Rambles in the United States and Canada During the Year 1845* (London, 1846), p. 22; Matilda C. Houstoun, *Hesperos; or, Travels in the West* (London, 1850), I:77–79; Fredrika Bremer, *Homes of the New World* (New York, 1853), I:15.

3. C. F. Bolduan, "Over a Century of Health Administration in New York City" (1916), quoted in Shryock, *Medicine and Society in America, 1660–1860* (New York, 1960), p. 167.

4. Catharine E. Beecher, *Physiology and Calisthenics for Schools and Families* (New York, 1856), pp. 10, 121–22, and *passim*. On the decline of health among women, see also Amy Louise Reed, "Female Delicacy in the Sixties," *The Century* 90 (1915):855–64.

5. Horace Greeley, *Hints Toward Reforms* (New York, 1853), pp. 59, 77, 115. R. T. Trall, *The Illustrated Family Gymnasium* (New York, 1857), pp. xi–xiv, also implored Americans to emulate the Greek spirit by restoring their health; W was familiar with this book, too.

6. Oliver Wendell Holmes, "Currents and Cross-Currents in Medical Science," in *Medical Essays, 1842–1882* (Boston, 1889), pp. 199–200. See also Francis A. Walker, "Our Population to 1900," *Atlantic Monthly* 32 (1873):487–95.

7. T. W. Higginson, "Saints and their Bodies," *Atlantic Monthly* 1 (1858):586.

8. Cited in Bremer, *Homes of the New World*, II:123.
9. Edward H. Dixon, "Hereditary Descent of Disease," *The Scalpel* 2 (1850):406–407.
10. *NYD*, 120; *LG*, 654–55; *LG1855*, 47.
11. W, *The Eighteenth Presidency!*, ed. Edward F. Grier (Lawrence, Kans., 1956), pp. 20, 22; *DV*, 371–72. See also "Whitman to Emerson, 1856," *LG*, 735.
12. *WWWC*, V:22; II:88.
13. *CW*, IX:95. For parallels, see *LG*, 342; W, *An 1855–56 Notebook Toward the Second Edition of Leaves of Grass*, ed. Harold W. Blodgett (Carbondale, Ill., 1959), p. 13.
14. *LG1860*, 451–52, 20.
15. *UPP*, II:172; *B D Eagle*, quoted in Mauricio González de la Garza, *Walt Whitman, Racista, Imperialista, Anti-Mexicana* (Mexico, D. F., 1971), pp. 193–94. W later called Mexico "the only one [country] to whom we have ever really done wrong" (*SD*, 93).
16. *DV*, 378–79; *LG*, 471.
17. Adam de Gurowski, *America and Europe* (New York, 1857), pp. 235–36.
18. *LG1860*, 368. W uses similar language in "Song of the Answerer," *LG1860*, 207; *An American Primer*, ed. Horace Traubel (Boston, 1904), p. 13.
19. Florence B. Freedman, ed., *Walt Whitman Looks at the Schools* (New York, 1950), p. 142; *LG*, 720.
20. W, *Manuscripts, Autograph Letters, First Editions and Portraits of Walt Whitman* (New York: American Art Association/Anderson Galleries, Inc., 1936), p. 35.
21. *Walt Whitman's Diary in Canada*, ed. William Sloane Kennedy (Boston, 1904), p. 71.
22. Oscar Cargill, *Intellectual America* (New York, 1954), p. 541.
23. Julius W. Pratt, "The Ideology of American Expansion," in *Essays in Honor of William E. Dodd*, ed. Avery Craven (Chicago, 1935), p. 543; *WWWC*, III:173–74.
24. *N&F*, 172.
25. *The Education of Henry Adams: An Autobiography* (New York, 1918), p. 237.
26. *LG*, 229–32.
27. *UPP*, II:8–10; *LG*, 173, 646, 318; Ellen Calder, quoted in Roger Asselineau, *The Evolution of Walt Whitman: the Creation of a Book* (Cambridge, Mass., 1962), p. 314.
28. *LG1860*, 254, 256–57 (italics mine). The "Hottentot with clicking palate" is a fair linguistic description of Hottentot speech.
29. Report of the United States Surgeon General: "Popular Errors Regarding the American Indians . . . The Statistical Report of the Sickness and Mortality of the United States Army from 1839 to 1855," cited in *The Scalpel* 9 (July, 1857):95–99.
30. Barrus, 335; *ISL*, 90; *WWWC*, II:283. For other expressions of W's racism, see *N&F*, 172; Cleveland Rodgers and John Black, eds., *The Gathering of the Forces* (New York and London, 1920), II:122–23; *W-Eagle*, 85–95, 161–65. For a reasoned assessment of W's racial views, see Oscar Cargill, "Walt Whitman and Civil Rights," in *Essays in American and English Literature Presented to Bruce Robert McElderry*, ed. Max F. Schulz (Athens, Ohio, 1970), pp. 48–58. On racial theories in W's day, see John S. Haller, *Outcasts from Evolution: Scientific Attitudes of Racial Inferiority, 1859–1900* (Urbana, Ill., 1971), pp. 28, 64–65, 72.

31. Basil De Selincourt, *Walt Whitman: A Critical Study* (London, 1914), pp. 228–30.
32. *LG*, 525, 740.
33. *WWWC*, III:94; *CW*, IX:208.
34. On W and secular evolution, see James T. F. Tanner, "Walt Whitman, Poet of Lamarckian Evolution" (Ph.D. diss., Texas Technical College, Lubbock, 1968); James T. F. Tanner, "The Lamarckian Theory of Progress in *Leaves of Grass*," *WWR* 9 (1963):3–11; Frederick W. Conner, *Cosmic Optimism: A Study of the Interpretation of Evolution by American Poets* (Gainesville, Fla., 1949), pp. 92–127.
35. These laws are summarized in F. Graham Cannon, *Lamarck and Modern Genetics* (Manchester, England, 1959), pp. 51–52.
36. *LG*, 165; "A Whitman Manuscript," *American Mercury* 3 (December, 1924):478.
37. *UPP*, II:66–69; P. Z. Rosenthal, "Dilation in Whitman's Early Writing," *WWR* 20 (1974):3–15.
38. Cited in Robert Dale Owen, *Moral Physiology; or, A Brief and Plain Treatise on the Population Question* (London, 1831 [pamphlet]).
39. John Greenleaf Whittier, "Peculiar Institutions in Massachusetts," *Prose Works* (Boston and New York, 1904), III:216–17; Elizabeth P. Peabody, *Memorial to Dr. William Wesselhöft* (Boston, 1859), pp. 33–34. A "dyscrasy" is a disproportionate mixture of body humors.
40. Orson S. Fowler, *Love and Parentage* (New York, 1844), p. viii. For similar ideas, see Bronson Alcott, *Table-Talk* (Boston, 1877), p. 146; Russell T. Trall, *Sexual Physiology* (New York, 1871), p. 234.
41. *B D Times*, May 24, 1859.
42. *UPP*, II:79; *LG*, 234–35.
43. John Burroughs, *Notes on Walt Whitman as Poet and Person* (1867; reprint New York, 1971), p. 28.
44. *UPP*, I:112–13.
45. *LG*, 96–97, 391, 103; *LG1860*, 368; *An American Primer*, p. 15.
46. *LG*, 107, 415.
47. Shaw is cited in Edward Carpenter, *Edward Carpenter, 1844–1920: Democratic Author and Poet* (London, 1970), p. 11; Odell Shepard, ed., *The Journals of Bronson Alcott* (Boston, 1938), p. 280. Good parentage is associated with the proper sowing of the seed in Fowler, *Love and Parentage*, p. xi; and Trall, *Sexual Physiology*, p. 254.
48. *CW*, IX:150.
49. Symonds, *Walt Whitman: A Study* (1893; reprint New York, 1967), p. 63.
50. *LG*, 90.
51. *LG*, 101–106.
52. J. G. Spurzheim, *Education: Its Elementary Principles* (New York, 1847), pp. 185, 215, and *passim*; Stephen Pearl Andrews, quoted in Ronald G. Watkins, "The Erotic South," *American Quarterly* 25 (1973):199; Charles Knowlton, *Fruits of Philosophy* (1831; reprint Mt. Vernon, N.Y., 1937), p. 19.
53. *Elizabeth Cady Stanton As Revealed in Her Letters, Diary and Reminiscences*, ed. Theodore Stanton and Harriot Stanton Blatch (New York, 1902), II:210.
54. Edward Carpenter, "Exfoliation," in *Civilization, Its Cause and Cure* (New York, 1891), p. 52.
55. *LG*, 262, 417.
56. *LG*, 236–38, 208, 226–27.

57. *LG*, 346; *LG1855*, 80.
58. *LG*, 156; Barbara Marinacci, *O Wondrous Singer! An Introduction to Walt Whitman* (New York, 1970), p. 325.
59. Laurence Sterne, *The Life and Opinions of Tristram Shandy* (London and Glasgow, 1955), p. 21.
60. Beecher, *Life Thoughts from Plymouth Pulpit* (Boston, 1858), p. 143.
61. *LG Inc.*, 557; *LG*, 59.
62. John S. Haller, Jr., and Robin M. Haller, *The Physician and Sexuality in Victorian America* (Urbana, Ill., 1974), pp. 97, 129, 201. See also Orson S. Fowler, *Amativeness* (New York, 1844), pp. 39–40; Fowler, *Love and Parentage*, pp. 37–39; Trall, *Sexual Physiology*, pp. 245–46, 254.
63. *LG1860*, 368; *LG*, 103, 105; *LG1860*, 325.
64. Trall, *Sexual Physiology*, p. 232; Frederick Hollick, *The Marriage Guide or Natural History of Generation* (1850; reprint New York, 1974), pp. vii–x, 211–12; Henry C. Wright, *Marriage and Parentage: or, The Reproductive Element in Man* (1855; reprint New York, 1974), p. 271.
65. An 1872 letter to W by Senator Matthew Hale Carpenter (*WWWC*, IV:119–20). On W and Dr. Gross, "the great doctor," see *WWWC*, IV:323.
66. L. A. Hink, "Relation of Marriage to Greatness," *Am Ph J* 12 (1850):60–63.
67. Fowler, *Love and Parentage*, p. 118; Fowler, *Amativeness*, pp. 71–72.
68. Alcott, *Table-Talk*, p. 74; Edward H. Dixon, *A Treatise on Diseases of the Sexual System* (New York, 1867), pp. 220–23. See also Trall, *Sexual Physiology*, pp. 256–57, 299; D. H. Jacques, *Hints Toward Physical Perfection* (New York, 1859), pp. 74–75.
69. *EPF*, 272, 321–23.
70. *LG*, 188, 193–94.
71. *UPP*, II:65; *LG*, 432. Compare "Salut au Monde!" sections 11–13 (*LG*, 145–48).
72. *LG*, 155.
73. *LG1860*, 139; *LG*, 268–69.
74. *LG*, 736, 342. W underlined passages in an article on "The Standard Civilized Head" on the factors which inhibit personal and national evolution; these included monotony, lack of spontaneity and "a fear of touching prejudices, which we are all taught to handle gingerly"; see *Trent*, 75. For a similar opinion, see *ISL*, 117.
75. *UPP*, I:192; *LG*, 599 (italics mine).
76. *LG*, 682.
77. *LG*, 439, 374, 724 (dots in original).
78. *DV*, 397.
79. Fowler, *Amativeness*, pp. 7–9, 29–31.
80. *DV*, 372.
81. Dixon, "Hereditary Descent of Disease," p. 411; Dixon, *Treatise on Diseases of the Sexual System*, pp. 230–37. See also Knowlton, *Fruits of Philosophy*, pp. 82–89; W. W. Sanger, *The History of Prostitution* (New York, 1857), p. 320.
82. Haller and Haller, *Physician and Sexuality*, pp. 296–97; Hollick, *Marriage Guide*, p. 331; Orson S. Fowler, *Creative and Sexual Science* (Philadelphia, 1870), p. 948.
83. *LG*, 424; *CW*, IX:152–53.
84. *LG1855*, 72. The symptoms are described in Frank C. Fowler, *Life: How to Enjoy and to Prolong It* (Modus, Conn., 1896), p. 114n.
85. *LG*, 57–58. The "solitary committer" appears only in *LG1856*.

86. G. S. Weaver, *Lectures on Mental Science* (New York, 1854), p. 114.

87. *SS*, 424; *Walt Whitman's Diary in Canada*, p. 54n.; Barrus, 9, 17.

Chapter 7. "Hardy and Well-Defined Women"

1. Hawthorne, *The Blithedale Romance* (New York, 1958), p. 59; *The Education of Henry Adams: An Autobiography* (New York, 1918), p. 384.

2. *DV*, 364.

3. *UPP*, I:202–205, II:185–88.

4. *LG*, 37, 430; *LC*, Item no. 91 (notebook ca. 1860–61).

5. Robert Dale Owen, *Moral Physiology; or, A Brief and Plain Treatise on the Population Question* (London, 1831), pp. 6, 13; Charles Knowlton, *Fruits of Philosophy* (1831; reprint Mt. Vernon, N.Y., 1937), pp. 79–80.

6. Richard Hildreth, *Theory of Morals* (Cambridge, Mass., 1844), p. 198.

7. George R. Drysdale, *Elements of Social Science* (London, 1886), pp. 172–74, 247. Originally published in 1854, this is labeled the "25th" edition.

8. *UPP*, II:98; "A Memorandum at a Venture," *PW1892*, 494.

9. *WWWC*, III:452–53. See also Emerson, "Swedenborg," *Representative Men: Seven Lectures*, ed. Edward Waldo Emerson (Boston and New York, 1903), p. 127.

10. *LG*, 212.

11. *LG*, 588–90.

12. *LG*, 741, 743.

13. *LG*, 208.

14. *UPP*, I:37, 117; Rubin, 154.

15. *W W Civ War*, 48; Rubin, 69; *W W Civ War*, 59; *NYD*, 19; *LC*, Item no. 93.

16. "Brooklyniana," *UPP*, II:293.

17. *WWWC*, II:205, 445, 500. On Frances Wright as a cult figure, see *SS*, 29–30; Walter C. Rivers, *Walt Whitman's Anomaly* (London, 1913), p. 48.

18. *SD*, 20; Rubin, 216. W first saw Fanny Kemble when she was thirteen and he was twenty-five; she was thirty when she resumed her career.

19. Clarence Gohdes and Rollo G. Silver, eds., *Faint Clews & Indirections: Manuscripts of Walt Whitman and His Family* (Durham, N.C., 1949), p. 19; *LG*, 407. See also Rubin, 280–81.

20. Allen Lesser, *Enchanting Rebel: Adah Isaacs Menken* (New York, 1947), p. 95; M. B. Gerson ("Samuel Edwards"), *Queen of the Plaza: A Biography of Adah Isaacs Menken* (London, 1965), pp. 97, 131, 145.

21. *WWWC*, I:235; III:309; Florence B. Freedman, "New Light on an Old Quarrel: Walt Whitman and William Douglas O'Connor—1872," *WWR* 11 (1965):44–46.

22. *WWWC*, IV:93; *LG*, 525. For a glimpse of the thirty-year-old W among the ladies, see "Letters from a Travelling Bachelor," in Rubin, 344–45. W's lovers in the 1860's possibly included the mysterious "Ellen Eyre" (*SS*, 279–80) and a French variety-hall entertainer in Washington (Edward F. Grier, "Whitman's Sexuality," *WWR* 22 [1976]:163–66).

23. D. H. Lawrence, *Studies in Classic American Literature* (1923; reprint New York, 1961), p. 167; Richard Chase, *Walt Whitman Reconsidered* (New York, 1955), p. 115.

24. Orson S. Fowler, *Tight Lacing; or, The Evils of Constricting the Organs of Animal Life* (New York, 1847), p. 16; Edward H. Dixon, *Woman and Her Diseases; From the Cradle to the Grave* (1847; reprint New York, 1867), p. 227;

Dixon, *A Treatise on the Diseases of the Sexual System* (New York, 1867), p. 222; Dixon, *Scenes in the Practice of a New York Surgeon* (New York, 1855), pp. 72–80; R. T. Trall, *The Illustrated Family Gymnasium* (New York, 1857), pp. 25–27.

25. *W-Eagle*, 186–87. On a later reaction to such dress, see *DV*, 372.

26. *B D Times*, May 24, 1859; Russell T. Trall, *Sexual Physiology* (New York, 1871), p. 189. On W's approval of the statuary, see Rubin, 260; *W-Eagle*, 215–16.

27. D. H. Jacques, *Hints Toward Physical Perfection*, (New York, 1859), pp. 44–50, 84–85, 125, 147–63. On the aesthetics of women fit for conception, see also Orson S. Fowler, *Creative and Sexual Science* (Philadelphia, 1870), pp. 133–46; Trall, *Illustrated Family Gymnasium*, p. 38.

28. *Corr.* I:80.

29. *CW*, IX:5; *UPP*, II:189; *LG*, 243, 245; *N&F*, 34. As "the first step toward a perfect marriage," urged the sexual reformer Dr. John Cowan, a thirty-year-old man, "full grown, perfectly developed, and desirous of marrying," should choose a woman of "twenty-four, perfectly developed, ripe and lovable": Cowan, *The Science of a New Life* (1874; reprint New York, 1970), p. 25.

30. *LG1860*, 302–303.

31. *LG*, 97; "Living Magnetism: Full Confirmation of Magnetism in the Human Body," *Am Ph J* 5 (1843):8–24. On the folklore of birth control, see Marie Carmichael Stopes, *Contraception (Birth Control): Its Theory and Practice* (London, 1927), pp. 56–130; on sex determination during conception, see Trall, *Sexual Physiology*, pp. 149–200.

32. Quoted in Arthur W. Calhoun, *A Social History of the American Family*, (Cleveland, 1918), II:114. Other examples of this commonplace sentiment are Clifton Furness, ed., *Walt Whitman's Workshop: A Collection of Unpublished Manuscripts* (New York, 1961), pp. 63–64; Trall, *Illustrated Family Gymnasium*, p. 19 and *passim*; Frances Wright, cited in David Goodale, "Some of Whitman's Borrowings," *American Literature* 10 (1938):208.

33. *LG*, 175. On the bloomer, see Madeleine B. Stern, *Heads & Headlines: The Phrenological Fowlers* (Norman, Okla., 1971), pp. 170–71.

34. *LG*, 96–97.

35. *LG*, 91–93.

36. *LG*, 466–67; William Sloane Kennedy, *The Fight of a Book for the World* (West Yarmouth, Mass., 1926), p. 184.

37. *LG*, 671–72. Compare: "What is Beauty? / Beauty is simply health" (fragment in Feinberg Collection).

38. *LG Inc.*, 566. These portraits appear in "Song of Myself," sections 8, 31, 15, and 26.

39. Compare the sexual fantasy in "From Pent-Up Aching Rivers" (*LG1860*, 289): "The swimmer swimming naked in the bath, or motionless on his back lying and floating, / The female form approaching—I, pensive, love-flesh tremulous, aching * * * *"

40. *CW*, IX:37.

41. *LG*, 594; *LG1860*, 290.

42. *LG*, 401; *SD*, 225–26; *WWWC*, II:151–52.

43. *LG*, 437; *ISL*, 116–17. On changes in the American household, see Arthur C. Cole, *The Irrepressible Conflict, 1850–1865* (New York, 1934), p. 162. On the decline in women's health and sexual development because of their soft

living, indulgence in dancing parties, and reading of romantic novels, see Frederick Hollick, *The Marriage Guide; or, Natural History of Generation* (1850; reprint New York, 1974), p. 106; Jacques, *Hints Toward Physical Perfection*; Catharine E. Beecher, *Physiology and Calisthenics for Schools and Families* (New York, 1856), pp. 120–22.

44. *ISL*, 111; *UPP*, I:137.

45. *ISL*, 114–16, 171; *NYD*, 141; *W-Eagle*, 146. On contraception in urban households, see Karl Theodor Griesinger, *Lebende Bilder aus Amerika* (Stuttgart, 1858), pp. 39, 47, 264–65; Cole, *Irrepressible Conflict*, pp. 169–71.

46. *UPP*, II:5–8; *NYD*, 95–96; W. W. Sanger, *The History of Prostitution* (New York, 1857), pp. 450–606, *passim.* Sanger estimated New York City's prostitutes at eight thousand and New Yorkers treated yearly for venereal disease at fifty thousand. W commented on the book in *B D Times*, December 11, 1858.

47. *ISL*, 82; *W-Eagle*, 133–34; *ISL*, 118–20; *LG*, 657.

48. *NYD*, 121–22, 129.

49. Rubin, 192, 299; *LG*, 387, 367. Compare "The City Dead-House" to Henry Ward Beecher, "The Strange Woman" (1845), the parable of a once-beautiful house whose successive chambers are Pleasure, Satiety, Discovery, Disease, and Death (*Lectures to Young Men on Various Important Subjects* [New York, 1873], pp. 145–53).

50. *LG1860*, 261.

51. *LC*, Item no. 61; *LG1860*, 375. For what seems to be a sympathetic gloss of "Calamus 38," see D. H. Lawrence, "Whitman," in *LG*, *Norton Critical Edition*, ed. Sculley Bradley and Harold W. Blodgett (New York, 1973), pp. 849–50.

52. *LC*, Item no. 91; *CW*, X:24; *LG*, 48, 511.

53. *LG*, 194–95 (italics mine); W, *An 1855–56 Notebook Toward the Second Edition of Leaves of Grass*, ed. Harold W. Blodgett (Carbondale, Ill., 1959), pp. 12, 39.

54. Barbara M. Cross, ed., *The Educated Woman in America: Selected Writings of Catharine Beecher, Margaret Fuller, and M. Carey Thomas* (New York, 1965), pp. 8–11, 81–82.

55. "A Legend of Life and Love," *EPF*, 118.

56. *UPP*, I:128; Fredrika Bremer, *Homes of the New World* (New York, 1853), I:190.

57. Barrus, 324.

58. *UPP*, I:217; *WWWC*, III:439. Compare Dr. Trall, *Sexual Physiology*, p. 202: "Woman's equality in all the relations of life implies her absolute supremacy in the sexual relation. . . . It is her absolute and indefeasible right to determine when she will, and when she will not, be exposed to pregnancy."

59. J. A. Symonds, *Walt Whitman: A Study* (1893; reprint New York, 1967), pp. 60–62.

60. W's self-review of *LG* and *Maud*, in Milton Hindus, ed., *Walt Whitman: The Critical Heritage* (New York, 1971), p. 43.

61. Eliza W. Farnham, *Woman and Her Era* (New York, 1864), 2 vols. Trall, *Sexual Physiology*, pp. 292–94, praises Mrs. Farnham's book and expresses a feminist position like that of *DV*.

62. *DV*, 370, 372n.–73n.

63. *DV*, 372, 389. Trall, *Sexual Physiology*, pp. 260–67, makes a similar case against frivolity.

64. *DV*, 396, 393n., 401.
65. *DV*, 400–401.
66. *WWWC*, I:332.
67. *LG*, 380, 365, 180–81, 467; George Drummond, *Ascent of Man* (1894), quoted in Alice B. Stockham, *Karezza: Ethics of Marriage* (Chicago, 1896), p. 70, reprinted in Charles Rosenberg and Carroll Smith-Rosenberg, eds., *Sexual Indulgence and Denial* (New York, 1974).
68. *The Annotated Uncle Tom's Cabin*, ed. Philip Van Doren Stern (New York, 1964), p. 197. For tributes to the postmenopausal woman, see Samuel Sheldon Fitch, *Six Lectures on the Uses of the Lungs* (New York, 1847), pp. 199–200; Farnham, *Woman and Her Era*, I:71–72.
69. Lowenfels, 133; *LG*, 747, 497.

Chapter 8. *"Thy Ensemble Including Body and Soul"*

1. Henry Thoreau, quoted in Bliss Perry, *Walt Whitman His Life and Work* (New York, 1906), p. 96n.; *WWWC*, I:372.
2. The phrase is by Sherman Paul, *Emerson's Angle of Vision* (Cambridge, Mass., 1952), p. 212.
3. Richard G. Lillard, *The Great Forest*, (New York, 1948), p. 29.
4. *LG1856*, 383.
5. *Letters of Charles Eliot Norton*, ed. Sara Norton and M. A. De Wolfe Howe (1913; reprint New York, 1973), I:135.
6. Edwin H. Miller, ed., *A Century of Whitman Criticism* (Bloomington and London, 1969), pp. 12, 88.
7. "The Apostle of Chaotism," anonymous review quoted in William M. Guthrie, *Walt Whitman (The Camden Sage) as Religious and Moral Teacher* (Cincinnati, 1897), p. 105.
8. Edmund C. Stedman, "Walt Whitman," *Scribner's Monthly* 21 (November, 1880):54.
9. W, *Poems by Walt Whitman*, ed. William Michael Rossetti (London, 1868), p. 11.
10. *WWWC*, IV:385–86.
11. Robert Ingersoll, "Liberty in Literature," in *In Re W W*, 256.
12. "The Poet Walt Whitman," in *The America of Jose Martí*, ed. Juan de Onís (New York, 1964), pp. 240–44, 249–50.
13. George Moore, *The Use of the Body in Relation to the Mind* (New York, 1847), pp. vi, 58ff., 94.
14. Odell Shepard, ed., *The Journals of Bronson Alcott* (Boston, 1938), pp. 33, 73, 77, 204.
15. *An American Primer*, ed. Horace Traubel (Boston, 1904), pp. 27–28.
16. Henry Ward Beecher, *Life Thoughts from Plymouth Pulpit* (Boston, 1858), pp. 40, 42, 75–76; Henry Ward Beecher, *Lectures to Young Men on Various Important Subjects* (New York, 1873), pp. 203, 205. W reviewed *Life Thoughts* in *B D Times*, July 26, 1858. Edward Dahlberg, *Alms for Oblivion* (Minneapolis, 1964), pp. 85, 96, calling *LG* "marvelous crank verse on human physiology," observes that Beecher "was delivering hot, amative sermons, some of which sound like lines out of Whitman's *Leaves of Grass*." On W and Beecher, see also Rubin, 130.
17. George R. Drysdale, *Elements of Social Science* (London, 1886), pp. 5, 191.
18. *LG*, 712, 722, 724, 726, 728.

19. *LG*, 737–38.
20. Burroughs, *Notes on Walt Whitman as Poet and Person* (1867; reprint New York, 1971), p. 172; Burroughs, *Walt Whitman: A Study* (Boston, 1896), pp. 224–25.
21. *WWWC*, III: 582; "Notes on . . . Elias Hicks," *PW1892*, 648.
22. *SD*, 295.
23. William Sloane Kennedy, *Reminiscences of Walt Whitman* (London, 1896), p. 2.
24. Edward Carpenter, *Days with Walt Whitman* (London, 1906), p. 26; Grace Gilchrist, "Chats With Walt Whitman," *Temple Bar Magazine* 103 (February, 1898): 204–205; *Corr.*, V: 172.
25. John Johnston and J. W. Wallace, *Visits to Walt Whitman in 1890–1891 by Two Lancashire Friends* (New York, 1918), pp. 150–51.
26. *WWWC*, II: 168–69.
27. Arthur E. Briggs, *Walt Whitman as Thinker and Artist* (New York, 1952), p. 90. See also "A Memorandum at a Venture," *PW1892*, 491–97; *Corr.*, IV: 70.
28. *LG*, 456.
29. *LG*, 741; *Corr.*, II: 151, 154.
30. *LG*, 750–51.
31. *LG*, 572.

Index

*Physicians with whom W was acquainted.

homeopathy, 42–43; mentioned, 56, 121

Buchanan, Joseph Rodes, 133, 268n72

Bucke, Richard Maurice*: *Walt Whitman,* 9, 13–14, 48, 63; *Cosmic Consciousness,* 14–15; as W's physician, 30–31, 99–102, 104; on W's medical knowledge, 37, 96–97; mentioned, 80, 207–8, 272n64

Bulwer-Lytton, Edward, 44, 231

Burns, Robert, 122

Burroughs, John: impressions of W, 7–9, 10, 13, 25, 208–9; comments on *Leaves of Grass,* 55, 195, 245

"By Blue Ontario's Shore," 62, 80, 118, 124, 129, 205

Byron, Lord, 150, 164

"By the Bivouac's Fitful Flame," 87

Calamus grass, 70, 239

"Calamus": group of poems, 23, 52, 70, 188; "Calamus 5," 160; "Calamus 38," 228–29

Calvin, John, 178–79

Cargill, Oscar, 189

Carlyle, Thomas: as a sickly writer, 19, 105; *Life of John Sterling,* 133; "Characteristics," 253n47

"Carol Closing Sixty-nine," 14

Carpenter, Edward, 29, 198, 208

"Cavalry Crossing a Ford," 87

"Centenarian's Story, The," 53

Channing, William Francis*: *Notes on the Medical Application of Electricity,* 145

Channing, William H., 154

"Chanting the Square Deific," 18

Chase, Richard, 218

"Child and the Profligate, The" (tale), 48

Childhood, 19, 122, 131–33

"Children of Adam" (group of poems), 52, 70, 195

Christian Commission, 261n4

"City Dead-House, The," 95, 227

"City Photographs" (sketches), 71–75

Clairvoyance: in W's writings, 162–64, 166, 169, 171–76; defined, 167–70; communication with the dead, 176–78, 272n80. *See also* Mesmerism; Spiritualism

Coleridge, Samuel T., 164

Columbus, Christopher, 10–13

Combe, George: *The Constitution of Man,* 113; *Lectures on Phrenology,* 115; mentioned, 111, 120, 128, 130

"Come Up From the Fields Father," 86

Conway, Moncure D., 22–23

Cooper, James Fenimore, 188, 212

Cornaro, Ludovico, 52

Cosmic consciousness, 14–15. *See also* Clairvoyance; Spiritualism

Cowan, John, 278n29

Creamer, Hannah G.: *Delia's Doctors,* 116

"Crossing Brooklyn Ferry," 118, 177, 178, 192, 208

Dahlberg, Edward, 280n16

Dale, Philip Marshall, 24, 26

Dante, 14, 89

Darwin, Charles, 192

Davis, Andrew Jackson: visions of, 162, 164; on spiritualism, 169–70, 173, 176–78

"Death's Valley," 14

"Debris" (group of poems), 69–70

Degeneration of American masses (theory of), 183–86, 191–92, 203. *See also* Evolution

Deleuze, J. P. F., 158–59, 176

Democratic Vistas: discussion of women in, 231–34; mentioned, 5, 95, 206–7, 211, 228

De Selincourt, Basil, 192

Dickens, Charles, 154

Digestion: W advocates hearty diet, 51, 60; as key to health, 104–5

Diseases and ailments: epilepsy, 18, 207; tuberculosis in W's family, 18, 33, 44; venereal disease, 18, 57, 204, 259n67; cholera, 46, 48, 56; opium eating, 56–57; tuberculosis, 65–67, 207; typhus, 66; accidents and wounds, 71–73, 88, 91; diarrhea, 90–91; gangrene, 92. *See also* Insanity; Women (physical fitness of)

"Dismantled Ship, The," 32

Dixon, Edward H.*: medical and health opinions of, 42, 46–47, 59–61, 63, 66, 146–47, 185, 202, 207, 218, 259n67; W's reactions to his

Index

key to national greatness, 187, 189, 193–95, 201–3. *See also* Evolution; Motherhood

Parton, James, 120

Parton, Sarah Payson ("Fanny Fern"), 22, 117, 267n54

"Passage to India," 11, 96, 195

Pathognomy, 133–34, 268n72. *See also* Phrenology; Physiognomy

Patmore, Coventry, 199

"Patrolling Barnegat," 12

Perry, Bliss, 19

Peters, George Absalom*, 75

Phrenological examination: of W, 20–21; W relates it to his poetry, 124–31; of other writers, 267n54

Phrenology: defined, 109–12; popularity of, 112–13; W's knowledge of, 113–17; used in *Leaves of Grass,* 117–24, 131–32, 136–41; and the "gift" of poetry, 122–24, 127

Physiognomy: defined, 133–35, 266n33; in W's poetry, 136–41

"Pioneers! O Pioneers!": 140, 190

Plato, 179

Poe, Edgar Allan: chemistry and poetry, 64; "Mesmeric Revelation," 176, 178; mentioned, 13, 123–24, 135, 144, 154

Poetry: related to phrenology, 6–7, 122–24, 127; and physiological themes, 54–55, 95; related to "chemistry," 64; related to electricity, 150–51; related to the body, 239, 241–48

Pope, Alexander, 124

Post, C. Wright*, 72

Powers, Hiram, 218–19

"Prayer of Columbus," 11–12, 90

Price, Helen, 23, 25

Prostitution, 205, 226–27, 279n46

"Proud Music of the Storm," 65, 217

Quimby, Phineas Parker, 159

Race: idealized white race, 139–40, 187–90; nonwhite, 139–40, 190–92, 212. *See also* Evolution

Récamier, Joseph-Claude, 154

Redpath, James, 262n29

Reich, Wilhelm, 133

"Return of the Heroes," 95

"Revenge and Requital" (tale), 48–49, 58

Rhine, J. B., 163–64

Ridge, James M.*, 97–98, 263n58

Roberts, Robert*, 72

Rodgers, Kearney*, 72

Rogers, Samuel, 120

Rolleston, Thomas, 240–41

Roosa, D. B. St. John*, 71–74

Ross, Jacob S., 260n92

Rossetti, William: on body in *Leaves of Grass,* 4, 240

"Runner, The," 55

"Rurio" (Thomas Horton Jones), 183

Ruschenberger, W. S. W.*, 263n57

"Salut au Monde!": as clairvoyant journey, 171–72; and race, 190–91; mentioned, 118, 272n80

Sammis, O. K.*, 44

Sand, George, 231

Sanger, W. W., 226–27, 279n46

Schmidt, Rudolf, 247

Scott, Sir Walter, 120

Schyberg, Frederik, 235

Seeress of Prevost: clairvoyant experiences of, 166–67, 169, 178

Selfhood: W's theme of, 240–42, 247–48

Shakespeare, William, 14, 102, 120, 121

Shaw, George Bernard, 137, 195

Shelley, Mary Godwin, 144

Shelley, Percy B., 164

Shew, Joel*, 44

Shivers, George Hendry*, 263n58

Shryock, Richard, 84

"Sight in Camp in the Daybreak Gray and Dim, A," 87

Sizer, Nelson, 121, 126, 139–40, 267n56

"Sleepers, The": as clairvoyant journey, 171–75; and evolution, 203–4, 207–8; mentioned 17, 49, 55, 65, 168, 212

Sleepwaking, 172–74. *See also* Clairvoyance

Smith, Stephen*, 39

Socrates, 113, 138

"So Long!": 187

"Some Fact-Romances" (sketches), 49

"Song at Sunset," 6

288   *Index*

Wendell, Matthew*, 47
Wesselhöft, William, 193–94, 260n85
"We Two Boys Together Clinging,"
47, 228
Wharton, Henry R.*, 31
"When I Heard at the Close of Day,"
228
"When Lilacs Last in the Dooryard
Bloom'd," 86
Whitman, Walt: emotionalism, 13, 19,
27–29, 94; ancestry and family, 15–
19; tuberculosis, 18; physical condition, 19–25; athletic activities, 21–
22; attraction to suffering, 24, 48–
49, 57, 62, 73, 78, 100; paralysis and
decline, 25–32; autopsic analysis of,
32–33; attraction to women, 215–
17, 277n22
—and medicine: knowledge of medicine, 37–38, 41, 47–48, 68, 77; relations with doctors, 47, 58–60, 96–
98, 100–5; plans physical culture
propaganda, 49–53; critic of hospital care, 70–71, 81–82. *See also*
Doctors; Drugs and medicines;
Hospitals
—attitudes: phrenology, 111–19, 125–
27; mesmerism and spiritualism,
144–45, 154–55, 164; eugenics and
racial improvement, 184–90, 194,
199, 205; masturbation, 207–8; homosexuality, 208–9; women, 213–
15, 225, 229, 231–36; birth control,
225–26; complete selfhood, 243–44.
See also Poetry
Whitman, Walt (persona): shaping the
persona, 3–15; as proletarian poet,
6–7, 61; as mythic healer, 7–10, 41,

43, 61–62, 69–70, 78, 90, 150, 154;
as national reconciler, 9–10, 95; as
old-age hero, 10–15; as genetic new
Adam, 119–22, 124, 140, 147–53,
195–96, 202–3; childhood and parentage of, 131–35
Whitman family: Walter, Sr. (father),
16–18; Louisa Orr (mother), 16–17,
93–94, 235; Andrew, 18, 44, 60–61;
Edward, 18; George W., 18, 21, 77;
Jesse, 18; Thomas J. ("Jeff"), 18, 30;
Hannah, 19, 21, 32; John (putative
ancestor), 115, 266n22; Manahatta
(niece), 219; Nancy (sister-in-law),
227
Whittier, John Greenleaf, 193
"Who Learns My Lesson Complete,"
19
Willis, Nathaniel Parker, 120, 163
Winter, William, 24
"With Husky-Haughty Lips, O Sea!":
12
"Woman Waits for Me, A": the ge-
netic role of women in, 118–19,
147–48, 196–98, 220–21
Women: physical fitness of, 60, 219,
221; political-esthetic ideal of, 140–
41, 214–16, 222–23, 232–34,
279n58; status of, 211, 225; sexuality
and marriage, 212, 220–21, 278n29;
as nurses, 262n19
Wordsworth, William, 102
"Wound-Dresser, The": discussed, 89–
93; mentioned, 27, 86, 227
Wright, Frances, 6–7, 216, 257n39
Wright, Henry C., 201
Wrobel, Arthur, 124, 267n57